SCOTT®

CATALOGUE OF

ERRORS

ON U.S. POSTAGE STAMPS

17TH EDITION

Editor-In-Chief .... Jay Bigalke

Editor ....Charles Snee

Editor Emeritus .... James E. Kloetzel

Ad Design Supervisor .... Dini Hampton

Senior Designer ....Cinda McAlexander

Printing and Image Coordinator... Stacey Mahan

Advertising/Sales .... David Pistello, Eric Roth

A division of Amos Media Co., 911 S. Vandemark Road, Sidney, OH 45365,
publisher of the Scott line of catalogs, *Linn's Stamp News* and *Coin World*.

SCOTT CATALOGUE MISSION STATEMENT

The Scott Catalogue Team exists to serve the recreational, educational and commercial hobby needs of stamp collectors and dealers. We strive to set the industry standard for philatelic information and products by developing and providing goods that help collectors identify, value, organize and present their collections.

Quality customer service is, and will continue to be, our highest priority.

We aspire toward achieving total customer satisfaction.

LETTER FROM THE EDITOR-IN-CHIEF

Dear Scott error catalog user:

Continuing the tradition of offering a catalog devoted to United States errors, we present the 17th edition of the Scott *Catalogue of Errors on U.S. Postage Stamps*. Stephen R. Datz, a highly respected collector and specialist of errors for half a century, was the author of the 16th edition of the Scott U.S. Errors catalog. Datz, who resided in Colorado, died in 2015, at age 71.

The new 17th edition includes a multitude of enhancements. One of the most substantial is the number of new illustrations shown for the first time. Our editorial team contacted numerous error collectors, dealers and specialists, who either provided images we needed or directed us to others who could do so.

Many new and updated images have been added to the listings of color-omitted postal stationery. Most of the new color-omitted postal card images are from the collection of William R. Weiss (1943-2015). A handful of new images of color-omitted stamped envelopes also are included.

In addition to new images, numerous values have been updated. Overall, hundreds of errors changed in value since the previous Scott U.S. Errors catalog was published in 2014.

Specific values for imperforate plate-number coil strips have replaced previously dashed entries (—). A dash indicates that insufficient valuing information exists. These strips are valued only in the Scott U.S. Errors catalog. Additional listings with dashes have been updated with values throughout the catalog.

Overall, imperforate errors have held their catalog values quite well. Conversely, there has been a softening of values for color-omitted errors.

Values for some classic-era and rare errors remain steady, while some show substantial increases. For example, the used single, imperforate horizontally 1875 special printing 15¢ brown and blue Columbus stamp (Scott 129a) soared from $7,000 to $30,000. The imperforate pair of the 1954 3¢ Statue of Liberty stamp (Scott 1035f) increased from $2,450 to $3,000.

Among the color-omitted errors, the possibly unique pane of 15 of the Celebrate the Century 1900s stamps with the red engraving omitted on the Gibson Girl stamp (Scott 3182p) increased from $2,530 to $3,000.

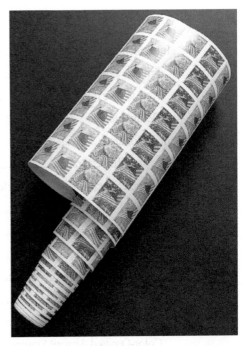

Inverts remain enduringly popular, and demand is strong. A few inverts showed robust increases, such as the 1901 2¢ Train stamp (Scott 295a), which jumped from $32,500 to $50,000.

Dozens of new listings have been added in this edition, including the 2013 Four Flags coil stamps with no horizontal slits between the coil rolls (Scott 4777b). Shown nearby is an example of this eye-catching coil error in its multi-roll format. A part of this error is pictured with the new listing.

Footnotes and other helpful information have been reviewed and updated accordingly.

If you have an image of a stamp error that is not pictured in this catalog, we would appreciate receiving an image for our files and for potential inclusion in a future edition. Updates or suggestions also are welcome. Send an email to jbigalke@amosmedia.com or write to P.O. Box 4129, Sidney, OH 45365-4129.

We hope you enjoy the 17th edition of the Scott *Catalogue of Errors on U.S. Postage Stamps.*

Jay Bigalke
Editor-in-Chief

CONTENTS

ACKNOWLEDGMENTS

Many individuals generously assisted in the preparation of this book. Sincere thanks are extended to all who contributed. Special thanks are due Jacques C. Schiff, Jr. for his encouragement and resources in originally making this book a reality. Special thanks also to Marvin Frey for his help and guidance in editing the section on Freaks, Oddities & Other Unusual Stamps. Among those who have helped with this or previous editions are:

Ken Beiner	Mark Eastzer	John Hotchner	D. James Samuelson
Larry Bustillo	Thomas Galloway	James E. Kloetzel	Jay Smith
Robert Dowiot	Henry Gitner	James McDevitt	Dan Undersander
Dr. Allen M. Dresher	Stan Goldfarb	Bruce H. Mosher	Martin Wilkinson
Bob Dumaine	John Greenwood	Jack Nalbandian	Wayne Youngblood

Those now deceased whose contributions have been part of this book since early editions include:

Mike Charles	Howard P. Gates Jr.	James B. Peterson	John Tison
Marvin Frey	Herman Herst Jr.	Jacques C. Schiff, Jr.	William Wallerstein
Stephen R. Datz	Jack S. Molesworth	Robert A. Siegel	William R. Weiss

Auction price results and retail price lists surveyed for valuing in this edition include those from:

Cherrystone Auctions, Inc.
Daniel F. Kelleher Auctions LLC
Dutch Country Auctions
Eric Jackson
Gary Posner, Inc.
Harmer-Schau Auction Galleries
Henry Gitner Philatelists, Inc.
H.R. Harmer LLC

Jack Nalbandian, Inc.
James E. Lee
Matthew Bennett, Inc.
Momen Stamps, Inc.
Regency-Superior Auctions
Richard Friedberg Stamps
Robert A. Siegel Auction
  Galleries, Inc.

Sam Houston Philatelics
Schuyler Rumsey Philatelic Auctions
Spink Shreves Philatelic Galleries, Inc.
Stan Goldfarb
Stanley M. Piller & Associates
Stuart Katz

PRINTERS

Abbreviations for printers appearing in the listings. Before 1980, most stamps were printed by the Bureau of Engraving and Printing. Printers are listed for stamps issued after 1980. Listings for twentieth-century stamps not mentioning a printer were printed by the Bureau of Engraving and Printing.

ABN.........................American Bank Note Company
APC..................... American Packaging Corporation
APU .... Ashton-Potter (USA) Ltd.
AVR .... Avery Dennison
BCA ....Banknote Corporation of America
BEP .... Bureau of Engraving and Printing
CCL... CCL Label Inc.
DBS... Dittler Brothers
DLR ....De La Rue Security Printing
GGI .... Guilford Gravure Inc.
JWF...J.W. Fergusson & Sons
KCS...KCS Industries
MCC .... Multi-Color Corporation
NBC ....National Bank Note Company
SSP...........................Sennett Security Products
SVS ....Stamp Venturers
UBN.......................................United Bank Note Co.
UCC ....Union Camp Corporation

ABBREVIATIONS

USB.. U.S. Bank Note
3M..3M Corporation
APS ....American Philatelic Society
btwn ....between
FDC ....first-day cover
hz ....horizontal
imperf ....imperforate
incl ....including
litho ....lithographed
misperf .... misperforated
perf ....perforation or perforated
PNC .... plate number coil
vrt ....vertical

INTRODUCTION

In general, an error stamp is one created unintentionally and by mistake. Technically, any stamp not properly prepared and inadvertently released can be regarded as an error. These improperly prepared stamps have come to be known as "EFOs" (errors, freaks, and oddities) by the error-collecting community.

All types of errors are collectible; however, this work focuses on imperforates, color-omitted errors, inverts, and certain allied types of errors, such as hologram-omitted errors and back inscriptions inverted or omitted errors. The omission of other types of error stamps should not be construed as a reflection on their desirability or collectibility.

More information about other types of errors is contained in the section **Freaks, Oddities, & Other Unusual Stamps.**

IMPERFORATES

To be considered an imperforate error, all traces of perforations (or die cutting) between two complete, adjacent stamps must be absent. The presence of even one perforation between stamps disqualifies the item from being considered an imperforate error. The presence of incompletely impressed perforations (known as "blind perforations") or die cuts also disqualifies a stamp as an imperforate error.

The presence of a row of perforations completely within the design of one of the stamps of a pair and parallel to the row of omitted perforations disqualifies the pair from being considered imperforate between, imperforate horizontally, or imperforate vertically, as the case may be. Perforations touching or cutting a design do not disqualify an error. Only when perforations are located completely inside the border of a design does disqualification occur.

It is generally accepted that a single stray perforation hole (not part of a row) within a design does not affect an item's status as an error. An example is Scott 1508a. Imperforate errors are described as follows:

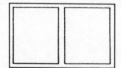

Imperforate. Lacking perforations. When used to describe a pair or multiple, imperforate means completely lacking perforations between stamps and on all sides. Stamps lacking die cuts are referred to as "die cutting omitted."

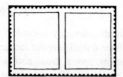

Imperforate Between. Lacking perforations between two stamps, but with perforations present on all outer sides. Pairs or multiples may be either horizontal or vertical. In the case of booklet panes, this description is applied only to error pairs (or panes) having perforations on all outer sides (as often results from a foldover). Booklet pane pairs having natural straight edges on two opposing exterior sides are described as imperforate vertically or horizontally in order to distinguish them from true imperforate betweens (i.e., possessing perforations on all outer sides). In some cases, both forms of errors exist for the same issue, and confusion arises where descriptions are not specific. Those with a natural straight edge at bottom can be described using the criteria set forth below in Imperforates—Other Configurations.

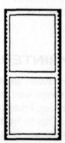

Vertical Pair, Imperforate Horizontally. A pair of stamps, one atop the other vertically, lacking horizontal perforations between stamps and with horizontal straight edges at top and bottom. Perforations are present all across left and right sides.

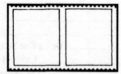

Horizontal Pair, Imperforate Vertically. A pair of stamps, side by side horizontally, lacking vertical perforations between stamps and with vertical straight edges at either side. Perforations are present all across top and bottom.

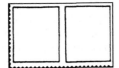

Imperforates—Other Configurations. Imperforates that do not conveniently fall into the above categories are described according to their appearance. The illustrated example is an imperforate horizontal pair with perforations at bottom and left, and straight edges at top and right.

The initial reference "imperforate" refers only to the omission of perforations between two stamps. Exterior sides are described according to the position and presence of perforations or straight edges. An item could have perforations on three sides and a straight edge on the fourth, or vice versa. This style is also appropriate for blocks or multiples and for items imperforate horizontally or vertically on which perforations appear only part way across the exterior top or bottom or sides.

In most cases, items with odd combinations do not constitute a separate listing category, but instead can be considered sub-varieties.

Stamps with perforations omitted between the stamp and the selvage are not listed because the omitted perforations do not occur between two adjacent stamps and, therefore, do not fall within the definition of an imperforate error. Their omission is not a reflection on their desirability or collectibility.

COLOR-OMITTED ERRORS

Color-Omitted Errors. A color-omitted error occurs when one or more colors is unintentionally omitted from a multicolored stamp. Color-omitted errors usually, but not always, occur as the result of an omission of one or more colors in process-color printing. In process-color printing, the image to be printed is broken down into a series of basic colors—usually black, yellow, cyan (blue) and magenta (red)—each of which is printed by a separate plate (or cylinder or sleeve). When printed, the dots mingle and yield a full-color result. Examine a lithographed or gravure-printed stamp under magnification, and you will be able to see the dot structure.

To be considered a color-omitted error, 100 percent of the affected color(s) must be absent from the design. The presence of even one dot of color disqualifies the stamp as an error. The stamp must be able to pass scrutiny under 30-power magnification.

Stamps that appear to have a color omitted as the result of shifted perforations are not considered to be color-omitted errors because it is the imprinted design that defines a stamp, not the location of perforations, which serve only to facilitate the separation of stamps. An otherwise properly prepared stamp containing all colors does not become a

color-omitted error simply because a shift in perforations eliminates part of the design. It is a color-missing error. Color-missing errors due to perforation shifts and other production anomalies are listed in the Scott *Specialized Catalogue of United States Stamps and Covers.*

Every attempt has been made to classify color-omitted errors according to accepted standards. In some cases, however, gray areas exist. In such cases, editorial discretion determines whether or not an item will be included in the listings.

For purposes of this work, the omission of an overprint or surcharge does not constitute a color-omitted error.

Albinos, stamps with all color(s) omitted, exist for some issues but are not included in this work. Their omission is not a reflection on their desirability or collectibility.

Tagging is applied by a separate printing plate and, although invisible to the naked eye, is considered by some to be a "color" for purposes of defining what constitutes a properly prepared stamp. Stamps with tagging omitted are not within the scope of this work and are not separately listed. In some cases, the omission of tagging is mentioned because it helps to authenticate the error.

INVERTS

An invert occurs when one of the elements of the design on a multicolored stamp is unintentionally inverted during printing.

HOLOGRAM OMITTED

A hologram-omitted error occurs when a hologram is omitted during production. Holograms are affixed with an adhesive. It may be possible to remove a hologram by dissolving the adhesive with a solvent. The result, of course, is not an error. It is wise to have hologram-omitted errors expertized.

BACK-INSCRIPTION ERRORS

A back-inscription-omitted error occurs when printing that would normally appear on the back side of a stamp is omitted during production. Some inscriptions, such as those on some waterfowl hunting stamps, are printed atop the gum. Removing the gum also removes the inscription. Cautions appearing with listings warn of potential problems.

A back-inscription-inverted error occurs when printing that appears on the back of a stamp is inverted during production.

ERROR-LIKE IMPERFORATES

Traditionally, to be regarded as a "legitimate" error, an imperforate must have found its way into public hands by being sold at a post office. Several kinds of imperforates have found their way into the philatelic domain by other means, which is to say that they were intentionally allowed to leave government hands, but not made available to the general public. On occasion, imperforate examples from government archives have been traded for services or rare items (such as the 1869 pictorial inverts) needed for the National Museum's collection.

While not errors in the traditional sense, they are similar in appearance and are included in their own section for reference and identification.

Arguably, some imperforates, especially early issues, are proofs prepared in issued colors on stamp paper, either gummed or ungummed.

PRINTER'S WASTE

Printer's waste is a term applied to production that, for whatever reason, is defective, improperly prepared, or lacks one or more elements that a properly prepared stamp should possess. In the broad sense, all errors are printer's waste because they should have been culled and discarded. In the narrower or philatelic sense, the term "printer's waste" refers to error-like items that have reached the market through the back door rather than across a post office counter. An error sold across the counter is deemed legitimate. Printer's waste is not. The term "printer's waste" implies that it was misappropriated from a printing plant or wastepaper destruction facility and illicitly sold into the hobby. Most collectors do not consider printer's waste to be errors—and rightly so, they are not.

Printer's waste is supposed to be destroyed. In rare cases, it inadvertently escapes destruction, blown off a truck on its way to a destruction facility or surviving as a partially incinerated scrap lifted up through a furnace smokestack. In most cases, however, printer's waste reaches the market illicitly through dishonest employees who sneak it out well aware of the value of error stamps.

In some cases it is not clear how imperfect stamps (either marked for destruction or generally faulty) reached public hands. Some legitimate errors are known with destruction marks. And in some cases, printer's waste has the appearance of a perfectly legitimate error but is known to have reached the market by having been misappropriated by someone inside a printing plant or destruction facility. In this catalogue, the term printer's waste takes the traditional connotation—that of stamps having reached the market by suspect means. These items appear in the section on **Printer's Waste.**

Errors purchased over a post office counter are legal to own. However, misappropriated stamps remain the property of the United States Government and are not legal to own. Stamps that could not have been purchased at a post office, such as full uncut sheets of booklet panes, should be avoided, as they remain government property.

FAKES

Fakes exist for some errors. While many are crude, some are excellent and difficult to detect. Cautionary notes appear in the listings where appropriate. From a practical standpoint, the collector's best protection is dealing with knowledgeable, reputable dealers, or requiring, at least for items of significant value, an expert certificate from a recognized expertizing body.

Imperforate Singles. Generally, imperforate singles should be avoided. Some nineteenth-century issues are known as imperforate singles. However, many nineteenth- and twentieth-century stamps exist with huge margins that can be trimmed to resemble imperforates. An expert certificate is necessary for imperforate singles.

Blind Perforations. Blind perforations sometimes can be ironed out and made invisible to the naked eye. This is especially true of stamps with gum soaked off. Imperforates lacking gum should be examined closely under magnification. The barest trace of even one perforation, even though not punched through, disqualifies the stamp from being imperforate. Pairs of stamps offered as imperforate should be carefully checked by a knowledgeable authority.

Colors Omitted. Certain dyes used in printing are susceptible to removal or alteration by exposure to light, heat, or chemicals. Many, such as the Copernicus yellow-omitted error, are easily created; therefore, expertizing is recommended. Be suspicious of "newly discovered" color-omitted errors on 20- or 30-year-old-stamps for which only a single example is purportedly known. This is especially true of used stamps.

Erasers have been used to remove colors from stamps, occasionally with treacherously deceptive results. Lithographed and gravure printed stamps are especially susceptible to this kind of tampering.

Used stamps are particularly susceptible to tampering. Fake used color-omitted "errors" are particularly abundant; therefore, our policy is to not list used color-omitted errors unless mint examples are also known.

Inverts. Clever fakes exist created by cutting a center design and inverting it in relation to its frame. The most clever of these do not cut entirely through the stamp's paper, so when viewed from the back, gum and paper appear intact.

Used Errors. Used errors should be checked carefully. Blind perfs can be ironed out and chemical treatments or other operations performed to remove colors without having to worry about disturbing original gum, tagging, or the pristineness of the stamp. Use caution.

Expertizing. The American Philatelic Expertizing Service (www.stamps.org), the Philatelic Foundation (www.philatelicfoundation.org), Professional Stamp Experts (www.gradingmatters.com) and Philatelic Stamp Authentication and Grading (www.stampauthentication.com) expertize error stamps. Visit their websites for information about their services. Obtain submission forms before submitting a stamp for an opinion.

HOW TO USE THE CATALOGUE

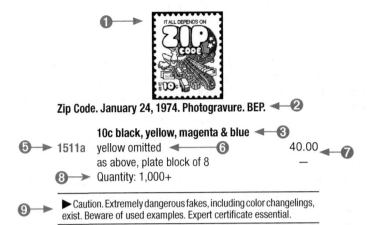

Zip Code. January 24, 1974. Photogravure. BEP.

10c black, yellow, magenta & blue

1511a   yellow omitted   40.00
         as above, plate block of 8   —
         Quantity: 1,000+

▶ Caution. Extremely dangerous fakes, including color changelings, exist. Beware of used examples. Expert certificate essential.

Listings are divided into sections according to type of error. Individual listings are arranged as follows:

1. Illustration

Illustrations bordered in black are those of error stamps. Most appear in color; however, in some cases where a color image was not available, a black-and-white image was used. In cases where we could not obtain the illustration of an error, the illustration of a normal stamp design—not bordered in black—is used. Illustrations of normal stamp designs are also used in cases where the image of the actual item does not adequately reveal a color-omitted error. Certain images were cropped from larger pieces, such as a block of four from a pane or a pair from a foldover booklet error. And in some cases, images were technically enhanced to better reveal the error, and images of some imperforate errors are simulations true to the actual error's appearance.

2. Description

Each error is described by the subject of the stamp, date of issue, form (se-tenant, souvenir sheet and so on) and method of printing. Perforation, watermark, and type are given only when necessary to distinguish one stamp from another of similar design. Printers are listed for stamps issued after 1980.

3. Description

Denomination and color(s) are given. Only color information necessary to identify the stamp is given for imperforate errors. For color-omitted errors, individual colors and the printing process used to apply them are given.

4. Designs

Where multiple stamp designs are contained se-tenant in an error, each individual design is identified.

5. Numbering

Errors are classified by category. Individual items within a category appear in numerical order.

A separate Scott catalogue number is assigned to each error or variety. Multiples, such as plate blocks, ZIP blocks and so on, are not separately numbered; they are regarded as varieties in form of the basic type.

Editor's Note. In this edition, some items appear with an asterisk (*) suffix. Such listings arise as a result of unresolved inconsistencies between listings in the *Scott Specialized Catalogue of United States Stamps & Covers* and listings in previous editions of *Errors on U.S. Postage Stamps*, as this catalogue was formerly known. The editor seeks documentable verification of these items, as indicated by the footnotes that accompany the asterisked listings.

6. Form

Following the catalogue number is a listing of the error in its basic or most commonly encountered form. Other forms of the error (such as plate blocks, used examples, covers and so on) are listed where known. The omission of a form does not necessarily imply that it does not exist, but only that it has not come to the attention of the editor.

7. Catalogue Value

Catalogue values are in U.S. dollars and are based on the best information available at press time. Auction prices, advertised retail prices, and editors' judgments have been weighed and blended in an attempt to reflect a reasonable idea of value.

Catalogue values are intended to reflect net retail prices, the price a consumer would expect to pay a dealer for stocking an item and making it available on demand. Retail prices reflect a dealer's cost of overhead and investment in inventory.

Auction prices are often either higher or lower than listed values and vary from sale to sale. In general, auction prices tend to be lower than retail prices for plentiful items or items sold in bulk. And they tend to be higher than listed values for items that rarely come to market, especially classic errors of premium quality.

In any case, there are no absolutes, and listed values are not intended as such. They are intended to be a general guide. Note as well that because the market determines values, prices for individual items may vary—up or down—from those listed herein. This is especially true for newly discovered errors. Actual market prices also vary according to condition.

Condition. Values are for sound stamps except where noted. Damaged or faulty examples usually sell for less, especially modern issues. Hinging is to be expected on issues before 1940, and values are for hinged examples in fine to very fine (F-VF) condition. Higher quality examples or never hinged (NH) examples usually command a premium—often substantial. For issues after 1940, values are for NH examples.

Italics. Catalogue values in italics are the editor's estimate where no precise information is available, such as newly discovered errors or infrequently traded errors. They should be regarded as tentative and subject to fluctuation. Actual market prices for these items may be either higher or lower.

Dash (—). A dash indicates that insufficient valuing information exists, e.g., infrequently traded items or varieties such as plate blocks and so on. Use of this symbol does not necessarily imply rarity.

Covers. Prices for used modern errors on cover are for timely usage. Philatelically inspired covers are usually worth much less.

Valuing anomalies. Errors frequently exist in similar quantities but with different catalogue values. Do not assume there is a consistent ratio of quantity to value. There is none. Classic errors, such as the 1869 inverts or the inverted Jenny, sell for much more than modern errors of similar quantity because values for classic rarities have been established over time.

Modern errors, as a group, are more plentiful. Generally, for modern errors—other factors being equal—the greater the eye appeal, the more dramatic and visually interesting the error, the greater its market price. Those with topical appeal also tend to sell for more. Plate or position error blocks tend not to command the premium that their normal counterparts do. Error plate or position multiples are generally not as much in demand among error collectors as their normal counterparts are among the general collecting community. Also, pressure often exists to break multiples, even plate blocks, because singles tend to be more salable than multiples.

8. Quantity

Quantities known or reliably reported to exist are given. The number given under quantity is for the number of error stamps irrespective of form (pairs, blocks and so on) unless otherwise stated. A quantity of 100 listed for an imperforate error means that 50 pairs could exist, or 25 blocks of four, or some combination. In many cases, the exact quantity existing is not ascertainable and, therefore, not given. Quantities given in italics are tentative and reflect the best information available at press time, which is often sketchy. Ranges are given, for example 50 to 100 pairs, where the general order of magnitude, but not the specific quantity, is acknowledged.

The term "reported" is used to indicate the quantity initially reported to exist. This number, especially for recently discovered errors, is subject to change. In addition, several general terms are used to indicate the quantity believed to exist where exact information is not available.

Unique. Only one example known.

Very Rare. Fewer than 10 examples.

Rare. Fewer than 25 examples.

Very Scarce. Fewer than 50 examples.

Scarce. Fewer than 100 examples.

Few Hundred. Generally, 100-300 examples.

Several Hundred. More than 300 examples.

Few Thousand. Generally, 1,000-3,000 examples.

Several Thousand. More than 3,000 examples.

N/A. Not available. No reliable information available.

9. Notes

Information of interest to the reader. Cautionary notes, for fakes and other potential problems, are given where appropriate and indicated by the symbol ▶.

DEFINITIONS

Blind Perforations

Incompletely or partially impressed perforations (or die cuts), often barely indented into the paper and giving stamps the appearance of being imperforate, or perforations incompletely cut (visible on one side of a pane of stamps but not visible on the other side) by the grinding technology employed for some issues in the 1990s.

Block

Four or more unseparated stamps arranged in a rectangle.

Booklet Pane

In the beginning, small sheetlets of stamps bound into booklets between card-stock covers by staples, thread or glue. More recently, panes containing self-adhesive stamps have been issued without separate covers. They can be folded and inserted into a wallet or purse, and are referred to as booklet panes.

Color Changeling

A stamp whose color(s) have been altered or eliminated by physical or chemical tampering. Certain stamp dyes are susceptible to alteration, especially bleaching by sunlight, heat, or chemicals. Color changelings are of no philatelic value.

EE Bars

Electric eye bars. Bars printed on margins of press sheets to guide them into position for perforating. These markings are normally trimmed off finished coil stamps.

Engraving

Also known as intaglio. A method of printing in which the design is engraved (recessed) into a metal plate. Ink fills the recesses and when printed, forms small ridges on the paper. Engraving can be identified by magnifying glass or by running your finger over the surface of the stamp and feeling the ridges.

Flat Press

A printing press that utilizes flat plates and prints paper one sheet at a time.

Imprint

A marginal inscription such as "American Bank Note Company." On modern issues "Use Zip Code," "Mail Early in the Day" and "Copyright USPS" often appear in margins.

Line Pair

On engraved, rotary-press coil stamps, a line is created by ink that fills the small space where the curved plates join and is printed in the same fashion as ink from the recessed stamp design.

Lithography

Also known as planographic or surface printing. This process is based on the antipathy of water and oil. A photographic image is exposed to a photosensitive plate. The area exposed becomes water insoluble. The unexposed, water-soluble area is washed away leaving an image that is receptive to ink. In some cases the inked image on the plate is transferred to a rubber-like blanket before being impressed on paper, hence the term "offset printing."

Images are broken up into a series of dots in order to achieve tonal gradation. Color lithography involves the mingling of areas of dots from several plates, each printing a separate color, in order to achieve the effect of full color. Because each printing plate lays down only a single color, passes beneath several plates are necessary in order to achieve the final, full-color result. These passes may occur in several press runs or in a single press run through a large press capable of mounting and running multiple plates. Lithographic stamp production typically involves from four to seven plates (colors). Color-omitted errors are produced when one or more plate impressions are omitted.

You can observe the dot structure of lithography by examining any black-and-white or color printing, for example from a magazine or stamp, under a 10-power or stronger glass. You will see how the dots are used to achieve tonal gradations and blend to make a variety of colors. In commercial printing, four plates (colors) are typically used to achieve the full-color effect: black, yellow, magenta (red) and cyan (blue). Stamp printing frequently employs additional plates, with a variety of specially mixed inks, in order to achieve a higher quality result.

Miscut

Cut abnormally so that portions of adjoining stamps appear together in the area normally occupied by a single design.

Pair

Two unseparated stamps.

Pane

A separate section of stamps, variously a quarter, half, or one-sixth sheet, as cut from a press sheet for retail sale.

Photogravure

Like lithography, the gravure plate is made by a photosensitive process; however, unlike lithography, the ink lies in small recesses and is very thinly applied. Tones are achieved by varying the depth of the recesses and thickness of the ink. The image is broken up into a series of fine points that keep the paper from being pressed into the recesses. The dot structure in photogravure is usually much finer than that used in lithography. You can see the difference by comparing a magazine illustration with a photogravure stamp under a 10-power magnifying glass.

Plate Number

A serial number usually appearing in the margin of a pane of stamps and, infrequently, on miscut coil or booklet stamps. Since about 1981, small plate numbers have appeared on coil stamps. They appear at predetermined intervals at the bottom of a stamp. The intervals vary from issue to issue; for example, every 24th or 52nd stamp or, depending on the issue, any of a number of other intervals. Multicolored stamps usually, but not always, have a separate plate number for each color used in printing.

Rotary Press

A printing press on which the plates are curved in the form of a cylinder to facilitate continuous printing on a web of paper.

Se-tenant

Two or more different designs printed next to one another on a regular pane of stamps, a souvenir sheet, a booklet, or a coil.

Splice

The splicing or joining of paper by glue or tape during stamp manufacture, typically in webfed rotary printing. Tape splices are known in a variety of colors and types of tape, including paper and plastic. Splices are often referred to as pasteups, a term originating from a time when most splices were made using glue or paste. At present, most, but not all, splices are made with tape. Splices on modern issues usually occur where paper from two web rolls has been joined during the printing process.

Strip

Three or more unseparated stamps arranged side by side or end to end.

Tagging

A luminescent coating applied during printing, used to facilitate the facing and handling of mail by automated machinery. Usually invisible to the naked eye, it can be observed under shortwave ultraviolet light. Tagging may cover all or part of a stamp.

Transition Multiple

A pair, strip, or block containing one or more error stamps, one or more normal stamps and, in the case of color-omitted errors, occasionally one or more stamps with color(s) partially omitted. Transition multiples usually sell for a premium.

Double Line Watermark

USPS

Single Line Watermark

Watermark

Letters impressed on paper during manufacture to discourage counterfeiting. Paper is thinner where the watermark has been impressed and, therefore, appears darker when immersed in watermark detecting fluid.

IMPERFORATE ERROR STAMPS

Typically, nineteenth century stamps are heavily hinged, contain only partial original gum and, often, small faults. Values are for stamps in such condition unless otherwise indicated. Sound stamps, stamps with full original gum, and lightly hinged examples sell for a premium.

SERIES OF 1857/61

Benjamin Franklin. July 1857. Engraved.

1c blue, type III

21a	hz pair, imperf between, used	*20,000.00*
	Quantity: 2 reported	

NOTE: A unique used vertical strip of 5 of No. 24, the 1c blue Franklin, type V of the Series of 1857, exists imperforate horizontally with a sixth stamp to the left of the next to bottom position. Each stamp in the strip has been irregularly torn between and hinged together. Because an unseparated-between pair does not exist, the item has not been accorded a separate listing. It is, nevertheless, a rarity and highly collectible. It is mentioned in Brookman, Volume I.

3c WASHINGTON TYPES - SERIES OF 1857/61

Type I. The outer frame line is intact on all four sides. The inner frame line is not recut.
Type II. Same as Type I, but inner frame lines are recut.
Type III. No outer frame lines at top and bottom. The side frame lines are continuous from stamp to stamp.
Type IV. Same as Type III, but side frame lines are not continuous from stamp to stamp, being broken between stamps.

George Washington. 1857. Engraved.

3c rose, type I

25b	vrt pair, imperf hz, used	*10,000.00*
	single on cover, used	*2,650.00*
	severed pair on cover	*3,000.00*
	Quantity: 1 pair and 2 on cover,	
	as listed above	

The severed pair on cover is postmarked "Hermon, NY, Nov. 10."

Beware of examples with blind perfs. No. 25b was printed from the same plates as the imperforate 1851 series. Regularly issued imperforate stamps of the 1851 series should not be confused with errors of the 1857 series. Also, proofs of the 1851 series in issued colors were printed on bond paper very similar in appearance to stamp paper. The two are so similar that it is very difficult, especially for the unpracticed eye, to distinguish one from another.

3c dull red, type III

26b	hz pair, imperf vrt	*14,000.00*
	imprint margin single, imperf vrt	*6,100.00*
	Quantity: very rare	

26c	vrt pair, imperf hz	16,000.00
	vrt pair, imperf hz, used	18,000.00
	vrt pair and single, imperf hz, on piece	14,000.00
	strip of 3, imperf hz, used on cover	24,000.00
	Quantity: very rare	

| 26d | used hz pair, imperf between | — |
| | Quantity: very rare | |

3c dull red, type IV

26Af	hz strip of 3, imperf vrt, on cover	14,500.00
	single, imperf vrt	—
	Quantity: the two items as listed	

The example listed on cover is postmarked "Boston, Ms. Apr. 20, 1859," in red, contains two black grid cancels, and is addressed to St. Louis. The left stamp in the strip has a closed tear.

George Washington. 1857. Engraved.

12c black

36c	hz pair, imperf between, used	12,500.00
	Quantity: very rare	

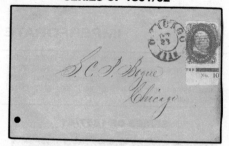

Benjamin Franklin. August 17, 1861. Engraved.

1c blue

63d	vrt pair, imperf hz, used	—
	margin single on cover	—
	Quantity: the used pair is possibly unique;	
	the margin single used on cover is unique	

The unique margin single used on cover contains a blue circular postmark reading "Chicago, Ills. Oct. 23" together with a blue grid. It is addressed to "S. C. P. Bogue, Chicago." The selvage contains part of the marginal inscription, including "No. 10."

George Washington. August 17, 1861. Engraved.

3c rose

65d	vrt pair, imperf hz	15,000.00
	upper left margin block of 4, without gum	14,500.00
	vrt pair, imperf hz, used	1,500.00
	Quantity: rare	

See also Nos. 65Pc and 66TCa in the Error-Like Imperforates section.

George Washington. August 17, 1861. Engraved.

10c yellow green

68b	vrt pair, imperf hz, used	30,000.00
	Quantity: very rare, possibly unique	

STAMPS WITH GRILLS

Grills, wafflelike in appearance, were impressed on stamps to break their paper fibers and permit better ink absorption, preventing washing and reuse. Several types of grills exist.

A grill: points up, grill covers entire stamp.
C grill: points up, grill measures about 13x16 mm.
F grill: points down, grill measures about 9x13 mm.

George Washington. 1867. Engraved.

	3c red, F grill	
94c	vrt pair, imperf hz	*15,000.00*
	bottom left margin block of 4	*43,500.00*
	Quantity: very rare	

See also Nos. 79P, 83P and 94P in the Error-Like Imperforates section.

▶ Caution: Nineteenth century stamps often occur with large margins that can be trimmed to resemble imperforates. Single stamps, even margin examples, should be regarded with suspicion. Imperforate singles without expert certificate should be avoided.

SERIES OF 1869
SPECIAL PRINTING OF 1875

Columbus. 1875. Engraved. National Bank Note Co.

	15c brown & blue	
129a	single, imperf hz	*5,000.00*
	used single, imperf hz	*30,000.00*
	Quantity: 10-15 unused; 2 used	

Often without gum and typically scissors separated along at least one perforated edge. Value is for an example without gum. Those with gum sell for a premium of 50% or more depending on the state of the gum. A premium quality unused example sold at auction for $20,125 in September 2010. No multiples exist. See also the Series of 1869 in the Error-Like Imperforates section.

SERIES OF 1873

Benjamin Franklin. 1873. Engraved. Secret mark.

	1c ultramarine	
156f	imperf pair	—
	imperf pair, used	*1,500.00*
	imperf strip of 3, used	—
	Quantity: approx 15 pairs, including	
	2 unused pairs	

Many are toned and creased. Value is for toned and creased pair. May not have been regularly issued.

George Washington. 1873. Engraved. Secret mark.

	3c green	
158h	hz pair, imperf vrt, used	—
	Quantity: n/a	
158i	hz pair, imperf between, used	*1,300.00*
	Quantity: rare	

Thomas Jefferson. 1873. Engraved. Secret mark.

	10c brown	
161d	hz pair, imperf between	—
	hz pair, imperf between, used	*15,000.00*
	Quantity: 2 pairs reported	

SERIES OF 1894

This series is similar to the Series of 1890 except that triangles were added to the upper corners. Printed on unwatermarked paper.

George Washington. October 5, 1894. Engraved.

2c pink, type I

248a	vrt pair, imperf hz	5,500.00
	Quantity: 3-4 pairs	

2c carmine, type I

250d	hz pair, imperf between	2,000.00
	Quantity: rare	

2c carmine, type III

252b	hz pair, imperf vrt	5,000.00
	Quantity: rare	

252c	hz pair, imperf between	5,500.00
	Quantity: rare	

Ulysses S. Grant. September 28, 1894. Engraved.

5c chocolate

255c	vrt pair, imperf hz	3,500.00
	vrt strip of 3, imperf hz	—
	block of 4, imperf hz	—
	vrt block of 6, imperf hz	4,500.00
	block of 9 with plate No. 130	
	and imprint	15,000.00
	Quantity: uncertain, but less	
	than one pane of 100	

Often heavily hinged or with disturbed gum. Values are for sound examples. Faulty examples sell for less.

James A. Garfield. July 18, 1894. Engraved.

6c brown

256a	vrt pair, imperf hz	3,000.00
	block of 4, imperf hz	—
	vrt block of 6, imperf hz	6,000.00
	top block of 9 with plate No. 28	
	and imprint	—
	bottom block of 6 with plate	
	No. 28 and imprint	30,000.00
	Quantity: 100	

Usually with disturbed gum or faults. Values are for sound examples. Faulty examples sell for less.

NOTE: See also the Error-Like Imperforates section for other issues of the Series of 1890/93, the Series of 1894, and the Series of 1895.

Hinging. Values for stamps preceding No. 899a are for hinged examples. Never hinged examples sell for a premium ranging from 25% to 100% or more depending on the scarcity of the item, and the scarcity of never hinged examples of the item. These guidelines do not apply to values for ultra-rare or unique items, which may not exist never hinged.

Troops Guarding Train. June 1898. Engraved.

8c violet brown

289a	vrt pair, imperf hz	27,500.00
	as above, line pair	—
	vrt strip of 4, imperf hz	—
	block of 4, top or bottom plate	
	No. 609, imperf hz	160,000.00
	Quantity: 25 pairs, including those	
	in blocks	

Value is for a sound example.

George Washington. November 12, 1903. Engraved.

2c carmine

319d	vrt pair, imperf hz	7,500.00
	vrt strip of 3, imperf hz	—
	block of 4, imperf hz	—
	Quantity: 1 pair, 1 strip of three,	
	2 blocks of four, and one block of 6	

319e	vrt pair, imperf between	—
	Quantity: 10 pairs	

▶ Caution. Do not confuse Nos. 319d and 319e with similar stamps of 1906 that were regularly issued imperforate. Expert certificate recommended.

Pairs similar to No. 319e exist rouletted between. Panes lacking perforations between the top two rows were rouletted by the postmaster in San Francisco and sold over the counter in the normal course of business. Value for a pair rouletted between: $3,250.00.

Thomas Jefferson. April 30, 1904. Engraved.

2c carmine

324a	vrt pair, imperf hz	25,000.00
	as above, line pair	—
	block of 4, imperf hz	55,000.00
	plate block of 4, imperf hz	75,000.00
	margin block of 4, arrow at lower	
	left, imperf hz	—
	Quantity: 19 pairs & 3 blocks as listed	

Well-centered examples sell for a premium.

William H. Seward. June 1909. Engraved.

2c carmine

370a	block of 6, imperf, P#5209	
	Quantity: n/a	

No. 370a comes from error panes found in perforated stock. No. 370a can only be collected as a plate-number stamp or multiple. Without attached plate number, stamps from the error panes cannot be differentiated from No. 371.

George Washington. February 12, 1912. Engraved. Single-line watermark. Perf 12.

1c green

405a	vrt pair, imperf hz	2,000.00
	vrt strip of three, imperf hz	—
	Quantity: rare	

▶ Caution. Do not confuse No. 405a with stamps of identical design that were regularly issued imperforate. Expert certificate recommended.

George Washington. 1914. Engraved. Single-line watermark. Perf 10.

1c green

424c	vrt pair, imperf hz	3,000.00
	used vrt pair, imperf hz	2,750.00
Quantity: very rare		

▶ Research has proven beyond doubt that all examples of the previously listed No. 424e, booklet pane of 6, imperforate and without gum, are unissued fabrications made from an ungummed press sheet on stamp paper once undoubtedly housed in the Smithsonian philatelic collection.

424f   vrt pair, imperf between   *13,000.00*
        Quantity: unique

No. 424f results from a foldover in which the upper right pair on a pane is imperf between and contains a straight edge at the top.

George Washington. 1917. Engraved. Unwatermarked. Perf 11.

     1c green
498a   vrt pair, imperf hz   800.00
        block of 4, imperf hz   *1,500.00*
        Quantity: 1 pane of 100 reported
Often in strips of 3.

498b   hz pair, imperf between   600.00
        block of 8, including 2 error pairs
          and plate No. 10656 in right selvage   —
        block of 15, including 3 error
          pairs and plate No. 10656
          in right selvage   *2,550.00*
        Quantity: scarce

Blocks with plate numbers occur in varying sizes.

498c   vrt pair, imperf between   *700.00*
        Quantity: scarce

▶   Caution. Beware of fakes of Nos. 498a-499c fabricated by adding perforations to completely imperforate regularly issued stamps of identical design. Expert certificate strongly advised.

George Washington. 1917. Engraved. Unwatermarked. Perf 11.

     2c rose, type I
499a   vrt pair, imperf hz   1,000.00
        block of 6, including 2 error
          pairs and plate No. 7945
          in left selvage   —
        Quantity: n/a

499b   hz pair, imperf vrt   *550.00*
        hz pair, imperf vrt, used   *600.00*
        Quantity: 100 pairs reported

499c   vrt pair, imperf between   900.00
       vrt pair, imperf between, used   300.00
       Quantity: very scarce

▶ Caution. Pairs are known with blind perfs that can be ironed out and eliminated to the naked eye, resulting in dangerous fakes. Pairs are also known with blind perfs occurring in the upper stamp due to a wandering perforating wheel. Pairs should be checked carefully. Examples lacking gum should be regarded with special caution. Expert certificate strongly advised.

George Washington. 1917. Engraved. Unwatermarked. Perf. 11.

3c light violet, type I

501c   vrt pair, imperf hz   2,100.00
       Quantity: 25 pairs

3c dark violet, type II

502c   vrt pair, imperf hz   1400.00
       vrt pair, imperf hz, used   850.00
       as above, on cover   1,400.00
       Quantity: 40-50 pairs reported

George Washington. 1917. Engraved. Unwatermarked. Perf 11.

5c blue

504a   hz pair, imperf between   20,000.00
       hz pair, plate No. 8902 in top
         margin, imperf between   25,000.00
       Quantity: 2 pairs

Benjamin Franklin. 1917. Engraved. Umwatermarked. Perf 11.

8c olive bister

508b   vrt pair, imperf between   —
       vrt pair, imperf between, used   —
       Quantity: 1 pair unused and
        2 pair used reported

▶ Caution. Beware of blind perfs.

Benjamin Franklin. 1917. Engraved. Unwatermarked. Perf 11.

20c light ultramarine

515b   vrt pair, imperf between   1,750.00
       as above, used   3,250.00
       Quantity: rare, used pair
        possibly unique

Usually poorly centered. Value is for a poorly centered example.

▶ Caution. No. 515b is often encountered with blind perfs that can be ironed out and eliminated to the naked eye, resulting in dangerous fakes. Examples lacking gum should be regarded with special caution. The discovery panes contained mostly pairs with blind perforations and yielded only about 5 truly imperf pairs per pane. Blind-perf pairs are comparatively plentiful and deceptive.

Benjamin Franklin. 1917. Engraved. Unwatermarked. Perf 11.

50c red violet
517b   vrt pair, imperf between and with
natural straight edge at bottom;
precanceled AKRON, OHIO   *6,000.00*
Quantity: unique

▶ Caution. Beware of pairs with blind perfs.

George Washington. 1918. Offset lithography.
Unwatermarked. Perf 11.

1c gray green
525c   hz pair, imperf between   *750.00*
as above, used   *650.00*
Quantity: rare, at least 3 used pairs

George Washington. 1920. Offset lithography.
Unwatermarked. Perf 11.

2c carmine, type V
527b   vrt pair, imperf hz   *850.00*
Quantity: 2-3 pairs reported

527c   hz pair, imperf vrt   *1,000.00*
hz pair, imperf vrt, used   —
Quantity: n/a

2c carmine, type Va
528g   vrt pair, imperf between   *3,250.00*
Quantity: rare

2c carmine, type VI
528Af   vrt pair, imperf hz   —
Quantity: very rare

528Ah   vrt pair, imperf between   *5,000.00*
left margin block of 4, imperf
between, with plate No. 11641   —
Quantity: very rare

▶ Caution. Do not confuse Nos. 527b-528Ah with the regularly
issued imperforates of the same design.

George Washington. 1919. Offset lithography.
Unwatermarked. Perf 12½.

1c gray green
536a   hz pair, imperf vrt   *1,000.00*
block of 4, imperf vrt   *4,500.00*
Quantity: n/a

540b   hz pair, imperf vrt   *2,000.00*
Quantity: 25 pairs

George Washington. 1921. Engraved. Rotary press.
Unwatermarked. Design 19 by 22½mm. Perf 10.

1c green
543a   hz pair, imperf between   *4,500.00*
Quantity: rare

Often occurs in a multiple containing two pairs.

SERIES OF 1922/26

Stamps of 1922/26 series were printed by flat plate press and were normally perforated 11. Designs measure 18½ to 19mm by 22mm.

George Washington. January 15, 1923. Engraved. Flat plate press.

2c carmine

554a	hz pair, imperf vrt	250.00
	plate block of 6, imperf vrt	—
	Quantity: few hundred	

Exists misperfed horizontally.

554b	vrt pair, imperf hz	*6,000.00*
	Quantity: 3 pairs reported	

▶ Caution. Beware of fakes of Nos. 554a and 554b fabricated from regularly issued imperforate stamps of the same design. Expert certificate advised.

Martha Washington. January 15, 1923. Engraved. Flat plate press.

4c yellow brown

556a	vrt pair, imperf hz	*12,500.00*
	Quantity: unique	

The listed example occurs in a block of 9. Another pair is known in a block of 8, but the pair lacking perforations is torn and has been repaired.

Theodore Roosevelt. October 27, 1922. Engraved. Flat plate press.

5c dark blue

557a	imperf pair	*2,000.00*
	plate block of 6, imperf	*29,000.00*
	Quantity: 1 pane of 100; 2 plate blocks	

Never hinged pairs are rare and sell for 200%-300% more.

557b	hz pair, imperf vrt	—
	Quantity: 10 pairs reported	

James Monroe. January 15, 1923. Engraved. Flat plate press.

10c orange

562a	vrt pair, imperf hz	*2,000.00*
	block of 4	—
	Quantity: 50 pairs	

Sound lightly hinged examples sell for a premium of 100% or more. Never hinged examples are rare and sell for a premium of 200%-300% or more. Most are poorly centered. Well-centered pairs sell for a premium. Twenty-seven pairs contain splicing paper on the reverse or blue pencil marks on the front. All pairs originally contained penciled position numbers on the reverse. The numbers are absent on regummed pairs.

562b	imperf pair	*1,750.00*
	block of 4, imperf	*6,250.00*
	plate block of 6	*24,000.00*
	Quantity: 2 panes	

Both panes contained large areas defaced by inspector's blue pencil marks. It is estimated that only 40 to 50 unmarked pairs exist. Blue pencil marked pairs sell for less. No. 562b was issued without gum.

Rutherford Hayes. October 4, 1922. Engraved. Flat plate press.

11c light blue
563d   imperf vert pair, precanceled
     SAN FRANCISCO, CALIFORNIA   *20,000.00*
    imperf vrt strip of 3, precanceled
     as above   —
    Quantity: 1 pair nearly severed by scissors
     cut and 1 strip of 3 reported

Grover Cleveland. May 20, 1923. Engraved. Flat plate press.

12c brown violet
564a   hz pair, imperf vrt   *3,750.00*
    block of 4, imperf vrt   —
    hz transition strip of 4, imperf vrt   —
    Quantity: 15 pairs reported
     including those in the multiples

Often without gum or with government splicing paper on the reverse. Exists misperfed horizontally. Value is for an impaired example. Sound examples sell for a premium of 100% or more.

Imperforate pairs of No. 564 almost certainly are trimmed from pairs of No. 564a that occurred at the top of the pane and contained a natural straight edge along the top edge.

Golden Gate. May 1, 1923. Engraved. Flat plate press.

20c carmine rose
567a   hz pair, imperf vrt   *2,500.00*
    pair with plate No. 19646 at left,
     imperf vrt   —
    block of 4, imperf vrt   —
    Quantity: 50 pairs

Niagara Falls. November 11, 1922. Engraved. Flat plate press.

25c yellow green
568b   vrt pair, imperf hz   *3,250.00*
    vrt strip of 3, imperf hz   *3,600.00*
    block with plate No. 14063 at right,
     imperf hz   *14,500.00*
    Quantity: rare

Refer to the Printer's Waste section for imperforate, underinked and ungummed examples of the Series of 1922/26.

Theodore Roosevelt. 1925. Engraved. Rotary press. Perf 10.

5c blue
586a   hz pair, imperf vrt precanceled
     PORTLAND, OREGON   *7,500.00*
    Quantity: very rare, possibly unique

Warren G. Harding. September 1, 1923. Engraved. Flat plate press. Design measures 19¼mm by 22¼mm.

2c black
610a   hz pair, imperf vrt   *2,000.00*
    Quantity: one pane of 100

▶ Caution. Beware of fakes fabricated from regularly issued imperforate stamps of the same design. Expert certificate strongly advised. Most pairs are centered to bottom. Value is for an example centered to bottom. Well-centered pairs sell for more.

610b   block of 12, plate No. 14870
         in left selvage, imperf   *25,000.00*
         block of 15, plate No. 14870
         in top selvage, imperf   —
         Quantity: 2-3 blocks

Plate No. 14870 was not used to print the regularly issued imperforate stamp (No. 611) and thus blocks with this plate number can be distinguished as an error.

NOTE: A spliced block of 20 with left selvage and plate number exists for No. 629, the White Plains commemorative of 1926, that gives the appearance of containing two pairs lacking perforations between. The omission of perforations occurs at the splice, which was made during production. For that reason, the pairs have not been accorded a catalogue listing as an error. The block is, nevertheless, a unique and collectible item.

Benjamin Franklin. June 10, 1927. Engraved. Rotary press. Perf 11x10½.

1c green

632b   vrt pair, imperf between   *3,000.00*
         as above, used   *3,250.00*
         Quantity: rare

Never hinged examples have sold for as much as $10,000.00.

632c   hz pair, imperf between   *5,000.00*
         Quantity: very rare, possibly unique

George Washington. December 10, 1926. Engraved. Perf 11x10½.

2c carmine

634c   hz pair, imperf between   *6,000.00*
         Quantity: very rare

William McKinley. March 24, 1927. Engraved. Rotary press. Perf 11x10½.

7c black

639a   vrt pair, imperf between   550.00
         as above, used   400.00
         block of 4, imperf between hz   —
         Quantity: 20 pairs, 2 blocks of 4

639a   vrt pair, imperf between,
         precanceled MOBILE, ALA.   *225.00*
         Quantity: n/a

▶ Caution. Both the regular and the precanceled varieties of No. 639a are known with blind perfs that can be ironed out and eliminated to the naked eye, resulting in dangerous fakes. Examples lacking gum should be regarded with special caution. Expert certificate advised.

Sullivan Expedition. June 17, 1929. Engraved.

2c carmine rose

657b	vrt pair, imperf between	*4,000.00*
	Quantity: unique	

No. 657b is the result of a foldover and exists in a block of 6.

General Von Steuben. September 17, 1930. Engraved.

2c carmine rose

689a	imperf pair	*2,000.00*
	block of 4, imperf	*4,500.00*
	plate block of 6, imperf	*12,500.00*
	Quantity: 1 pane of 100	

Yorktown Sesquicentennial. October 19, 1931. Engraved.

2c carmine rose & black

703c	hz pair, imperf vrt	7,000.00
	block of 4, imperf vrt	—
	hz block of 6, imperf vrt	—
	hz center line block of 10	*35,000.00*
	top plate block of 10	*37,500.00*
	bottom plate block of 10	*35,000.00*
	Quantity: 1 pane of 50 of which 15 pairs are in the 3 large position blocks individually listed above	

George Washington Bicentennial. June 16, 1932. Engraved.

3c deep violet

720c	vrt pair, imperf between	*725.00*
	used pair, imperf between	*1,750.00*
	Quantity: several unused pairs, several used pairs	

720c	as above, precanceled
	PHILADELPHIA, PENNSYLVANIA —

Quantity: 3 precanceled pairs

▶ Caution. Pairs exist with blind perforations that can be ironed out and eliminated to the naked eye, resulting in dangerous fakes. Examples lacking gum should be regarded with special caution.

William Penn. October 24, 1932. Engraved.

3c violet

724a	vrt pair, imperf hz	—
	Quantity: very rare	

General Tadeusz Kosciuszko. October 13, 1933. Engraved.

5c blue

734a	hz pair, imperf vrt	*1,750.00*
	block of 4, imperf vrt	*4,500.00*
	bottom plate block of 8, imperf vrt	*35,000.00*
	Quantity: 1 pane of 100 stamps	

Often with heavy natural gum creases or bends.

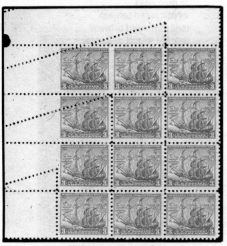

Maryland Tercentenary. May 23, 1934. Engraved.

3c carmine rose

736a	hz pair, imperf between	*4,000.00*
	Quantity: unique	

A single unique pair of No. 736a exists in an upper left block of 12 stamps, the error resulting from a foldover.

Wisconsin Tercentenary. July 7, 1934. Engraved.

3c deep violet

739a	vrt pair, imperf hz	*575.00*
	Quantity: n/a	

739b	hz pair, imperf vrt	*1,000.00*
	bottom plate block of 10, imperf vrt	*6,500.00*
	Quantity: approx 80 pairs reported	

NATIONAL PARK SERIES OF 1934

The items listed below are errors of the fully gummed, perforated stamps of National Parks issue. They are similar in appearance to the Farley Special Printing, which was issued fully imperforate and without gum. Refer to the Error-Like Imperforates section for Farley/Roosevelt favor items.

▶ Caution. Beware of fakes of Nos. 739a-746a fabricated from completely imperforate stamps of identical designs from the Farley Special Printing of 1935, which were issued without gum. In 1940, the Bureau of Engraving & Printing offered to gum Farley Special Printing sheets submitted by collectors. Therefore, presence of government gum on part-perforate stamps is not necessarily an indication of genuineness. Expert certificate advised for part-perforate error stamps that have Farley Special Printing counterparts.

Yosemite. July 16, 1934. Engraved.

1c green

740a	vrt pair, imperf hz, with gum	*1,750.00*
	Quantity: 16 pairs or strips of three	

▶ Caution. Fakes exist. All known genuine examples are signed "S.A." (Spencer Anderson) on the reverse in indelible pencil. Those rubber stamped "Sloane" are fakes.

Grand Canyon. July 24, 1934. Engraved.

2c red

741a	vrt pair, imperf hz, with gum	800.00
	plate block of 6, imperf hz, with gum	—
	Quantity: 2-3 panes	

741b	hz pair, imperf vrt, with gum	1,000.00
	plate block of 6, imperf vrt, with gum	*3,500.00*
	Quantity: 2-3 panes	

741c	block of 20, imperf, P#21261	*7,500.00*
	Quantity: unique	

No. 741c is a unique bottom margin plate #21261 block of 20. This plate was not used to print the imperforate Farley special printing, No. 757. Loose stamps separated from this block or from other possible imperforate No. 741 Plate #21261 blocks are indistinguishable from gummed examples of No. 757.

▶ Caution. Fakes exist. See the note following 740a.

Mt. Rainier. August 3, 1934. Engraved.

3c deep violet

742a	vrt pair, imperf hz, with gum	1,000.00
	plate block of 6, imperf hz, with gum	—
	Quantity: 1 pane	

▶ Caution. Fakes exist. See the note following No. 740a.

Mesa Verde. September 25, 1934. Engraved.

4c brown

743a	vrt pair, imperf hz, with gum	*3,500.00*
	Quantity: 15 pairs	

Approximately 6 to 9 of the 15 known pairs have brown Post Office paper affixed to the reverse. Examples without brown paper sell for a 50% to 100% premium or more.

Yellowstone. July 30, 1934. Engraved.

5c blue

744a	hz pair, imperf vrt, with gum	*1,500.00*
	plate block of 6	—
	Quantity: 50 pairs	

▶ Caution. Fakes exist. See the note following No. 740a.

Acadia. October 2, 1934. Engraved.

7c black

746a	hz pair, imperf vrt, with gum	*1,250.00*
	plate block of 6, imperf vrt, with never hinged gum	*6,000.00*
	Quantity: 50 pairs	

▶ Caution. Fakes exist. See the note following No. 740a.

PRESIDENTIAL SERIES OF 1938

Martha Washington. May 5, 1938. Engraved.

1½c bister brown
805b   hz pair, imperf between   100.00
        Quantity: n/a

805b   hz pair, imperf between,
        precanceled SAINT LOUIS, MO.   20.00
        Quantity: few thousand

Thomas Jefferson. June 16, 1938. Engraved.

3c deep violet
807b   hz pair, imperf between   *2,000.00*
        block, with 1 error pair   *2,500.00*
        Quantity: several pairs known

No. 807b occurs in sheet stamps, one error pair at a time. It exists in individual pair form, as well as within a block. Blocks typically range in size from 12 to 20 stamps, which illustrate how the error pair occurs as a result of defective or missing perforating pins.

807c   imperf pair   *3,500.00*

▶ Caution. The 3c Jefferson was counterfeited to defraud the post office. Counterfeits were lithographed and thus can be distinguished from engraved genuine stamps. Gum on counterfeits lacks the gum breaking ridges found on genuine stamps and is much more yellow than gum on genuine stamps.

807d   booklet pane, imperf vrt btwn   *5,000.00*
        booklet pane, imperf vrt btwn,
            vrt gutter btwn   —
        Quantity: very rare

▶ The booklet pane with the vertical gutter contains 3 error pairs plus 6 additional stamps or parts of stamps, one on either side of each error pair.

Woodrow Wilson. August 29, 1938. Engraved.

$1 purple & black
832a   vrt pair, imperf hz   *1,100.00*
        top plate block of 8, imperf hz *7,500.00*
        arrow block of 6, imperf hz   —
        Quantity: 50 pairs reported, including
            the unique plate block

832e   vrt pair, imperf between   *7,500.00*
        Quantity: very rare

Woodrow Wilson. August 31, 1954. Engraved.

$1 red violet & black
832d   vrt pair, imperf hz   *900.00*
        Quantity: 1-2 panes of 100 reported

832f   vrt pair, imperf between   10,000.00
       block of 4, imperf hz between   —
       Quantity: 10 pairs

No. 832d and No. 832f were printed by the dry process on somewhat thicker paper than that of No. 832a and No. 832e. The gum of the 1954 stamps is smooth and clear, and the purple color is decidedly more reddish than that of the 1938 issue.

HINGING. Catalogue values from this point forward are for never hinged examples. Hinged examples sell for less.

NATIONAL DEFENSE SERIES OF 1940

Statue of Liberty. October 16, 1940. Engraved.

      1c bright blue green
899a   vrt pair, imperf between   600.00
       vrt pair, imperf between, used   —
       Quantity: 100-200 pairs reported

899b   hz pair, imperf between   32.50
       Quantity: several thousand pairs

899b   hz pair, imperf between, precanceled
       GLENDALE, CALIF.   75.00
       Quantity: n/a

899b   hz pair, imperf between,
       precanceled BROCKTON, MASS.   —
       Quantity: n/a

▶ Caution. Often with blind perfs or a few punched perf holes.

Anti-aircraft gun. October 16, 1940. Engraved.

      2c rose carmine
900a   hz pair, imperf between   37.50
       Quantity: several thousand

▶ Caution. Often with blind perfs or few punched perf holes.

Torch. October 16, 1940. Engraved.

      3c bright violet
901a   hz pair, imperf between   22.50
       Quantity: several thousand

▶ Caution. Often with blind perfs or a few punched perf holes.

Mt. Palomar. August 30, 1948. Engraved.

      3c blue
966a   vrt pair, imperf between   300.00
       plate block of 4, imperf vrt between 700.00
       Quantity: 450+ pairs, 15+ plate
         blocks (each with 2 pairs) reported

LIBERTY SERIES OF 1954

Statue of Liberty. June 24, 1954. Engraved.

3c deep violet
1035f	imperf pair	*3,000.00*
	block of 6, imperf	—
	Quantity: 5-10 pairs reported	

Statue of Liberty. June 30, 1954. Booklet pane of 6. Engraved.

3c deep violet
1035b	booklet pane with hz pair,	
	imperf between	*5,000.00*
	Quantity: very rare	

No. 1035b occurs as the result of a foldover or, in at least one case, as the result of a miscut.

1035g	vrt pair, imperf between	*1,000.00*
	Quantity: 5-10 pair	

Abraham Lincoln. July 31, 1958. Booklet pane of 6. Engraved.

4c red violet
1036c	booklet pane of 6, imperf hz	*10,000.00*
	Quantity: very rare, possibly unique	
1036d	hz pair, imperf between	*4,000.00*
	Quantity: very rare, possibly unique	

No. 1036d occurs as the result of a booklet pane foldover.

Theodore Roosevelt. March 1957. Engraved. Dry printing. BEP.

6c carmine
1039b	imperf block of 4 LRS (7/00)	*23,000.00*
	Quantity: 1 block of 4	

COIL STAMPS

George Washington. October 8, 1954. Coil. Engraved.

1c dark green
1054c	imperf pair	*3,000.00*
	as above, used	*1,000.00*
	strip of 4, unused on cover,	
	including 3 error stamps	*3,500.00*
	Quantity: 13 unused pairs, strip of 4 on cover	

The strip of 4 on cover is affixed to an unused DAV reply envelope.

Palace of the Governors. June 17, 1960. Engraved. BEP.

1¼c turquoise
1054Ad imperf pair, precanceled
SEATTLE, WASH. —
line pair or strip —
Quantity: 13 stamps

The discovery strip contained 13 stamps including a line pair. The listing contemplates that the discovery strip may be broken into a multiple containing the line, either as a pair or strip of 4.

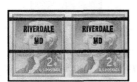

Thomas Jefferson. October 22, 1954. Coil. Engraved.

2c carmine rose
1055c imperf pair, precanceled
RIVERDALE, MD *325.00*
line pair, imperf *1,200.00*
Quantity: 200 pairs reported

1055d imperf pair *425.00*
line pair, imperf *1,100.00*
spliced pair or strip, imperf —
Quantity: 100 pairs reported

Transition multiples exist.

Statue of Liberty. July 20, 1954. Coil. Engraved.

3c deep violet
1057b imperf pair *1,250.00*
as above, used *800.00*
line pair, imperf *2,750.00*
used strip of 3, imperf —
Quantity: 30 pairs reported

Abraham Lincoln. July 31, 1958. Coil. Engraved.

4c red violet

1058a imperf pair 75.00
line pair, imperf *225.00*
spliced pair or strip, imperf —
imperf pair, used 70.00
Quantity: 500+ pairs

Exists miscut and miscut with EE bars showing at top. Transition multiples exist and sell for a premium.

1058a imperf pair, precanceled
SEATTLE, WASH.
Quantity: rare —

Paul Revere. February 25, 1965. Coil. Engraved.

25c green
1059Ac imperf pair, untagged, shiny gum —
line pair, imperf —
Quantity: n/a

The editors question the existence of No. 1059Ac.

1059Ad imperf pair, tagged, shiny gum 30.00
line pair, imperf 65.00
spliced pair or strip, imperf —
Quantity: n/a

No. 1059Ac is identical to No. 1059Ad except for tagging.

No. 1059Ad exists miscut. Most examples are poorly centered. Values are for poorly centered examples. Well-centered examples sell for 50% more. Transition multiples exist and sell for a premium.

Jose de San Martin. February 25, 1959. Engraved.

4c blue
1125a hz pair, imperf between *900.00*
Quantity: 20 pairs reported

Often poorly centered. Value is for a poorly centered example. Occasionally occurs in transition strips of 5.

Ephraim McDowell. December 3, 1959. Engraved.

4c rose lake

1138a	vrt pair, imperf between	375.00
	Quantity: 75+ pairs reported	

1138b	vrt pair, imperf hz	200.00
	plate block of 4, imperf hz	—
	Quantity: 210 pairs reported	

Thomas G. Masaryk. March 7, 1960. Engraved.

4c blue

1147a	vrt pair, imperf between	1,900.00
	Quantity: 10 pairs	

Thomas G. Masaryk. March 7, 1960. Engraved.

8c carmine, ultramarine & ocher

1148a	hz pair, imperf between	—
	Quantity: 3 pairs reported	

SEATO. May 31, 1960. Engraved.

4c blue

1151a	vrt pair, imperf between	125.00
	plate block of 4, imperf hz between	—
	Quantity: 100-200 pairs reported	

Appomattox. April 9, 1965. Engraved.

5c Prussian blue & black

1182a	hz pair, imperf vrt	3,500.00
	Quantity: very rare	

▶ Caution. Pairs exist with nearly invisible blind perfs. Expert certificate advised.

Winslow Homer. December 15, 1962. Engraved.

4c multicolored

1207a	hz pair, imperf between	7,000.00
	hz pair with plate No.,	
	imperf between	—
	Quantity: 4 pairs reported	

▶ Caution. Pairs exist with blind perfs. Expert certificate advised.

U. S. Flag. January 9, 1963. Engraved.

5c blue & red
1208b hz pair, imperf between　　　　2,250.00
Quantity: 3-4 pairs reported

▶ Caution. Pairs exist with blind perfs. Expert certificate advised.

George Washington. November 23, 1962. Booklet pane. Engraved.

5c dark blue gray
1213d hz pair, imperf between　　　　1,750.00
hz pair (1 stamp, 1 label),
　imperf between　　　　　　　　—
booklet pane, imperf vrt between　—
Quantity: rare

No. 1213d results from foldovers or miscut booklet panes and also exists se-tenant with label containing slogan. At least half a dozen individually unique panes exist, including at least one that contains two error pairs. Recent auction prices for panes have ranged between $1,400 and $4,000.

George Washington. November 23, 1962. Coil. Engraved.

5c dark blue gray

1229b imperf pair　　　　　　　　　300.00
line pair, imperf　　　　　　　　900.00
spliced strip of 8 with 2 line pairs　—
Quantity: 50+ pairs reported

Transition multiples exist and sell for a premium. Exists tagged and untagged. Often with gum problems. Value is for example with sound gum.

Christmas. November 1, 1963. Engraved.

5c multicolored
1240b hz pair, imperf between　　　　7,500.00
Quantity: unique

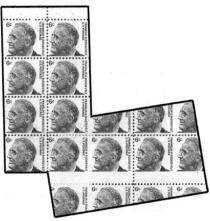

Franklin D. Roosevelt. December 28, 1967. Booklet pane. Engraved.

6c gray brown
1284d hz pair, imperf between　　　　2,250.00
Quantity: very rare

No. 1284d results from a foldover.

Oliver Wendell Holmes. June 28, 1978. Booklet pane of 8. Engraved. Perf 10.

15c magenta

1288Be	booklet pane of 8, imperf vrt between	*1,500.00*
	Quantity: n/a	

Francis Parkman. November 4, 1975. Coil. Engraved.

3c violet

1297a	imperf pair (shiny gum)	22.50
	line pair, imperf	45.00
	Quantity: 1,000+ pairs	
1297a	imperf pair (dull gum)	22.50
	line pair, imperf	45.00
	Quantity: 1,000+ pairs	

1297c	imperf pair, precanceled	
	Non-Profit ORG CAR-RT SORT	8.00
	line pair, imperf	20.00
	spliced pair or strip, imperf	—
	Quantity: several thousand	

Exists miscut. Transition multiples exist.

Franklin D. Roosevelt. December 28, 1967. Coil. Engraved.

6c gray brown

1298a	imperf pair	*1,500.00*
	line pair, imperf	*4,500.00*
	line strip of 4, imperf	—
	Quantity: 25-30 pairs reported	

Thomas Jefferson. January 12, 1968. Coil. Engraved.

1c green

1299b	imperf pair	*22.50*
	line pair, imperf	*50.00*
	Quantity: 1,000+ pairs	

Abraham Lincoln. May 28, 1966. Coil. Engraved.

4c black

1303b	imperf pair	*600.00*
	line pair, imperf	*1,300.00*
	spliced pair or strip, imperf	—
	Quantity: 100 pairs reported	

Transition multiples exist and sell for a premium.

1304b
Original Design

1304Cd
Revised Design

George Washington. September 8, 1966. Original design. Coil. Engraved.

5c blue

1304b	imperf pair	110.00
	line pair, imperf	250.00
	spliced pair or strip, imperf	—
	used pair, imperf	—
	Quantity: 200 pairs reported	

Often with faults. Value is for a sound example. Exists miscut. Transition multiples exist and sell for a premium.

1304e	imperf pair, precanceled	
	MOUNT PLEASANT, IA	250.00
	line pair, imperf	800.00
	imperf pair or strip, gap in bars	500.00
	Quantity: n/a	

1304e	imperf pair, precanceled	
	CHICAGO, IL	1,500.00
	line pair, imperf	—
	Quantity: 6 pairs and unique line pair reported	

George Washington. Revised design; clean shaven. Coil. Engraved.

5c blue

1304Cd	imperf pair	375.00
	line pair, imperf	675.00
	Quantity: 50-60 pairs reported	

Franklin D. Roosevelt. February 28, 1968. Coil. Engraved.

6c gray brown

1305a	imperf pair	55.00
	line pair, imperf	115.00
	Quantity: approx 1,000 pairs	

Exists miscut. Transition multiples exist.

1305m	pair, imperf between	250.00
	line pair, imperf	500.00
	Quantity: n/a	

Eugene O'Neill. January 12, 1973. Coil. Engraved.

$1 dull purple

1305Cd	imperf pair	1,250.00
	line pair, imperf	3,000.00
	spliced pair or strip, imperf	—
	Quantity: 50 pairs, 3 line pairs reported	

Exists miscut. Transition multiples exist and sell for a premium.

Oliver Wendell Holmes. June 14, 1978. Coil. Engraved. Exists with shiny or dull gum.

15c magenta; type I, shiny gum

1305Eg	imperf pair	20.00
	line pair, imperf	50.00
	imperf pair, used	—
	Quantity: 600-800 pairs	

Exists miscut. Transition multiples exist and sell for a premium.

Type I	Type II

Type I. The tip of the tie touches or almost touches the coat. The downward sloping hatch lines in the tie are more pronounced. The upper bar of the cents symbol is aligned slightly to the left of the "E" of "POSTAGE."

Type II. The tip of the tie is well clear of the coat. The downward sloping hatch lines in the tie are almost eliminated. The third upward sloping line of the tie stops well short of the right side of the tie. The upper bar in the cents symbol is aligned almost directly under the "E" of "POSTAGE."

15c magenta; type I, dull gum

1305Eg	imperf pair	22.50
	line pair, imperf	60.00
	Quantity: several hundred pairs	

1305Eh	pair, imperf between	125.00
	line pair, imperf between	*400.00*
	Quantity: 200-250 pairs reported	

15c magenta; type II, dull gum

1305Ej	imperf pair	*55.00*
	line pair, imperf	*150.00*
	Quantity: 150+ pairs	

Transition multiples exist and sell for a premium.

Davy Crockett. August 17, 1967. Engraved, lithographed. BEP.

5c black, yellow & green

1330a	vrt pair, imperf between	*7,500.00*
	Quantity: 3-5 pairs reported	

U.S. Flag. January 24, 1968. Engraved. Design 19x22mm. Perf 11. BEP.

6c dark blue, red & green

1338k	vrt pair, imperf between	*250.00*
	as above, used	*150.00*
	Quantity: 50+ pairs	

▶ Caution. Many offered as errors have traces of perforations. Check carefully.

1338u	vrt pair, imperf hz	*275.00*
	as above, used	—
	Quantity: very scarce	

▶ Caution. Beware of regumming. Most pairs lack gum, which was removed to eliminate faint perforation impressions. So long as impressions do not affect a stamp's paper, the stamp is considered imperforate. Check carefully for blind perfs. Value is for pair with original gum. Those without gum sell for less.

U.S. Flag. May 30, 1969. Coil. Engraved. BEP.

6c dark blue, red & green

1338Ab imperf pair   *350.00*
    spliced pair or strip, imperf   —
    Quantity: 50-100 pairs reported

Often with faults. Value is for a sound example.

U.S. Flag. August 7, 1970. Engraved. Design 18¼ by 21mm. Perf 11x10½. BEP.

6c dark blue, red & green

1338De hz pair, imperf between   *115.00*
    Quantity: 100-200 pairs

Often with clipped perfs, a normal result of trimming at the Bureau of Engraving & Printing.

U.S. Flag. May 10, 1971. Engraved. Perf 11x10½. BEP.

8c dark blue, red & slate green

1338Fi imperf, vertical pair   35.00
    top or bottom plate block
      of 20, imperf   *600.00*
    Quantity: 500+ pairs reported

Value is for an example with gum. Pairs without gum sell for less. Collected in vertical pairs or blocks to distinguish it from the coil imperforate of similar design.

1338Fj hz pair, imperf between   45.00
    Quantity: 600 pairs

1338Ft hz pair, imperf vrt   —
    Quantity: n/a

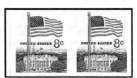

U.S. Flag. May 10, 1971. Coil. Engraved. BEP.

8c dark blue, red & slate green

1338Gh imperf pair   *45.00*
    spliced pair or strip, imperf   —
    Quantity: 750-1,000 pairs reported

Exists miscut, including 3 strips with complete plate number showing at bottom. Transition multiples exist and sell for a premium. Although it is generally accepted that line pairs, in the traditional sense, are not created on Huck press printed stamps, pairs with coloration between stamps resembling lines exist and are collected. They sell for about double the price of regular pairs.

Historic Flags. July 4, 1968. Se-tenant pane of 50. Engraved, lithographed. BEP

6c multicolored

a) Ft. Moultrie	b) Ft. McHenry
c) Washington's Cruisers	d) Bennington
e) Rhode Island	f) First Stars & Strips
g) Bunker Hill	h) Grand Union
i) Philadelphia Light Horse	j) First Navy Jack

1354c   strip of 10 (a-j), imperf   4,500.00
         Quantity: unique

Walt Disney. September 11, 1968. Photogravure. UCC.

6c multicolored
1355b   vrt pair, imperf hz   575.00
         plate block of 4, imperf hz   —
         Quantity: 50 pairs

1355c   imperf pair   425.00
         block of 4, imperf   —
         Quantity: 100 pairs

1355e   hz pair, imperf between   *5,000.00*
Quantity: 5 pairs

▶ Caution. Expert certificate essential. Beware of fakes fabricated from No. 1355c.

Waterfowl Conservation. October 24, 1968. Engraved, lithographed. BEP.

6c multicolored
1362a   vrt pair, imperf between   *250.00*
strip of 20, 2 pairs imperf between   —
full pane, 5 pairs imperf between   —
Quantity: 150+ pairs

No. 1362a occurs on pairs comprising the 6th and 7th rows, thus yielding 5 error pairs per pane of 50 stamps. Some margin pairs contain an inspector's red crayon mark in the selvage. Its presence does not detract from value.

Christmas. November 1, 1968. Engraved, lithographed. BEP.

6c multicolored
1363b   imperf pair, tagged   *140.00*
plate block of 10, imperf, tagged   —
Quantity: 500 pairs

1363d   imperf pair, untagged   *200.00*
Quantity: 250 pairs

No. 1363d often occurs with mottled gum. Those with flawless gum sell for a premium.

Grandma Moses. May 1, 1969. Engraved, lithographed. BEP.

6c multicolored
1370a   hz pair, imperf between   *140.00*
Quantity: 250 pairs reported, see note

▶ Caution. Many pairs have faint traces of blind perfs. Frequently, perf traces can be seen only on the gummed side. Pairs on cover have been reported; however, it is thought that they may have been thus used to disguise the presence of blind perfs and, therefore, when encountered, should be examined carefully. Of the quantity reported, it is not known how many pairs contain faint blind perfs.

Football. September 26, 1969. Engraved, lithographed.

6c red & green
1382b   vrt pair, imperf hz   *5,750.00*
Quantity: unique

Christmas. November 3, 1969. Engraved, lithographed. BEP.

6c multicolored
1384b   imperf pair   *700.00*
Quantity: 25 pairs reported

Dwight D. Eisenhower. January 28, 1972. Booklet pane. Engraved.

8c deep claret

1395e	vrt pair, imperf between	*750.00*
	Quantity: at least 4 panes are confirmed, more may exist	

No. 1395e occurs as the result of a foldover. Some panes include the "Use Zip Code" label, although not as part of an error pair. Recent auction prices have ranged from the $750 to $1,250. Refer to the Printer's Waste section for other imperforates of this issue.

Dwight D. Eisenhower. August 6, 1970. Coil. Engraved.

6c dark gray blue

1401b	imperf pair	*2,500.00*
	line pair, imperf	—
	Quantity: 20-30 pairs reported	

Sometimes encountered with incomplete gum or without gum. Value is for pair with full gum, never hinged.

Dwight D. Eisenhower. May 10, 1971. Coil. Engraved.

8c dark claret

1402a	imperf pair	37.50
	line pair, imperf	70.00
	spliced pair or strip, imperf	—
	used pair, imperf	—
	Quantity: 1,000+ pairs	

Exists miscut. Transition multiples exist and sell for a premium.

1402c	pair, imperf between	*6,250.00*
	Quantity: 1 pair	

Christmas. November 5, 1970. Se-tenant block of 4. Photogravure. GGI.

6c multicolored

a) Doll Carriage   b) Toy Horse

1416c	used vrt margin pair (a & b) with plate No. 31907, imperf	—
	used vrt margin pair (a & b) with Mail Early slogan, imperf	*2,500.00*
	Quantity: each pair listed is unique	

Each listed pair is postmarked Washington, DC, Nov. 5, 1970.

Tom Sawyer. October 13, 1972. Engraved, lithographed. BEP.

8c multicolored

1470a	hz pair, imperf between	*6,750.00*
	plate block of 4, imperf vrt between	—
	Quantity: 7 pairs reported (one of which is damaged)	

Pharmacy. November 10, 1972. Engraved, lithographed. BEP.

8c multicolored

1473e	vrt pair, imperf hz	*2,000.00*
	Quantity: 2 pairs	

George Gershwin. February 23, 1973. Photogravure. BEP.

8c multicolored

1484a	vrt pair, imperf hz	*160.00*
	plate block of 12, imperf hz	—
	Quantity: 160-200 pairs	

Robinson Jeffers. August 13, 1973. Photogravure. BEP.

8c multicolored

1485a	vrt pair, imperf hz	*160.00*
	Quantity: 80-100 pairs reported	

Willa Cather. September 20, 1973. Photogravure. BEP.

8c multicolored

1487a	vrt pair, imperf hz	*175.00*
	plate block of 12, imperf hz	—

Lyndon B. Johnson. August 27, 1973. Photogravure. BEP.

8c multicolored

1503a	hz pair, imperf vrt	*200.00*
	plate block of 12, imperf vrt	—
	Quantity: 128-160 pairs	

Rural America. October 5, 1973. Engraved, lithographed. BEP.

8c multicolored

1504b	used vrt pair, imperf between	*5,000.00*
	Quantity: unique	

▶ Caution. Many pairs exist with blind perforations. Expert certificate essential. The listed pair is comprised of stamps 2 and 3 in a vertical strip of 5.

Christmas. November 7, 1973. Photogravure. BEP.

8c multicolored
1508a vrt pair, imperf between   225.00
        Quantity: 100+ pairs

Pairs often contain a misplaced perforation in the design due to the nature of the error. Transition multiples exist and sell for a premium.

Crossed Flags. December 8, 1973. Engraved. BEP.

10c red & blue
1509a hz pair, imperf between   40.00
        top or bottom plate strip of 20   —
        Quantity: several hundred pairs

1509a hz pair, imperf between,
        precanceled SALEM, IND.   100.00
        Quantity: n/a

1509d hz pair, imperf vrt   900.00
        hz strip of 4, imperf vrt   2,000.00
        Quantity: 8 pairs reported

Most often encountered as a strip of 4 containing two error pairs.

1509c vrt pair, imperf   450.00
        block of 4, imperf   —
        plate block of 6, imperf   —
        Quantity: 60+ pairs

Collected in vertical pairs or blocks to distinguish it from coil stamps of the same design.

1509f vrt pair, imperf between   —
        Quantity: unique, see note

The error pair occurs in a block. Only one example has been certified and reported.

Jefferson Memorial. December 14, 1973. Engraved. BEP.

10c blue
1510e vrt pair, imperf hz   300.00
        Quantity: n/a

No. 1510e is poorly centered. Value is for poorly centered example. Often with mottled gum.

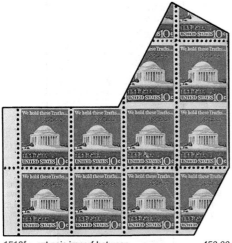

1510f vrt pair, imperf between   *450.00*
      Quantity: rare

No. 1510f occurs from miscut booklet panes or from foldover panes.

1510i booklet pane of 5, including 2 hz
      pairs imperf between & 1 hz
      pair consisting of a stamp
      a label imperf between   *1,750.00*
      Quantity: likely unique

No. 1518i is the result of a foldover.

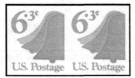

Liberty Bell. October 1, 1974. Coil. Engraved. BEP.

6.3c brick red

1518b imperf pair   *130.00*
      line pair, imperf   *375.00*
      Quantity: 200+ pairs reported

Transition multiples exist.

1518c imperf pair, precanceled
      WASHINGTON, DC   *75.00*
      line pair, imperf   *175.00*
      imperf pair or strip, gap in bars   —
      spliced pair or strip, imperf   —
      Quantity: 300-500 pairs reported

Exists miscut. Transition multiples exist and sell for a premium.

1518c imperf pair, precanceled
      COLUMBUS, OH   *400.00*
      line pair, imperf   —
      imperf pair or strip, gap in bars   —
      spliced pair or strip, imperf   —
      Quantity: rare

1518c imperf pair, precanceled
      GARDEN CITY, NY   *850.00*
      line pair, imperf   —
      Quantity: rare

Flags. December 8, 1973. Coil. Engraved. BEP.

10c red & blue

1519a imperf pair   35.00
      line pair, imperf   50.00
      spliced pair or strip, imperf   —
      Quantity: 1,000+ pairs

Refer to the note following No. 1338Gh. Exists miscut. Transition multiples exist and sell for a premium.

Jefferson Memorial. December 14, 1973. Coil. Engraved. BEP.

10c blue

1520b	imperf pair	30.00
	line pair, imperf	50.00
	spliced pair or strip, imperf	—
	used pair, imperf	—
	Quantity: 750+ pairs	

Exists miscut. Transition multiples exist and sell for a premium.

Skylab. May 14, 1974. Engraved, lithographed. BEP.

10c multicolored

| 1529a | vrt pair, imperf between | — |
| | Quantity: n/a | |

| 1529c | vrt pair, imperf hz | — |
| | Quantity: n/a | |

UPU. June 6, 1974. Se-tenant block of 8. Photogravure. BEP.

10c multicolored (block of 8)

a) Terboch   e) Raphael
b) Chardin   f) Hokusai
c) Gainsborough   g) Peto
d) Goya   h) Liotard

1537b	block of 8, imperf vrt	2,500.00
	plate block of 16	—
	Quantity: 4 blocks of 8, including the	
	plate block	

Paul Laurence Dunbar. May 1, 1975. Photogravure. BEP.

10c multicolored

1554a	imperf pair	*800.00*
	plate block of 10, imperf	—
	Quantity: 15+ pairs	

Some pairs exist with blind perfs at top, which do not affect the desirability of the error. Of these, some pairs are known to have had the blind perfs trimmed off to create the appearance of a fully imperforate pair. Such pairs tend to have a tight top margin.

Lexington & Concord. April 19, 1975. Photogravure. BEP.

10c multicolored

| 1563a | vrt pair, imperf hz | *300.00* |
| | plate block of 12, imperf hz | — |

Apollo-Soyuz. July 15, 1975. Se-tenant pair. Photogravure. BEP.

10c multicolored

a) Spacecraft & Emblem
b) Spacecraft & Globe

1570c	vrt pair, imperf hz	*800.00*
	Zip block of 4, imperf hz	—
	Quantity: 24-36 pairs	

▶ Completely imperforate examples of No. 1570 occur from printer's waste. Refer to the Printer's Waste section.

World Peace Through Law. September 29, 1975. Engraved. BEP.

10c multicolored

1576b	hz pair, imperf vrt	*7,500.00*
	Quantity: 2 pairs in unique plate block	

The plate block (plate No. 36535) consists of 2 pairs plus parts of 2 additional stamps at left, giving it the appearance of containing nearly six stamps.

Christmas. October 14, 1975. Photogravure. BEP.

10c multicolored

1579a	imperf pair	*75.00*
	plate block of 12, imperf	*525.00*
	Quantity: several hundred pairs	

Christmas. October 14, 1975. Photogravure. BEP.

10c multicolored

1580a	imperf pair	*85.00*
	plate block of 12, imperf	—
	Quantity: several hundred pairs	

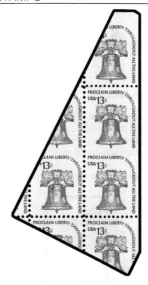

Liberty Bell. October 31, 1975. Booklet pane. Engraved. BEP.

13c brown

1595e	booklet pane containing one or two vertical pairs, imperf between	*1,100.00*
	Quantity: rare	

No. 1595e results from a foldover and must be collected in that form in order to distinguish it from printer's waste. Complete unfolded booklet panes with the label "Paying Bills" in the lower left corner are printer's waste. Likewise, detached individual vertical pairs, imperf between, must be regarded as printer's waste. Refer to the Printer's Waste section.

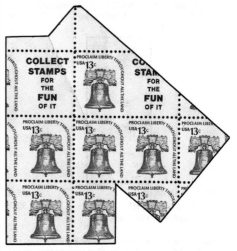

1595g	hz pair, imperf between	—
	Quantity: rare	

No. 1595g results from a foldover.

Eagle & Shield. December 1, 1975. Photogravure. BEP.

13c multicolored

1596a	imperf pair	*40.00*
	block of 4, imperf	*80.00*
	Quantity: approx 500 pairs	

Exists with color shift. Used pairs exist on philatelically inspired covers.

U.S. Flag. June 30, 1978. Engraved. BEP.

15c gray, dark blue & red

1597c	vrt pair, imperf between	*350.00*
	Quantity: rare	

No. 1597c contains a natural straight edge at bottom. It is usually encountered in a strip of 3 or more. Vertical pairs, imperf horizontally exist fabricated by trimming perforations off the top and bottom of No. 1597c.

1597e	vrt pair, imperf	*15.00*
	block of 4, imperf	*30.00*
	Quantity: 1,000+ pairs	

Collected in vertical pairs or blocks to distinguish it from coil imperforate of the same design. Transition multiples exist and sell for a premium.

Oil Lamp. September 11, 1979. Engraved, lithographed. BEP.

50c tan, black & orange

1608b	vrt pair, imperf hz	*1,200.00*
	Quantity: very rare	

▶ Caution. Most pairs contain faint blind perfs and, therefore, do not qualify as errors. The blind perfs can be very deceptive. Extreme caution advised. Expert certificate necessary.

Guitar. October 25, 1979. Coil. Engraved. BEP.

3.1c brown (yellow paper)

1613b	imperf pair	*850.00*
	line pair, imperf	—
	Quantity: 30-50 pairs, 2 line pairs	

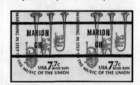

Saxhorns. November 20, 1976. Coil. Engraved. BEP.

7.7c brown (yellow paper)

1614b	imperf pair, precanceled MARION, OH	*1,950.00*
	Quantity: 7-10 pairs reported	

1614b	imperf pair, precanceled WASHINGTON, DC	*1,250.00*
	line pair, imperf LRS (6/08)	*3,000.00*
	imperf pair or strip, gap in bars	—
	Quantity: 40-50 pairs reported	

Drum. April 23, 1976. Coil. Engraved. Shiny Gum. BEP.

7.9c carmine (yellow paper)
1615b	imperf pair	*300.00*
	line pair, imperf	—
	spliced pair or strip, imperf	—
	Quantity: 100+ pairs reported	

Transition multiples exist and sell for a premium.

Piano. July 13, 1978. Coil. Engraved. Shiny gum. BEP.

8.4c dark blue (yellow paper)
1615Ce	pair, imperf between, precanceled bars	45.00
	line pair, imperf between	110.00
	pair, imperf between, gap in bars	65.00
	Quantity: several hundred pairs	

1615Cf	imperf pair, precanceled bars	15.00
	line pair, imperf	35.00
	imperf pair or strip, gap in bars	35.00
	Quantity: few thousand pairs	

Exists miscut. Some miscut pairs contain EE bars at top.

1615Cf	imperf pair, precanceled NEWARK, NJ	25.00
	line pair, as above	50.00
	imperf pair or strip, gap in bars	40.00
	Quantity: several hundred pairs	

Exists miscut.

1615Cf	imperf pair, precanceled	
	BROWNSTOWN, IN	*900.00*
	line pair, imperf	—
	imperf pair or strip, gap in bars	—
	spliced pair or strip, imperf	—
	Quantity: rare, spliced strip unique	

1615Cf	imperf pair, precanceled	
	OKLAHOMA CITY, OK	*1,500.00*
	line pair, imperf	*5,250.00*
	imperf pair or strip, gap in bars	—
	Quantity: rare	

1615Cf	imperf pair, precanceled	
	WASHINGTON, DC	*900.00*
	line pair, imperf	—
	imperf pair or strip, gap in bars	—
	Quantity: rare	

Capitol Dome. March 5, 1976. Coil. Engraved. BEP.

9c slate green (gray paper)
1616a	imperf pair	*125.00*
	line pair, imperf	*260.00*
	Quantity: few hundred pairs	

Exists miscut to varying degrees. Value is for a well-centered pair. Slightly miscut pairs sell for about half the well-centered pair value. Drastically miscut pairs sell for about 66% of well-centered pair value. Three line strips of six exist showing two full plate numbers at bottom.

1616c	imperf pair, precanceled	
	PLEASANTVL, NY	*600.00*
	line pair, imperf	—
	Quantity: scarce, 2 line pairs reported	

Justice. November 4, 1977. Coil. Engraved. BEP.

10c violet (gray paper)

1617b	imperf pair (shiny gum)	80.00
	line pair, imperf (shiny gum)	*150.00*
	spliced pair or strip, imperf	—
	Quantity: few hundred pairs	

1617c	imperf pair (dull gum), precanceled	
	bars	*3,750.00*
	line pair, imperf	*4,750.00*
	Quantity: 2 pairs, 1 line pair	

Exists miscut. Transition multiples exist and sell for a premium.

Liberty Bell. November 25, 1975. Coil. Engraved. Shiny gum. BEP.

13c brown

1618b	imperf pair	22.50
	line pair, imperf	45.00
	spliced pair or strip, imperf	—
	Quantity: few thousand pairs	

Exists miscut. Transition multiples exist and sell for a premium.

| 1618g | pair, imperf between | *600.00* |
| | Quantity: scarce | |

| 1618h | imperf pair, precanceled bars | *5,000.00* |
| | Quantity: possibly unique | |

No. 1618h is miscut.

U.S. Flag. June 30, 1978. Coil. Engraved. BEP.

15c gray, dark blue & red

1618Cd	imperf pair	20.00
	spliced pair or strip, imperf	—
	Quantity: several thousand pairs	

Exists miscut. Transition multiples exist and sell for a premium.

| 1618Ce | pair, imperf between | 100.00 |
| | Quantity: 75-100 pairs | |

Flag & Independence Hall. November 15, 1975. Engraved. Huck Press. Perf 11x10½. BEP.

13c dark blue, red & brown red

| 1622a | hz pair, imperf between | 40.00 |
| | Quantity: approx 1,000 pairs | |

1622b	vrt pair, imperf	*300.00*
	block of 4, imperf	—
	top plate strip of 20	—
	Quantity: 110-130 pairs	

1622e hz pair, imperf vrt   —
      Quantity: 9 pairs reported

Flag & Independence Hall. 1981. Engraved. Combination Press. Perf 11. BEP.

    13c red, blue & brown
1622Cd vrt pair, imperf   100.00
      block of 4, imperf   *225.00*
      Quantity: 150-200 pairs reported

No. 1622b was printed on the Huck Press; plate numbers appear at the top or bottom of a pane. No. 1622Cd was printed on the Combination Press; plate numbers appear on the left or right of the pane. In addition, No. 1622b and No. 1622Cd can be distinguished from one another as follows: No. 1622b has visible gum-breaking ridges on the reverse, and tagging is usually in the form of a well-defined block. No. 1622Cd has smooth gum without ridges, and tagging, which is in block form, tends to be very irregular.

No. 1622b and No. 1622Cd are collected in vertical pairs or blocks to distinguish them from coil imperforates of the same design.

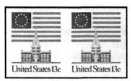

Flag & Independence Hall. November 15, 1975. Coil. Engraved. BEP.

    13c dark blue, red & brown red
1625a imperf pair   20.00
      line pair, imperf   *50.00*
      spliced pair or strip, imperf   —
      Quantity: several thousand pairs

Refer to note following No. 1338Gh. Transition multiples exist and sell for a premium.

The Spirit of '76. January 1, 1976. Se-tenant strip of 3. Photogravure. BEP.

    13c multicolored

    a) Drummer Boy
    b) Old Drummer
    c) Fifer

1631b imperf strip of 3 (a-c)   *700.00*
      plate block of 12, imperf   —

1631c vertical pair (c), imperf   *500.00*
      imperf single (c), white border
        all around   250.00
      Quantity: 3 panes of 50 yielding 45
        possible strips of 3 and 15 stamps
        as singles or pairs.

BICENTENNIAL SOUVENIR SHEETS

A variety of perforation and color-omitted errors exist for this series. Some sheets contain multiple errors. Those that exist imperforate are listed below, including those that also contain color-omitted errors. Refer to the color-omitted section for other varieties.

The Surrender of Lord Cornwallis at Yorktown
From a Painting by John Trumbull

Surrender at Yorktown. May 29, 1976. Souvenir sheet of 5. Lithographed. BEP.

13c multicolored

1686f   imperf souvenir sheet, tagging omitted, USA 13c omitted on "b," "c" & "d" stamps, with 5/29/76 PHILADELPHIA, PA precancel postmark   *1,750.00*
Quantity: 2-3 reported

1686h   imperf souvenir sheet, tagging omitted, tied by postmark (5/29/76) to first day display card   *2,500.00*
Quantity: 1-2 reported

1686m   imperf souvenir sheet, tagging omitted, USA 13c omitted on all stamps, with 5/29/76 PHILADELPHIA, PA precancel postmark   —
Quantity: 1-2 reported

1686n   imperf souvenir sheet, tagging omitted, USA 13c omitted on "a" & "e"   —
Quantity: very rare

1686n   imperf souvenir sheet, tagging omitted, USA 13c omitted on "a" & "e," with 5/29/76 PHILADELPHIA, PA first day postmark   —
Quantity: very rare, possibly unique

1686r   imperf souvenir sheet, tagged   —
Quantity: possibly unique

The Declaration of Independence, 4 July 1776 at Philadelphia
From a Painting by John Trumbull

Declaration of Independence. May 29, 1976. Souvenir sheet of 5. Lithographed. BEP.

18c multicolored

1687k   imperf souvenir sheet, tagging omitted, USA 18c omitted on all stamps   *1,500.00*
Quantity: very rare

1687p   imperf souvenir sheet, tagged   *1,000.00*
Quantity: very rare

Washington Crossing the Delaware. May 29, 1976. Souvenir sheet of 5. Lithographed. BEP.

24c multicolored

1688f   imperf souvenir sheet, tagging omitted, USA 24c omitted on all stamps   *950.00*
Quantity: 2-3 reported

Washington Crossing the Delaware
From a Painting by Emanuel Leutze / Eastman Johnson

1688j   imperf souvenir sheet, tagging omitted   *1,250.00*
Quantity: very rare

1688l   imperf souvenir sheet, tagging omitted, USA 24c omitted on "a," "b" & "c"   *3,250.00*
Quantity: very rare

1688s   imperf souvenir sheet, tagged   *1,250.00*
Quantity: n/a

Washington at Valley Forge. May 29, 1976. Souvenir sheet of 5. Lithographed. BEP.

31c multicolored

1689f   imperf souvenir sheet, tagging omitted, USA 31c omitted from all stamps   *950.00*
      Quantity: 6-8 reported

1689k   imperf souvenir sheet, tagging omitted, tied by 5/29/76 PHILADELPHIA, PA precancel postmark to first day display card   *2,000.00*
      Quantity: very rare

1689n   imperf souvenir sheet, tagging omitted, USA 31c omitted on "a," "c" & "e"   —
      Quantity: possibly unique

1689p   imperf souvenir sheet, tagging omitted, USA 31c omitted on "b," "d" & "e"   *1,250.00*
      Quantity: very rare

1689q   imperf souvenir sheet, tagging omitted, USA 31c omitted on "a" & "c"   *2,500.00*
      Quantity: very rare

Olympics. July 16, 1976. Se-tenant block of 4. Photogravure. BEP.

13c multicolored

a) Diving   b) Skiing
c) Running   d) Skating

1698b   imperf block of 4 (a-d)   *375.00*
      plate block of 12, imperf   —
      Zip block of 4, imperf   —
      imperf pair (a-b) or (c-d)   —
      Quantity: 200+ blocks of 4 reported

Clara Maass. August 18, 1976. Photogravure. BEP.

13c multicolored

1699a   hz pair, imperf vrt   *350.00*
      Quantity: 60-80 pairs reported

Christmas. October 27, 1976. Photogravure. BEP.

13c multicolored

1701a   imperf pair   *85.00*
      plate block of 12, imperf   —
      Quantity: few hundred pairs

CHRISTMAS 1976

Stamps of the following design exist in two varieties, each printed by a different press. Type II is more gray and is washed out in overall appearance. The varieties also can be distinguished under UV light. Type I is completely tagged. Type II is tagged with rectangles that cover only the design area.

Christmas. October 27, 1976. Photogravure. BEP.

13c multicolored, type I

1702a	imperf pair	*75.00*
	plate block of 12, imperf	—
	Quantity: few hundred pairs	

13c multicolored, type II

1703a	imperf pair	*75.00*
	plate strip of 20, imperf	—
	Quantity: few hundred pairs	

1703b	vrt pair, imperf between	*275.00*
	Quantity: 40-60 pairs	

Pairs often show blind perfs at outer edges.

Washington at Princeton. January 3, 1977. Photogravure. BEP.

13c multicolored

1704a	hz pair, imperf vrt	*425.00*
	plate block of 12, imperf	—
	Quantity: 40-60 pairs	

Pueblo Art. April 13, 1977. Se-tenant block or strip of 4. Photogravure. BEP.

13c multicolored

a) Zia Pottery   b) San Ildefonso Pottery
c) Hopi Pottery   d) Acoma Pottery

1709b	block of 4 (a-d), imperf vrt	*1,100.00*
	strip of 4 (a-d), imperf vrt	*1,100.00*
	Quantity: 16 blocks of 4, 4 strips of 4 reported	

Panes of the Pueblo Pottery stamp are arranged so that the four designs are se-tenant (a-b-c-d) in a row. Additionally, rows alternate so that it is possible for the four designs to appear in a se-tenant block of four.

Spirit of St. Louis. May 20, 1977. Photogravure. BEP.

13c multicolored

1710a	imperf pair	*700.00*
	plate block of 12, imperf	—
	Quantity: 85-100 pairs reported	

Colorado. May 21, 1977. Photogravure. BEP.

13c multicolored

1711a	hz pair, imperf between and with natural straight edge at right	*650.00*
	Quantity: scarce	

1711b   hz pair, imperf vrt   *500.00*
         Quantity: 35 pairs

**Butterflies. June 6, 1977. Se-tenant block of 4.
Photogravure. BEP.**

13c multicolored

a) Swallowtail   b) Checkerspot
c) Dogface   d) Orange-Tip

1715b   block of 4 (a-d), plate numbers
            at left, imperf hz   9,500.00
         block of 4 (a-d), perfs slightly in
            at lower right, imperf hz   —
         Quantity: the 2 blocks as listed

Christmas. October 21, 1977. Photogravure. BEP.

13c multicolored
1729a   imperf pair   *50.00*
         plate strip of 20, imperf   —
         Quantity: 1,000+ pairs

Christmas. October 21, 1977. Photogravure. BEP.

13c multicolored
1730a   imperf pair   *175.00*
         plate block of 10, imperf   —
         Quantity: few hundred

**Captain James Cook. January 20, 1978. Pane of 50 arranged
so that each half pane contains 25 stamps of the same
design. Five se-tenant pairs exist at the center of each pane.
Engraved. BEP.**

13c dark blue (a), green (b)

a) Captain Cook   b) Ships at Anchor

1733a   vrt pair (b), imperf hz   *1,000.00*
         strip of 10 containing Nos. 1733a & 1733c   —
         Quantity: very rare

▶ Caution. Pairs of the Captain Cook portrait design exist with
blind perforations that give the appearance of being imperforate.

1733c   se-tenant pair (a-b), imperf between   *4,000.00*
         Quantity: fewer than 5 pairs reported

Although No. 1733c appears to be imperf vertically, it is properly
described as imperf between because of the presence of blind
perfs at left and right.

Indian Head Penny. January 11, 1978. Engraved. BEP.

13c brown & blue green (bister paper)
1734a   hz pair, imperf vrt   *175.00*
         Quantity: 300-375 pairs

Eagle & A. May 22, 1978. Photogravure. BEP.

A (15c) orange

1735a	imperf pair	*70.00*
	plate block of 4, imperf	—
	Quantity: few hundred pairs	

The sheet variety of this stamp was printed by photogravure; the coil stamp was engraved. Therefore, horizontal pairs of the sheet stamp are collectible because they can be distinguished from coil stamps.

1735b	vrt pair, imperf hz	*500.00*
	plate block of 4, imperf hz	—
	Quantity: 20+ pairs reported	

Most pairs exist with faint vertical perfs. Pairs with distinct perforations are much rarer.

Eagle & A. May 22, 1978. Booklet pane. Engraved. BEP.

A (15c) orange

1736c	vrt pair, imperf between	*1,000.00*
	Quantity: 3-4 reported	

No. 1736c results from a foldover.

Roses. July 11, 1978. Booklet pane of 8. Engraved. BEP.

15c multicolored

1737b	imperf pair	*450.00*
	Quantity: 20+ pairs reported	
1737c	booklet pane, imperf	*2,250.00*
	Quantity: 9 panes reported	

Pairs often show blind perfs at outer edges.

Eagle & A. May 27, 1978. Coil. Engraved. BEP.

A (15c) orange

1743a	imperf pair	65.00
	line pair, imperf	140.00
	spliced pair or strip	—
	Quantity: 150-200 pairs	

Well-centered examples are scarcer and sell for more.

CAPEX. June 10, 1978. Souvenir sheet of 8. Engraved, lithographed. BEP.

13c multicolored

a) Cardinal	e) Moose
b) Mallard	f) Chipmunk
c) Canada Goose	g) Red Fox
d) Blue Jay	h) Raccoon

1757j	strip of 4 (a-d), imperf vrt	*5,000.00*
	Quantity: 2 strips of 4	

1757k	strip of 4 (e-h), imperf vrt	*2,000.00*
	as above, in souvenir sheet	—
	Quantity: 6 strips of 4, including those within souvenir sheets	

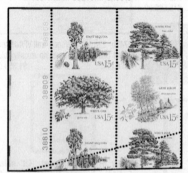

Trees. October 9, 1978. Se-tenant block of 4. Photogravure. BEP.

15c multicolored

a) Giant Sequoia	b) White Pine
c) White Oak	d) Gray Birch

1767b	block of 4 (a-d), imperf hz	*17,500.00*
	Quantity: unique	

Madonna. October 18, 1978. Photogravure. BEP.

15c multicolored

1768a	imperf pair	*70.00*
	plate block of 12, imperf	—
	Quantity: 300-400 pairs	

Value is for an uncreased pair.

Hobby Horse. October 18, 1978. Photogravure. BEP.

15c multicolored

1769a	imperf pair	*75.00*
	plate block of 12, imperf	—
	Quantity: 400-500 pairs	

1769b	vrt pair, imperf hz	*1,000.00*
	Quantity: 4-6 pairs or strips of 3	

No. 1769b contains traces of blind vertical perfs at top and bottom that may give it the appearance of being completely imperforate.

Martin Luther King. January 13, 1979. Photogravure. BEP.

13c multicolored

1771a	imperf pair	*900.00*
	Quantity: 10 pairs reported	

▶ Caution. Many exist with blind perfs.

Folk Art. April 19, 1979. Se-tenant block of 4. Photogravure. BEP.

15c multicolored

a) Coffeepot b) Tea Caddy
c) Sugar Bowl d) Coffeepot

1778b block of 4 (a-d), imperf hz *2,000.00*
plate block of 8, imperf hz —
Quantity: 1 pane reported

Endangered Flora. June 7, 1979. Se-tenant block of 4. Photogravure. BEP.

15c multicolored

a) Persistent Trillium
b) Hawaiian Wild Broadbean
c) Contra Costa Wallflower
d) Antioch Dunes Evening Primrose

1786b block of 4 (a-d), imperf *200.00*
plate block of 12, imperf —
Quantity: 100+ blocks of 4; 50+ pairs

Seeing for Me. June 15, 1979. Photogravure. BEP.

15c multicolored

1787a imperf pair *325.00*
Quantity: 100 pairs

John Paul Jones. September 23, 1979. Photogravure. Two perforation varieties; Type I perf 11x12, Type II perf 11x11. JWF.

15c multicolored

1789c vrt pair, type I, perf 12 vrt,
imperf hz *125.00*
plate block of 10, imperf hz —
Zip block of 4, imperf hz —
Quantity: 60-100 pairs

No. 1789c exists on first day cover.

1789Ad vrt pair, type II, perf 11 vrt,
 imperf hz   *115.00*
 plate block of 10, imperf hz   *600.00*
 Zip block of 4, imperf hz   *250.00*
 Quantity: 200-300 pairs

Completely imperforate pairs and multiples are proofs. Refer to the Error-Like Imperforates section.

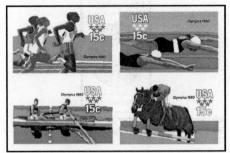

Summer Olympics. September 5, 1979. Se-tenant block of 4. Photogravure. BEP.

15c multicolored

a) Running b) Swimming
c) Rowing   d) Horse Jumping

1794b block of 4 (a-d), imperf   *900.00*
 plate block of 12, imperf   —
 vrt pair (a & c), imperf   *300.00*
 vrt pair (b & d), imperf   *300.00*
 Quantity: 20 blocks of 4, 10 pairs

Christmas Madonna. October 18, 1979. Photogravure. BEP.

15c multicolored

1799a imperf pair   70.00
 Quantity: 300-500 pairs

1799b vrt pair, imperf hz   *450.00*
 Quantity: at least 20-25 pairs

1799c vrt pair, imperf between   *950.00*
 Quantity: reportedly very rare

Will Rogers. November 4, 1979. Photogravure. BEP.

15c multicolored

1801a imperf pair   *135.00*
 Quantity: several hundred pairs

W.C. Fields. January 29, 1980. Photogravure. BEP.

15c multicolored

1803a imperf pair   —
 Quantity: n/a

Benjamin Bannecker. February 15, 1980. Photogravure. ABN.

15c multicolored
1804a hz pair, imperf vrt   *275.00*
      plate block of 12, imperf   —
      Quantity: 50+ pairs reported

▶ Caution. Fakes exist from printer's waste fraudulently perforated to simulate No. 1804a. Genuine examples of No. 1804a do not have misregistered colors. Expert certificate strongly advised. Completely imperforate pairs or multiples are from printer's waste. Refer to the Printer's Waste section.

Inkwell & Quill. March 6, 1981. Coil. Engraved. Shiny gum. BEP.

1c dark blue (greenish paper)
1811a imperf pair   *60.00*
      line pair, imperf   *150.00*
      spliced pair or strip, imperf   —
      Quantity: 600+ pairs

Transition multiples exist and sell for a premium.

Violins. June 23, 1980. Coil. Engraved. BEP.

3.5c purple (yellow paper)
1813b imperf pair   *125.00*
      line pair, imperf   *375.00*
      Quantity: 250 pairs reported

Values are for well-centered examples. Poorly centered examples sell for about half. Exists miscut. Transition multiples exist and sell for a premium.

Torch. April 8, 1981. Coil. Engraved. BEP.

12c red brown (gray paper)
1816b imperf pair   135.00
      line pair, imperf   275.00
      Quantity: 250 pairs

Eagle & B. March 15, 1980. Coil. Engraved. BEP.

B (18c) violet
1820a imperf pair   *75.00*
      line pair, imperf   *120.00*
      spliced pair or strip, imperf   —
      used pair, imperf   —
      Quantity: 300-400 pairs

Well-centered pairs sell for a premium.

Emily Bissell. May 31, 1980. Engraved. BEP.

15c black & red
1823a vrt pair, imperf hz   *250.00*
      plate block of 4, imperf hz   —
      Quantity: 40-60 pairs

Veterans Administration. July 21, 1980. Photogravure. ABN.

15c carmine & violet blue
1825a hz pair, imperf vrt   *375.00*
      Quantity: 50 pairs

Coral Reefs. August 26, 1980. Se-tenant block of 4. Photogravure. BEP.

15c multicolored

a) Brain Coral   b) Elkhorn Coral
c) Chalice Coral   d) Finger Coral

1830b	block of 4 (a-d), imperf	*350.00*
	any pair, imperf	*175.00*
	plate block of 12, imperf	*1,350.00*
	Zip block of 4, imperf	—
	Quantity: 60-80 blocks of 4, 30-40 pairs	
1830c	block of 4 (a-d), imperf between vrt	*1,750.00*
	as above, any pair	—
	Quantity: 2 blocks of 4 and 2 pairs reported	
1830d	block of 4 (a-d), imperf vrt	*2,750.00*
	Quantity: 4 blocks reported	

▶ Caution. Blind perfs may exist. Examine carefully.

Organized Labor. September 1, 1980. Photogravure. BEP.

15c multicolored

1831a	imperf pair	*275.00*
	Zip block of 4, imperf	—
	Quantity: 100-150 pairs reported	

Learning Never Ends. September 12, 1980. Photogravure. ABN.

15c multicolored

1833a	vrt pair, imperf vrt	150.00
	plate block of 8, imperf vrt	*1,000.00*
	Quantity: approx 100 pairs	

Madonna. October 31, 1980. Photogravure. BEP.

15c multicolored

1842a	imperf pair	40.00
	plate block of 12, imperf	300.00
	Quantity: 1,000+ pairs	

Examples without gum sell for a substantial discount.

Drum. October 31, 1980. Photogravure. BEP.

15c multicolored

1843a	imperf pair	40.00
	plate block of 20, imperf	500.00
	Quantity: 1,000+ pairs	
1843c	vrt pair, imperf hz	—
	Quantity: 3+ pairs reported	
1843d	hz pair, imperf between	*3,250.00*
	Quantity: 2 pairs	

The two listed pairs of No. 1843d are contained in a block of 15 and occupy positions 4 & 5 and 9 & 10.

GREAT AMERICANS SERIES OF 1980

Dorothea Dix. September 23, 1983. Engraved. BEP.

1c black
1844a   imperf pair   *250.00*
Quantity: at least 100 pairs

1844b   vrt pair, imperf between   *1,000.00*
Quantity: 5-7 pairs

Pairs of No. 1844b contain a natural straight edge at bottom. Perfs at top should be clear of the design. Slightly disturbed gum is typical.

1844e   vrt pair, imperf hz   *1,000.00*
Quantity: 4-7 pairs reported

Walter Lippmann. September 15, 1985. Engraved. BEP.

6c orange vermilion
1849a   vrt pair, imperf between   *1,000.00*
plate block of 4   —
Quantity: 10 pairs

Pairs of No. 1849a contain a natural straight edge at bottom.

Richard Russell. May 31, 1984. Engraved. BEP.

10c Prussian blue
1853b   vrt pair, imperf between   *550.00*
Quantity: 10-20 pairs

Most pairs of 1853b contain a natural straight edge either at top or bottom. At least one pair exists with a few perforations at top in the natural straight edge, clear of the design. They occur due to slanting misperforation of the pane.

1853d   vrt pair, imperf hz   —
Quantity: 10-17 pairs reported

Do not confuse Nos. 1853b and 1853d. Vertical pairs of No. 1853d exist with perforations well into the stamp above the error pair. Such error pairs are considered to be imperforate horizontally, because the perforations in the third stamp do not occupy space between any stamps and are, therefore, completely extraneous to the error pair.

1853c   hz pair, imperf between   *1,250.00*
Quantity: 10 pairs

Completely imperforate examples of No. 1853 are printer's waste. Refer to the Printer's Waste section.

Sinclair Lewis. March 21, 1985. Engraved. BEP.

14c slate green
1856b   vrt pair, imperf hz   *90.00*
Quantity: 200-250 pairs reported

1856c   hz pair, imperf between   8.00
         Quantity: several thousand pairs

1856d   vrt pair, imperf between   *1,250.00*
         Quantity: 15-20 pairs reported

NOTE: See Nos. 2182d and 2940a for other Great Americans imperforate errors.

John J. Audubon. April 23, 1985. Engraved. BEP.

22c dark chalky blue

1863d   vrt pair, imperf hz   *1,300.00*
         Quantity: 10 pairs

Transition multiples exist.

1863f   hz pair, imperf between   *1,300.00*
         Quantity: 10 pairs

Transition multiples exist. Beware of blind perfs, especially shifted into the stamps.

1863g   vrt pair, imperf between   —
         Quantity: n/a

Grenville Clark. May 20, 1985. Engraved. BEP.

39c rose lilac

1867a   vrt pair, imperf hz   *350.00*
         strip of 3, imperf hz   —
         Quantity: 30-50 pairs reported

Some examples exist with horizontal folds between stamps. Value is for an example without fold. Examples with fold sell for about one-third the price of those without folds.

1867b   vrt pair, imperf between   *1,500.00*
         Quantity: 5+ pairs reported

Editor's Note. The American Wildlife booklet pane (No. 1889a) has been reported imperforate vertically between; however, we are not aware of any example on which misplaced perforations at right are not entirely within the design, thus disqualifying the error. We would welcome documentation of a genuine example. Refer to the Printer's Waste section for completely imperforate examples.

Flag & Grain. April 24, 1981. Engraved. BEP.

18c red, blue & brown

1890a   imperf pair   75.00
         Quantity: several hundred pairs

1890b vrt pair, imperf hz   *550.00*
     block of 4, imperf hz   —
     Quantity: 10-15 pairs reported

1890c vrt pair, imperf between   *550.00*
     Quantity: n/a

Flag & Seashore. April 24, 1981. Coil. Engraved. BEP.

18c red, blue & brown

1891a	imperf pair	17.50
	imperf strip with plate No. 2	*750.00*
	imperf strip with plate No. 3	*5,500.00*
	imperf strip with plate No. 4	*750.00*
	imperf strip with plate No. 5	175.00
	spliced pair or strip, imperf	—
	Quantity: 1,000+ pairs	

Exists miscut. Value for plate No. 2 is for a strip of 4 (the longest known strip); price for plate No. 5 for strip of 6. Plate No. 2 is most commonly encountered in pairs: value $125.00. Plate number pairs of No. 5 sell for about half the price of plate strips of 6.

At the time plate number coils were first introduced, the practice of saving plate numbers in strips had not yet been established. Therefore, many early plate number imperfs are relatively plentiful in pair form, but genuinely rare in longer strips.

Imperforate vertical pairs and multiples are printer's waste. Refer to the Printer's Waste section.

1891b hz pair, imperf between   *1,750.00*
     Quantity: very rare

▶ Caution. Expert certificate necessary. The listing example is miscut.

Flag & Mountains se-tenant with numeral "6" in Circle of Stars. April 24, 1981. Booklet pane. Engraved. BEP.

6c Numeral in Circle of Stars
18c Flag & Mountains

1893b	booklet pane of 8 (6c & 18c), imperf vrt between	60.00
	pair (6c), imperf between	—
	pair (18c), imperf between	—
	Quantity: 1,000+ booklet panes	

U.S. Flag. December 17, 1981. Engraved. BEP.

20c black, dark blue & red

1894a	imperf vertical pair	30.00
	block of 4, imperf	75.00
	Quantity: 1,000+	

Collected in vertical pairs or blocks to distinguish it from the coil imperforate of the same design.

1894b vrt pair, imperf hz   *350.00*
     Quantity: very scarce

Transition multiples exist and sell for a premium.

U.S. Flag. December 17, 1981. Coil. Engraved. BEP.

20c black, dark blue & red

1895d	imperf pair	8.00
	imperf pair, used	—
	imperf strip with plate No. 1	—
	imperf strip with plate No. 2	350.00
	imperf strip with plate No. 3	450.00
	imperf strip with plate No. 4	400.00
	imperf strip with plate No. 5	300.00
	imperf strip with plate No. 6	1,150.00
	imperf strip with plate No. 8	160.00
	imperf strip with plate No. 9	160.00
	imperf strip with plate No. 10	140.00
	imperf strip with plate No. 11	900.00
	imperf strip with plate No. 12	850.00
	imperf strip with plate No. 13	950.00
	imperf strip with plate No. 14	1,250.00
	spliced pair or strip, imperf	—
	Quantity: several thousand pairs	

Exists miscut, some with EE bars at top or marginal markings at bottom. Transition multiples exist and sell for a premium. Exists untagged. Used pairs exist on philatelically inspired covers.

Values are for plate strips of 6; plate strips of 5 sell for similar prices. Generally, plate strips of 3 sell for about 50% of the plate strip of six price, and plate pairs sell for about 33% of the strip of six price. There are exceptions depending on the issue and the plate number. Refer to second note following No. 1891a.

1895e	pair, imperf between	*600.00*
	Quantity: 10-15 pairs	

▶ Caution. Fakes exist. Expert certificate necessary.

A unique strip exists containing three examples of No. 1895d spliced to three examples of No.1906c. The plate No. 3 is visible under the splicing tape on No. 1906c.

TRANSPORTATION SERIES OF 1982 COIL STAMPS

NOTE. Catalogue values for imperforate plate number coil (PNC) strips in this section are for strips of 6 unless otherwise noted. Generally, PNC strips of 5 sell for similar prices; PNC strips of 3 sell for about 50% of the strip of 6 price; and PNC pairs sell for about 33% of the strip of 6 price. There are exceptions, however, depending on issue and scarcity. Also, refer to the second note following No. 1891a.

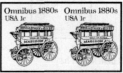

Omnibus. August 19, 1983. Coil. Engraved. BEP.

1c violet

1897b	imperf pair	*325.00*
	imperf strip with plate No. 5	*2,000.00*
	imperf strip with plate No. 6	*2,100.00*
	Quantity: 150-250 pairs	

Most plate No. strips of No. 1897b are 3 or 4 stamps in length. Longer strips are scarce.

See also No. 2225c.

Locomotive. May 20, 1982. Coil. Engraved. BEP.

2c black

1897Ac	imperf pair	45.00
	used strip of 3, imperf	—
	imperf strip with plate No. 3	200.00
	imperf strip with plate No. 4	225.00
	imperf strip with plate No. 8	275.00
	imperf strip with plate No. 10	275.00
	Quantity: few thousand pairs	

Transition multiples exist and sell for a premium. Values are for plate strips of 6 with plate numbers & lines. Plate pairs sell for 33% less. Refer to second note following No. 1891a.

Stagecoach. August 19, 1982. Coil. Engraved. BEP.

4c reddish brown

1898Ac	imperf pair, precanceled 2 bars & NON-PROFIT Org.	*375.00*
	imperf strip with plate No. 5	*1,250.00*
	imperf strip with plate No. 6	*1,250.00*
	imperf pair, gap in bars	—
	spliced pair or strip, imperf	—
	Quantity: 75+ pairs	

Exists miscut. Transition multiples exist. Plate No. 5 exists as pairs, strips of 3 and a unique strip of 4 (value, $2,500). Plate No. 6 exists only as pairs or strips of 3 on which the plate number always appears at the top.

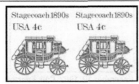

1898Ad imperf pair, without precancel — 400.00
imperf strip with line & plate No. 1 — 2,000.00
imperf strip with line & plate No. 2 — 2,000.00
spliced pair or strip, imperf — —
Quantity: 150 pairs reported

Exists miscut.

See also No. 2228b.

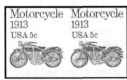

Motorcycle. October 10, 1983. Coil. Engraved. BEP.

5c gray green
1899a imperf pair — 1,750.00
imperf strip of 5 with plate No. 1 — 7,000.00
imperf strip of 5 with plate No. 2 — 7,000.00
spliced strip, imperf — —
Quantity: 32 pairs; the 2 plate strips,
each unique; unique spliced strip

A transition multiple exists.

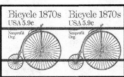

Bicycle. May 17, 1982. Coil. Engraved. BEP.

5.9c blue
1901b imperf pair, precanceled 2 bars — 140.00
imperf strip with plate No. 3 — 750.00
imperf strip with plate No. 4 — 750.00
imperf pair or strip, gap in bars — —
Quantity: 1,000+ pairs

Exists miscut, some with EE bars at top. Transition multiples exist and sell for a premium.

Refer to the introductory note preceding No. 1897b and the second note following No. 1891a for information about size and valuing of plate number coil strips.

Mail Wagon. December 15, 1981. Coil. Engraved. BEP.

9.3c carmine rose
1903b imperf pair, precanceled 2 bars — 90.00
imperf strip with plate No. 1 — 1,250.00
imperf strip with plate No. 2 — 1,250.00
imperf strip with plate No. 3 — 3,000.00
imperf strip with plate No. 4 — 3,000.00
imperf pair or strip, gap in bars — —
Quantity: 500 pairs; plate No. strips
3 and 4 are unique

Hansom Cab. March 26, 1982. Coil. Engraved. BEP.

10.9c purple
1904b imperf pair, precanceled 2 bars — 125.00
imperf strip with plate No. 1 — 1,100.00
imperf strip with plate No. 2 — 1,100.00
imperf pair or strip, gap in bars — —
Quantity: 250+ pairs reported

Electric Auto. June 25, 1981. Coil. Engraved. BEP.

17c ultramarine
1906b imperf pair — 130.00
imperf strip with plate No. 1 — 950.00
imperf strip with plate No. 2 — 950.00
imperf strip with plate No. 3 — 950.00
imperf strip with plate No. 4 — 950.00
imperf strip with plate No. 5 — 2,750.00
imperf strip with plate No. 7 — 2,750.00
used pair, imperf — —
spliced pair or strip, imperf — —
Quantity: 350-400 pairs; 2 plate
No. strips each of Nos. 5 and 7 known

Exists miscut. Plate numbers often appear at top of strip due to miscut. Transition multiples exist and sell for a premium.

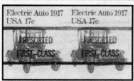

1906c   imperf pair, precanceled 2 bars
         & PRESORTED FIRST-CLASS   *400.00*
         imperf strip with plate No. 3   *1,750.00*
         imperf strip with plate No. 4   *1,750.00*
         imperf pair or strip, gap in bars   —
         spliced pair or strip, imperf   —
         Quantity: 80-100 pairs reported

Exists miscut. Refer to the note following No. 1895e for spliced combination strip containing No. 1906c.

Surrey. May 18, 1981. Coil. Engraved. BEP.

18c dark brown

1907a   imperf pair   95.00
         imperf strip with plate No. 1   *3,000.00*
         imperf strip with plate No. 2   *3,000.00*
         imperf strip with plate No. 8   *500.00*
         imperf strip with plate No. 9   *575.00*
         imperf strip with plate No. 10   *575.00*
         imperf strip with plate No. 13 *1,750.00*
         spliced pair or strip, imperf   —
         Quantity: 400-500 pairs

Exists miscut. Values are for strips of 5 or 6 with plate number and line, except plate No. 13, which exists only as a unique strip of 4. Also, refer to the second note following No. 1891a.

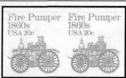

Fire Pumper. December 10, 1982. Coil. Engraved. BEP.

20c vermilion

1908a   imperf pair   75.00
         imperf strip with plate No. 1   *1,500.00*
         imperf strip with plate No. 2   *3,500.00*
         imperf strip with plate No. 3   *1,500.00*
         imperf strip with plate No. 4   *1,250.00*
         imperf strip with plate No. 5   *1,500.00*
         imperf strip with plate No. 9   *1,100.00*
         imperf strip with plate No. 10   *1,100.00*
         imperf strip with plate No. 15   *1,250.00*
         imperf strip with plate No. 16   *1,250.00*
         imperf pair, used   *75.00*
         Quantity: 600-800 pairs

Exists miscut. Transition multiples exist and sell for a premium. Values are for strips of 6 with plate number and line. Plate Nos. 1, 4 and 5 are most commonly encountered in plate number pairs: price $200-$375. Plate No. 2 exists only as a pair and is unique. Plate strips of 3 or 4 generally sell for about 33%-50% of plate strips of 6.

Refer to the introductory note preceding No. 1897b and the second note following No. 1891a for information about size and pricing of plate number coil strips.

NOTE: See Nos. 2126b-2136b, 2225c-2228b, 2252b-2265a, and 2451a-2468a for other Transportation Series coils.

Space Achievement. Se-tenant block of 8. May 21, 1981. Photogravure. BEP.

18c multicolored
         a) Exploring the Moon
         b) Space Shuttle
         c) Space Shuttle Launching Satellite
         d) Understanding the Sun
         e) Probing the Planets
         f) Space Shuttle Blasting Off
         g) Space Shuttle with Landing Gear Down
         h) Comprehending the Universe
1919b   block of 8 (a-h), imperf   *5,500.00*
         plate block of 8 (a-h), imperf   —
         Zip block of 8 (a-h), imperf   —
         Quantity: 4-6 blocks of 8 reported

Two blocks of 8 exist perforated horizontally at the top, and with vertical perforations extending about one-third the way down from the top. This creates four imperf stamps (e-h) along the bottom row and four imperf horizontally (a-e, b-f, c-g, and d-h) pairs. One sold at auction for $1,725 in December 2010.

1919c block of 8, imperf vrt   *2,000.00*
   Quantity: unique

The error block contains rows of blind horizontal perforations.

Year of the Disabled. June 29, 1981. Photogravure. BEP.

18c multicolored
1925a vrt pair, imperf hz   *1,500.00*
   plate block of 4   *5,000.00*
   Quantity: 10 pairs reported, including
   2 pairs in the plate block

▶ Caution. Beware of pairs with blind horizontal perfs. Error pairs contain blind vertical perforations, which are normal.

Beat Alcoholism. August 19, 1981. Engraved. BEP.

18c blue & black
1927a imperf pair   *325.00*
   Quantity: at least 50 pairs

Value is for pair without disturbed gum. Examples with disturbed gum sell for less.

1927b vrt pair, imperf hz   *2,000.00*
   Quantity: 3 pairs reported

Frederic Remington. October 9, 1981. Engraved. BEP.

18c gray, olive green & brown
1934a vrt pair, imperf between   *160.00*
   Quantity: 200 pairs reported

▶ Caution. Pairs or strips of 3 exist with blind perfs.

Madonna. October 28, 1981. Photogravure. BEP.

(20c) multicolored
1939a imperf pair   *90.00*
   Quantity: few hundred pairs

1939b vrt pair, imperf hz   *750.00*
   block of 4, imperf hz   —
   Quantity: 4-5 pairs reported

Christmas Toys. October 28, 1981. Photogravure. BEP.

(20c) multicolored
1940a imperf pair   *175.00*
   Quantity: 200-300 pairs

1940b vrt pair, imperf hz   *2,000.00*
   Quantity: 10-15 pairs

No. 1940b results from blind perfs at left and right.

**Cactus. December 11, 1981. Se-tenant block of 4.
Engraved, lithographed. BEP.**

20c multicolored
a) Barrel Cactus   b) Agave
c) Beavertail Cactus   d) Saguaro

1945c   vrt pair (d only), imperf   3,000.00
         single (d), imperf   —
         Quantity: 2 pairs, 1 single

The vertical imperf pair (d only) is contained in a block of 8.

Eagle & C. October 11, 1981. Coil. Photogravure. BEP.

C (20c) brown
1947a   imperf pair   700.00
         line strip of 4, imperf   —
         Quantity: 60-70 pairs, 6+ line strips

Gum along the edges of approximately half the known pairs
appears to have been slightly disturbed by moisture. Value is for
a pair without moisture disturbance. Those with the disturbance
sell for less.

**Bighorn Sheep. January 8, 1982. Booklet pane of 10.
Engraved. BEP.**

20c dark blue
1949b   booklet pane of 10, imperf vrt between   90.00
         complete booklet of 2 panes,
           imperf vrt between   180.00
         Quantity: at least 150 booklet panes

Love. February 1, 1982. Photogravure. BEP.

20c multicolored
1951b   imperf pair   200.00
         plate block of 4, imperf   —
         Quantity: 150-200 pairs

Horizontal pairs usually sell for more than vertical pairs.

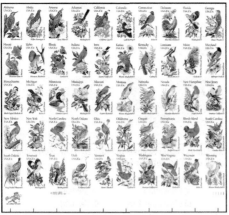

State Birds & Flowers. April 14, 1982. Se-tenant pane of 50. Photogravure. BEP.

20c multicolored.

2002d	pane of 50, imperf	*21,000.00*
	imperf pair	—
	Quantity: 4 panes	

Of the four panes, two are completely imperforate, one contains some blind perforations, and one was cut into pairs.

Netherlands/USA. April 20, 1983. Photogravure. BEP.

20c multicolored

2003a	imperf pair	*250.00*
	plate strip of 20, imperf	—
	Quantity: 94 pairs reported	

Consumer Education. April 27, 1982. Coil. Engraved. BEP.

20c sky blue

2005a	imperf pair	70.00
	imperf strip with plate No. 1	*750.00*
	imperf strip with plate No. 2	*750.00*
	imperf strip with plate No. 3	*1,750.00*
	imperf strip with plate No. 4	*1,750.00*
	Quantity: several hundred pairs	

Values are for strips of 6 with plate number and line. Plate strips of 5 sell for similar prices. Plate pairs are much more common: value $275.00. Plate strips of 3 sell for about 33% the plate strip of 6 price. Exists miscut. Transition multiples exist and sell for a premium.

America's Libraries. July 13, 1982. Engraved. BEP.

20c red & black

2015a	vrt pair, imperf hz	*200.00*
	Quantity: 100-120 pairs	

Touro Synagogue. August 22, 1982. Photogravure. BEP.

20c multicolored

2017a	imperf pair	*1,400.00*
	Quantity: 25 pairs	

Ponce de Leon. October 12, 1982. Photogravure. BEP.

20c multicolored

2024a	imperf pair	*250.00*
	plate block of 20, imperf	—
	Quantity: 125+ pairs reported	
2024b	vrt pair, imperf between and at top	*500.00*
	Quantity: rare	

Puppy & Kitten. November 3, 1982. Photogravure. BEP.

13c multicolored

2025a   imperf pair   *300.00*
         Quantity: 75-100 pairs reported

Some pairs are faulty. Value is for a sound pair. Faulty pairs sell for considerably less.

Madonna. October 28, 1982. Photogravure. BEP.

20c multicolored

2026a   imperf pair   90.00
         plate block of 20, imperf   —
         Quantity: few hundred pairs

2026b   hz pair, imperf vrt   *900.00*
         Quantity: 3-6 pairs reported

2026c   vrt pair, imperf hz   —
         plate block of 4, imperf hz   —
         Quantity: very rare

The plate block contains blind perforations on its sides and at bottom.

Christmas Winter Scenes. October 28, 1982. Se-tenant block of 4. Photogravure. BEP.

20c multicolored

         a) Snowman   b) Sledding
         c) Christmas tree   d) Skating

2030b   block of 4 (a-d), imperf   *1,250.00*
         Quantity: 20 blocks of 4

▶ Caution. Beware of blocks with blind perforations.

2030c   block of 4 (a-d), imperf hz   *700.00*
         Quantity: rare

Expect blind vertical perfs.

Balloons. March 31, 1983. Se-tenant block of 4. Photogravure. BEP.

20c multicolored

         a) Intrepid
         b) Hot Air Ballooning
         c) Hot Air Ballooning
         d) Explorer II

2035b   block of 4 (a-d), imperf   *2,750.00*
         plate block of 4, imperf   —
         Zip block of 4, imperf   —
         copyright block of 4, imperf   —
         Quantity: 10 blocks of 4

In addition to the above, five blocks of 4 (a-d) exist with perforations on the three exterior sides of the right stamp (d). Some, but not all, of the blocks contain a vertical row of blind perforations between stamps (b-c) and the right stamp (d). Value $2,000.

Civilian Conservation Corps. April 5, 1983. Photogravure. BEP.

20c multicolored
2037a imperf pair   *2,250.00*
       plate block of 4, imperf   —
Quantity: 17 pairs, including
         those in the plate blocks

The discovery pane contained seven error pairs, including two in a plate block. A second pane contains ten error pairs, including a plate block.

2037b vrt pair, imperf hz   —
       Quantity: unique

No. 2037b results from blind perfs at its sides.

Volunteer Lend A Hand. April 20, 1983. Engraved. BEP.

20c red & black
2039a imperf pair   *225.00*
       Quantity: 25-50 pairs reported

Some examples have an underinked appearance. Value is for underinked example. Solidly colored examples sell for much more.

Scott Joplin. June 9, 1983. Photogravure. BEP.

20c multicolored
2044a imperf pair   *300.00*
       Quantity: 50 pairs reported

Santa Claus. October 28, 1983. Photogravure. BEP.

20c multicolored
2064a imperf pair   *100.00*
       plate block of 6, imperf   450.00
       Quantity: 150+ pairs

Alaska Statehood. January 23, 1984. Photogravure. ABN.

20c multicolored
2066a used vrt pair, imperf hz   —
       Quantity: see note

No. 2086a occurs in an irregular used block of 13 stamps containing several pairs.

Love. January 31, 1984. Photogravure. BEP.

20c multicolored
2072a hz pair, imperf vrt   *125.00*
       plate strip of 20   —
       Quantity: 150-175 pairs

Carter G. Woodson. January 31, 1984. Photogravure. ABN.

20c multicolored

2073a hz pair, imperf vrt   *800.00*
Quantity: 25 pairs reported

Summer Olympics. May 4, 1984. Photogravure. BEP.

20c multicolored

a) Diving   b) Long Jump
c) Wrestling   d) Canoeing

2085b block of 4, imperf between vrt   *9,500.00*
pair c & d, imperf vrt   —
Quantity: 2 blocks of 4, 1 pair

The discovery pane contained the listed stamps in a strip of ten at right. The pane also contained a row of blind perfs between rows 6 and 7. The pane has since been broken up.

Douglas Fairbanks. May 23, 1984. Engraved, photogravure. BEP.

20c multicolored

2088b hz pair, imperf vrt   —
Quantity: reportedly unique

Preserving Wetlands. July 2, 1984. Engraved. BEP.

20c blue

2092a hz pair, imperf vrt   *275.00*
hz strip of 3, imperf vrt   *375.00*
Zip block, imperf vrt   —
Quantity: 100-125 pairs

Smokey. August 13, 1984. Photogravure. BEP.

20c multicolored

2096a hz pair, imperf between   *175.00*
plate block of 4, vrt imperf
between   —
Quantity: 100-125 pairs

2096b vrt pair, imperf between   *150.00*
Quantity: 160-200 pairs

2096c   block of 4, imperf hz & vrt
       (internally) between   *2,500.00*
       Quantity: 6 blocks of 4 (including
       1 faulty block) and 2 blocks of 6

2096d   hz pair, imperf vrt   *450.00*
       Quantity: 20-25 pairs

Roberto Clemente. August 17, 1984. Photogravure. BEP.

20c multicolored

2097a   hz pair, imperf vrt   *1,250.00*
       hz strip of 3, vrt imperf   —
       Quantity: 20 pairs, 3 strips of 3 reported

Dogs. September 7, 1984. Photogravure. BEP.

20c multicolored

a) Beagle, Boston Terrier
b) Chesapeake Bay Retreiver, Cocker Spaniel
c) Alaskan Malamute, Collie
d) Black & Tan Coonhound, American Foxhound

2101b   block of 4, imperf hz   *5,500*
       pair (b & d) imperf hz   —
       Quantity: 1 pane including 8 blocks of 4
       and 4 pairs (b & d)

Hispanic Americans. October 31, 1984. Photogravure. BEP.

20c multicolored

2103a   vrt pair, imperf hz   *1,250.00*
       Quantity: 20 pairs reported

Family Unity. October 1, 1984. Photogravure. BEP.

20c multicolored

2104a	hz pair, imperf vrt	*325.00*
	Quantity: 50 pairs	
2104c	vrt pair, imperf between	—
	Quantity: n/a	

No. 2104c occurs with a natural straight edge at bottom.

2104d	hz pair, imperf between	—
	Quantity: n/a	

Madonna. October 30, 1984. Photogravure. BEP.

20c multicolored

2107a	imperf pair	*1,750.00*

Christmas. October 30, 1984. Photogravure. BEP.

20c multicolored

2108a	hz pair, imperf vrt	*750.00*
	Quantity: 25 pairs	

Most examples are poorly centered. Value is for a poorly centered example.

Eagle & D. February 1, 1985. Photogravure. BEP.

D (22c) green

2111a	vrt pair, imperf	35.00
	block of 4, imperf	70.00
	plate block of 4, imperf	110.00
	Zip block of 4, imperf	100.00
	copyright block of 4, imperf	100.00
	Quantity: 1,000+	

2111b	vrt pair, imperf hz	*750.00*
	Quantity: 5 pairs reported	

▶ Caution. Beware of blocks with blind perforations.

Eagle & D. February 1, 1985. Coil. Photogravure. BEP.

D (22c) green

2112a	imperf pair	45.00
	imperf strip with plate No. 1	500.00
	imperf strip with plate No. 2	750.00
	spliced pair or strip, imperf	—
	Quantity: 1,000+	

Catalogue values are for plate strips of 6. Plate strips of 5 sell for similar prices. Plate strips of 3 or 4 for sell for 33%-50% the price of plate strips of 6. Strips exist spliced with a variety of kinds and colors of cellophane, masking, and paper tapes, and they sell for a premium. Exists miscut. Exists untagged; quantity 200 pairs; value $125.

Eagle & D. February 1, 1985. Booklet pane of 10. Photogravure. BEP.

D (22c) green

2113b	booklet pane of 10, imperf hz between	*1,850.00*
	Quantity: 2 panes	

Two examples of No. 2113b are reported, both in an unexploded booklet.

Flag & Capitol. March 29, 1985. Coil. Engraved. BEP.

22c red, blue & black

2115f	imperf pair	10.00
	imperf strip with plate No. 1	250.00
	imperf strip with plate No. 2	150.00
	imperf strip with plate No. 3	*1,000.00*
	imperf strip with plate No. 4	*750.00*
	imperf strip with plate No. 5	675.00
	imperf strip with plate No. 6	850.00
	imperf strip with plate No. 7	*450.00*
	imperf strip with plate No. 8	300.00
	imperf strip with plate No. 10	500.00
	imperf strip with plate No. 11	*1,250.00*
	imperf strip with plate No. 12	350.00
	imperf strip with plate No. 13	*650.00*
	imperf strip with plate No. 15	900.00
	imperf strip with plate No. 17	—
	imperf strip with plate No. 18	550.00
	imperf strip with plate No. 19	400.00
	imperf strip with plate No. 20	950.00
	imperf strip with plate No. 22	400.00
	spliced pair or strip, imperf	—
	Quantity: few thousand pairs	

Catalogue values are for plate strips of 5 or 6 of 2115f. Strips of 3 or 4 sell for 33%-50% of the strip of 6 price. Exists miscut, some with EE bars at top or marginal markings at bottom. Transition multiples exist and sell for a premium.

Sea Shells. April 4, 1985. Se-tenant booklet pane of 10. Engraved. BEP.

22c multicolored

a) Frilled Dogwinkle
b) Reticulated Helmet
c) New England Neptune
d) Calico Scallop
e) Lightning Whelk

2121c	booklet pane, imperf vrt between	*350.00*
	Quantity: 40-50 booklets reported	

Panes removed from booklets usually contain tab faults. Value is for pane with tab faults.

2121d	booklet pane, imperf	—
	Quantity: n/a	

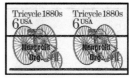

Tricycle. May 6, 1985. Coil. Engraved. BEP.

6c red brown

2126b	imperf pair, precanceled 2 bars & NON-PROFIT Org.	*175.00*
	imperf strip with plate No. 2	*1,250.00*
	Quantity: 250 pairs reported	

Oil Wagon. April 18, 1985. Coil. Engraved. BEP.

10.1c slate blue

2130b	imperf pair, service inscribed Bulk Rate Carrier Route Sort In red	15.00
	imperf strip with plate No. 2	200.00
	imperf strip with plate No. 3	200.00
	spliced pair or strip, imperf	—
	Quantity: a few thousand pairs	

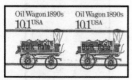

2130b	imperf pair, precanceled 2 bars & BULK RATE in black	70.00
	imperf strip with plate No. 1	*500.00*
	spliced pair or strip, imperf	—
	imperf pair or strip, gap in bars	—
	Quantity: 500 pairs reported	

Pushcart. April 18, 1985. Coil. Engraved. BEP.

12.5c olive green

2133b	imperf pair, precanc bars & Bulk Rate	40.00
	imperf strip with plate No. 1	200.00
	imperf pair or strip, gap in bars	—
	Quantity: 750-1,000 pairs	

Iceboat. March 23, 1985. Coil. Engraved. BEP.

14c sky blue

2134a	imperf pair	75.00
	imperf strip with plate No.1	350.00
	imperf strip with plate No.2	350.00
	Quantity: 350+ pairs reported	

Transition multiples exist and sell for a premium.

Note: See Nos. 1897b-1908a, 2225c-2228b, 2252b-2265a, and 2451a-2468a for other Transportation Series coils.

Dog Sled. August 20, 1986. Coil. Engraved. BEP.

17c sky blue

2135a	imperf pair	*300.00*
	imperf strip with plate No. 2	*1,500.00*
	used strip of 3, imperf	—
	Quantity: 100-125 pairs reported	

Catalogue values are the same for plate strip of 5 or 6. Exists miscut. Transition multiples exist and sell for a premium. A used strip of 3 on piece exists postmarked "Gardenville, PA, Jul 15, 1987."

Breadwagon. November 22, 1986. Coil. Engraved. BEP.

25c orange brown

2136a	imperf pair	10.00
	imperf strip with plate No. 1	*1,000.00*
	imperf strip with plate No. 2	175.00
	imperf strip with plate No. 3	225.00
	imperf strip with plate No. 4	225.00
	imperf strip with plate No. 5	*500.00*
	imperf pair, used	—
	spliced pair or strip, imperf	—
	Quantity: few thousand pairs; 3 plate No. 1 strips known	

Exists miscut, some with EE bars at top or marginal markings at bottom. Transition multiples exist and sell for a premium. Exists untagged.

2136b	pair, imperf between	*525.00*
	strip of three pairs with plate No. 2	—
	Quantity: 10 pairs reported	

Special Olympics. March 5, 1985. Photogravure. BEP.

22c multicolored
2142a   vrt pair, imperf hz   *300.00*
        Quantity: 60-80 pairs reported

Love. April 17, 1985. Photogravure. BEP.

22c multicolored
2143a   imperf pair   *800.00*
        Quantity: 15 pairs imperf, 5 pairs
        partially imperf, see note

Some pairs (often in transition strips) contain perfs at left, and on top and bottom of the left stamp. Often with paper crease. Value is for sound pair. Creased pairs sell for about 33% of sound pairs.

Rural Electrification. May 11, 1985. Engraved, photogravure. BEP.

22c multicolored
2144a   vrt pair, imperf between   —
        Quantity: reportedly unique

Abigail Adams. June 14, 1985. Photogravure. BEP.

22c multicolored
2146a   imperf pair   *200.00*
        Quantity: 150-200 pairs

Transition multiples exist and sell for a premium.

George Washington. November 6, 1985. Coil. Photogravure. BEP.

18c multicolored
2149b   imperf pair, without precancel   *750.00*
        imperf strip with plate No. 1112   *2,500.00*
        Quantity: 35-40 pairs reported

2149c   imperf pair, precanceled PRESORTED
        FIRST-CLASS   *575.00*
        imperf strip with plate No. 3333   —
        imperf strip with plate No. 1121   —
        imperf strip with plate No. 3333   *1,250.00*
        spliced pair or strip, imperf   —
        Quantity: 75-100 pairs reported. Exists miscut.

Transition multiples exist and sell for a premium.

Madonna. October 30, 1985. Photogravure. BEP.

22c multicolored
2165a   imperf pair   *55.00*
        plate block of 4, imperf   *110.00*
        Zip block of 4, imperf   *110.00*
        Quantity: 300-400 pairs

Poinsettia. October 30, 1985. Photogravure. BEP.

22c multicolored

2166a	imperf pair	50.00
	block of 4, imperf	100.00
	plate block of 4, imperf	—
	Zip block of 4, imperf	100.00
	Quantity: 250-300 pairs	

Arkansas. January 3, 1986. Photogravure. ABN.

22c multicolored

2167a	vrt pair, imperf hz	500.00
	Quantity: 25 pairs reported	

Jack London. May 3, 1988. Engraved. BEP.

25c blue

2182d	hz pair, imperf between	750.00
	Quantity: n/a	

Texas. March 2, 1986. Photogravure. ABN.

22c multicolored

2204a	hz pair, imperf vrt	600.00
	Quantity: 25 pairs	

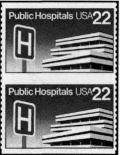

Public Hospitals. April 11, 1986. Photogravure. BEP.

22c multicolored

2210a	vrt pair, imperf hz	250.00
	Quantity: 50-75 pairs	

2210b	hz pair, imperf vrt	800.00
	Quantity: 20 pairs	

Duke Ellington. April 29, 1986. Photogravure. ABN.

22c multicolored

2211a	vrt pair, imperf hz	500.00
	plate block of 4, imperf hz	—
	use pair, imperf hz	—
	used strip of 3, imperf hz	—
	Quantity: 40-60 pairs	

Presidents of
the United States: I

AMERIPEX 86
International
Stamp Show
Chicago, Illinois
May 22-June 1, 1986

Presidents. May 22, 1986. Souvenir sheet of 9. Engraved, lithographed. BEP.

22c multicolored

2216l	imperf sheet of 9	*10,500.00*
	Quantity: very rare, possibly unique	

Omnibus. November 26, 1986. Coil. Engraved. BEP.

1c violet

2225c	imperf pair	*1,750.00*
	imperf strip with plate No. 2	*4,500.00*
	spliced pair or strip, imperf	—
	Quantity: 22-24 pairs	

Transition multiples exist. Plate No. 2 is known on a transition strip in which the plate number appears on a perforated stamp.

See also No. 1897b.

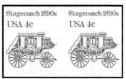

Stagecoach. August 15, 1986. Revised design. Coil. Engraved. BEP.

4c reddish brown

2228b	imperf pair	175.00
	imperf strip with plate No. 1	*1,250.00*
	Quantity: 250 pairs	

See also No. 1898Ad. No. 1898Ad contains a line on plate number pairs or strips. No. 2228b contains a plate number only. Transition multiples exist.

Wood Carving. October 1, 1986. Se-tenant block of 4. Photogravure. ABN.

22c multicolored

a) Highlander Figure	b) Ship Figurehead
c) Nautical Figure	d) Cigar Store Indian

2243b	block of 4 (a-d), imperf vrt	*750.00*
	pair (a-b or c-d), imperf vrt	*300.00*
	Quantity: 20 blocks of 4;	
	5 pairs each a-b & c-d	

Madonna. October 24, 1986. Photogravure. BEP.

22c multicolored

2244a	imperf pair	400.00
	Quantity: 25-50 pairs reported	

Conestoga Wagon. February 29, 1988. Coil. Engraved. Shiny gum. BEP.

3c claret, untagged

2252b	imperf pair	1,350.00
	imperf strip with plate No. 5	2,500.00
	Quantity: 2 transitional strips of 12 or 13 stamps	

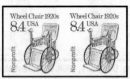

Wheel Chair. August 12, 1988. Coil. Engraved. BEP.

8.4c deep claret (red service inscription)

2256a	imperf pair	350.00
	imperf strip with plate No. 1	1,500.00
	imperf strip with plate No. 2	1,500.00
	Quantity: 100+ pairs reported	

Transition multiples exist and sell for a premium.

Canal Boat. April 11, 1987. Coil. Engraved. BEP.

10c blue

2257e	imperf pair	1,000.00
	imperf strip with Plate No. 1	6,500.00
	Quantity: 53 stamps; plate strip unique	

Coal Car. July 19, 1988. Coil. Engraved. BEP.

13.2c slate green (red service inscription)

2259a	imperf pair	75.00
	imperf strip with plate No. 1	275.00
	imperf strip with plate No. 2	500.00
	Quantity: several hundred pairs	

Transition multiples exist and sell for a premium.

Tugboat. July 12, 1988. Coil. Engraved. BEP.

15c violet

2260c	imperf pair	500.00
	imperf strip with plate No. 2	1,750.00
	Quantity: 80-100 pairs	

Transition multiples exist and sell for a premium.

Popcorn Wagon. July 7, 1988. Coil. Engraved. BEP.

16.7c rose (black service inscription)

2261a	imperf pair	125.00
	imperf strip with plate No. 1	1,200.00
	Quantity: several hundred pairs reported	

All known examples are miscut. Transition multiples exist and sell for a premium.

Note: For other imperforate Transportation Series coils see Nos. 1897b-1908a, 2126b-2136b, 2225c-2228b, and 2451a-2468a.

Racing Car. September 25, 1987. Coil. Engraved. BEP.

17.5c dark violet

2262b	imperf pair	1,250.00
	imperf strip with plate No. 1	3,500.00
	Quantity: 26 pairs; 3 plate strips of 6 reported	

Transition multiples exist and sell for a premium.

Cable Car. October 28, 1988. Coil. Engraved. BEP.

20c blue violet

2263a	imperf pair	50.00
	imperf strip with plate No. 2	275.00
	spliced pair or strip, imperf	—
	Quantity: 1,000+ pairs	

Transition multiples exist and sell for a premium.

Mail Car. August 16, 1988. Coil. Engraved. BEP.

21c olive green (red service inscription)

2265a	imperf pair	35.00
	imperf strip with plate No. 1	300.00
	imperf pair on first day cover	—
	Quantity: 1,000+ pairs;	
	36 first day covers reported	

Current Postal Service policy allows a grace period of 120 days unless stated otherwise after a stamp is issued during which covers may be submitted for first day cancellation. Because of this policy, controversy exists about the legitimacy of items that cannot conclusively be proved to have been postmarked on the actual first day of issue. Some regard imperforates on first day covers as contrived curiosities; others regard them as legitimately collectible. The editors take no position in this matter other than to report the existence of the covers.

Flag & Fireworks. November 30, 1987. Booklet pane of 20. Photogravure. BEP.

22c multicolored

2276b	vert pair, imperf btwn	*1,450.00*
	Quantity: unique	

No. 2276b occurs as a result of a foldover.

Earth. March 22, 1988. Coil. Photogravure. BEP.

E (25c) multicolored

2279a	imperf pair	60.00
	imperf strip with plate No. 1111	*375.00*
	imperf strip with plate No. 1211	*1,500.00*
	imperf strip with plate No. 1222	*950.00*
	imperf strip with plate No. 2222	*950.00*
	spliced pair or strip, imperf	—
	Quantity: 1,000+ pairs	

Catalogue values are for plate strips of 6. Exists miscut. The plate number on plate strips of No. 1222 appears at the top due to a miscut. Transition multiples exist and sell for a premium.

Flag Over Yosemite. May 20, 1988. Coil. Block tagging. Engraved. BEP.

25c red, ultramarine & cobalt green

2280b	imperf pair	25.00
	imperf strip with plate No. 2	600.00
	imperf strip with plate No. 3	425.00
	imperf strip with plate No. 4	*800.00*
	imperf strip with plate No. 5	700.00
	imperf strip with plate No. 7	500.00
	imperf strip with plate No. 8	550.00
	imperf strip with plate No. 9	700.00
	spliced pair or strip, imperf	—
	Quantity: several thousand pairs	

Exists miscut. Transition multiples exist and sell for a premium.

Flag Over Yosemite. February 14, 1989. Coil. Prephosphored paper. Engraved. BEP.

2280c	imperf pair	10.00
	imperf strip with plate No. 2	150.00
	imperf strip with plate No. 3	*550.00*
	imperf strip with plate No. 5	*550.00*
	imperf strip with plate No. 6	*750.00*
	imperf strip with plate No. 7	450.00
	imperf strip with plate No. 8	*550.00*
	imperf strip with plate No. 9	250.00
	imperf strip with plate No. 10	375.00
	imperf strip with plate No. 11	*450.00*
	imperf strip with plate No. 13	*1,100.00*
	imperf strip with plate No. 14	350.00
	imperf strip with plate No. 15	*1,100.00*
	imperf pair on first day cover	—
	spliced pair or strip, imperf	—
	Quantity: several thousand pairs	

Exists miscut, some with EE bands at top or marginal markings at bottom. Exists untagged. Transition multiples exist and sell for a premium. Values are for plate strips of 6.

Block tagging on No. 2280b is rectangular in shape covering the design. Prephosphored paper tagging on No. 2280c covers the entire stamp and has a mottled appearance. Refer to note following No. 2265a regarding first day covers.

2280f	pair, imperf between	*375.00*
	strip of 6 with plate No. 9	—
	strip of 6 with plate No. 14	—
	Quantity: 35+ pairs reported	

Expert certificate advised.

Honeybee. September 2, 1988. Coil. Engraved, lithographed. BEP.

25c multicolored

2281a	imperf pair	45.00
	imperf strip with plate No. 1	250.00
	imperf strip with plate No. 2	250.00
	imperf pair on first day cover	—
	spliced pair or strip, imperf	—
	Quantity: several hundred pairs;	
	at least 6 first day covers	

Exists miscut, some with EE bars at top. Some pairs contain lines that resemble Cottrell press lines. Values are for plate strips of 6. Refer to the note following No. 2265a regarding first day covers. Vertical pairs or blocks both imperforate and with engraved black omitted are printer's waste.

▶ Caution. Pairs exist with blind perfs.

2281d	pair, imperf between	*600.00*
	strip with plate No. 1, imperf between	—
	Quantity: 10 pairs, 1-2 plate	
	number strips reported	

Pairs may have blind perfs at left and right (see illustration).

Pheasant. April 29, 1988. Booklet pane of 10. Engraved, lithographed. ABN.

25c multicolored

2283d	vrt pair, imperf between	*275.00*
	Quantity: rare	

No. 2283d occurs as the result of a foldover. Non-foldover pairs and multiples are printer's waste and plentiful. Refer to the Printer's Waste section.

South Carolina. May 23, 1988. Photogravure. ABN.

25c multicolored

2343a	hz strip of 3, imperf vrt	*12,500.00*
	Quantity: unique strip of 3	

Love. July 4, 1988. Photogravure. BEP.

25c multicolored

2378a	imperf pair	*1,500.00*
	Quantity: 5-10 pairs or strips of 3	

Antarctic Explorers. September 14, 1988. Se-tenant block of 4. Photogravure. ABN.

25c multicolored
a) Nathaniel Palmer   b) Charles Wilkes
c) Richard Byrd   d) Lincoln Ellsworth

2389c   block of 4, imperf hz   *1,500.00*
         plate block of 4, imperf hz   —
         Quantity: 10 blocks of 4,
            5 singles (a & c)

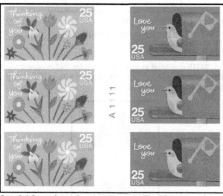

Special Occasions. October 22, 1988. Booklet pane of 6. Photogravure. ABN.

25c multicolored

a) Flowers   b) Bird in mailbox

2398b   booklet pane, imperf hz   *2,250.00*
         Quantity: very rare

2398c   booklet pane, imperf   —
         Quantity: unique

Ernest Hemingway. July 17, 1989. Photogravure. ABN.

25c multicolored
2418a   vrt pair, imperf hz   *800.00*
         Quantity: 24-36 pairs reported

Pairs are typically centered to the right or left and often with small faults. Value is for a sound example.

Astronauts on Moon. July 20, 1989. Engraved, lithographed. BEP.

$2.40 multicolored
2419b   imperf pair   *375.00*
         plate block of 4, imperf   —
         Quantity: 200 pairs

Madonna. October 19, 1989. Engraved, lithographed. BEP.

25c multicolored
2427c   imperf pair   —
         Quantity: n/a

Christmas. October 19, 1989. Photogravure. Perf 11. ABN.

25c multicolored

2428a   vrt pair, imperf hz   *500.00*
        Quantity: 20+ pairs reported

Christmas. October 19, 1989. Booklet pane of 10.
Photogravure. Perf 11½. BEP.

25c multicolored

2429b   vrt pair, imperf between   *500.00*
        Quantity: included below

2429c   booklet pane, imperf hz btwn   *2,250.00*
        Quantity: 2 panes reported

Nos. 2428a and 2429b can be distinguished in several ways.
The runners on the sleigh on No. 2429b are twice as thick as
those on No. 2428a. On No. 2429b the package at the upper left
in the sleigh has a red bow, whereas the same package on No.
2428a has a red and black bow; and the ribbon on the upper right
package on No. 2429b is green, whereas the same ribbon on No.
2428a is black.

2429e   imperf pair   —
        block of 4, imperf   —
        Quantity: rare

Eagle & Shield. November 10, 1989. Photogravure. Self-
adhesive. Straight die cut. ABN.

25c multicolored

2431b   pair, die cutting omitted between   *325.00*
        Quantity: 27-36 pairs

2431c   pair, die cutting omitted   *200.00*
        plate block of 4, die cutting omitted   —
        Quantity: n/a

No. 2431b is difficult to distinguish from No. 2431c once it has
been removed from a pane. Margin pairs with all die cutting
omitted, however, are No. 2431c.

Love. January 18, 1990. Photogravure. USB.

25c multicolored

2440a   imperf pair   *550.00*
        Quantity: 50 pairs

Steam Carriage. August 31, 1990. Coil. Engraved. BEP.

4c claret

2451a	imperf pair	450.00
	imperf strip with plate No. 1	1,800.00
	spliced pair or strip, imperf	—
	imperf pair on first day cover	—
	Quantity: 100+ pairs; at least 5	
	first day covers	

Transition multiples exist and sell for a premium. Refer to note following No. 2265a regarding first day covers. Some first day covers contain a "Glendale, AZ - Sta. No. 7" circular date cancel.

Circus Wagon. August 31, 1990. Coil. Engraved. BEP.

5c carmine

2452c	imperf pair	350.00
	imperf strip with plate No. 1	5,250.00
	spliced pair or strip, imperf	—
	Quantity: 72-88 pairs;	
	plate No. 1 strip is unique	

Transition multiples exist and sell for a premium. Wheels of the wagon are usually close to the bottom edge or touch it. Catalogue value is for such an example. Well-centered examples exist and sell for more.

Circus Wagon. March 20, 1995. Coil. Photogravure. SVS.

5c carmine

2452De	imperf pair	115.00
	imperf strip with plate No. S2	425.00
	imperf pair, used	—
	Quantity: a few hundred pairs	

Some pairs possess counting numbers on the back.

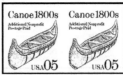

Canoe. May 25, 1991. Coil. Engraved. BEP.

5c brown (gray service inscription)

2453a	imperf pair	225.00
	imperf strip with plate No. 1	750.00
	imperf strip with plate No. 2	750.00
	imperf pair on first day cover	—
	Quantity: 250+ pairs; 5 first day	
	covers reported	

Exists miscut. Transition multiples exist. Refer to note following No. 2265a regarding first day covers.

Tractor Trailer. May 25, 1991. Coil. Engraved. BEP.

10c green (gray service inscription)

2457a	imperf pair	110.00
	imperf strip with plate No. 1	375.00
	Quantity: 1,000+ pairs	

Transition multiples exist and sell for a premium.

Cog Railway. June 9, 1995. Coil. Engraved. BEP.

20c green

2463a	imperf pair	75.00
	imperf strip with plate No. 1	225.00
	Quantity: 400+ pairs	

Lunch Wagon. April 12, 1991. Coil. Engraved. BEP.

23c dark blue

2464b	imperf pair	100.00
	imperf strip with plate No. 2	650.00
	imperf strip with plate No. 3	750.00
	spliced pair or strip, imperf	—
	Quantity: 400-500 pairs reported	

Exists miscut; some miscut pairs show EE bars at top. Transition multiples exist and sell for a premium. Plate No. 3 exists with both mottled and solid tagging.

Note: See Nos. 1897b-1908a, 2126b-2136b, 2225c-2228b, and 2252b-2265a for other Transportation Series coils.

Ferryboat. June 2, 1995. Coil. Engraved. BEP.

32c blue

2466a	imperf pair, shiny gum	*375.00*
	imperf pair, low gloss gum	*475.00*
	imperf strip with plate No. 2	*1,250.00*
	imperf strip with plate No. 3	*1,250.00*
	imperf strip with plate No. 5	*3,750.00*
	Quantity: 100+ pairs	

Exists miscut, some with EE bars at top or marginal markings at bottom. Examples from plate No. 2 possess shiny gum. Examples from plate Nos. 3 and 5 possess low gloss gum. The plate strip with plate No 5 is unique.

Seaplane. April 20, 1990. Coil. Engraved. BEP.

$1 blue & scarlet

2468a	imperf pair	*1,750.00*
	imperf strip with plate No. 1	*8,500.00*
	imperf pair, used	*1,150.00*
	Quantity: 54 unused stamps; 13 used	
	stamps in pairs and strips;	
	plate No. 1 strip is unique	

Bluebird. June 22, 1991. Lithographed. ABN.

3c multicolored

2478a	vrt pair, imperf hz	
	plate block of 4, plate No. A8588	—
	Quantity: at least 20+ pairs	

Imperforate examples are proofs. Refer to the Error-Like Imperforates section.

Fawn. March 11, 1991. Photogravure. BEP.

19c multicolored

2479c	imperf pair	*900.00*
	Quantity: n/a	

Blue Jay. June 15, 1995. Booklet pane of 10. Lithographed. Self-adhesive. Serpentine die cut. SVA.

20c multicolored

2483b	pane of 10, die cutting omitted	—
	Quantity: n/a	

Wood Duck. April 12, 1991. Booklet pane of 10. Photogravure. BEP.

29c multicolored & black numeral

2484b	vrt pair, imperf hz	*175.00*
2484c	booklet pane of 10, imperf hz	*875.00*
	Quantity: 20+ panes reported	

2484f	vrt pair, imperf between	*175.00*
2484g	booklet pane, imperf between	*875.00*
	Quality: n/a	

Examples of No. 2484f contain horizontal perforations at either top or bottom and a natural straight edge on the opposite edge. See illustration.

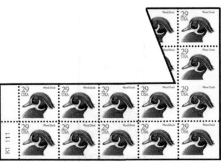

Wood Duck. April 12, 1991. Booklet pane of 10. Photogravure. KCS.

29c multicolored & red numeral
2485b   vrt pair, imperf between   *2,500.00*
         Quantity: 2-3 reported

No. 2485b results from a foldover.

2485c   imperf pair   *4,500.00*
         Quantity: 2 pairs reported

Squirrel. June 25, 1993. Booklet pane of 18. Self-adhesive. Straight die cut. Photogravure. DBS.

29c multicolored
2489b   pair, die cutting omitted   —
         Quantity: n/a

Pine Cone. November 5, 1993. Booklet pane of 18. Engraved. Self-adhesive. Straight die cut. BCA.

29c multicolored
2491b   pair, die cutting omitted between   *175.00*
         used pair, die cutting omitted between   *125.00*
         Quantity: 14-20 pairs reported

Pink Rose. June 2, 1995. Booklet pane of 20. Photogravure. Self-adhesive. Serpentine die cut. SVS.

32c black, pink & olive green
2492c   hz pair, die cutting omitted btwn   —
         hz pair, 1 stamp & 1 label, die cutting
           omitted between   —
         Quantity: 12 pairs, 2 pairs with label

2492h   vrt pair, die cutting omitted between   *400.00*
         Quantity: rare

2492k   booklet pane, hz die cutting omitted   —
         Quantity: n/a

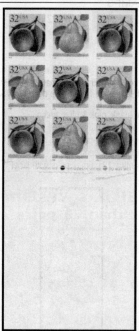

Peach & Pear. July 8, 1995. Se-tenant booklet pane of 20. Self-adhesive. Photogravure. AVR.

32c multicolored
2494c   booklet pane, die cutting
    omitted (see note)   —
    Quantity: unique

The listed and illustrated error block of 9 contains die-cutting omitted pairs of Nos. 2493 and 2494. The stamps in the bottom section possessed normal die cutting and were removed and used; the liner paper, however, was left intact.

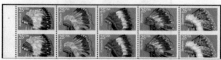

American Indian Headdresses. July 6, 1990. Se-tenant booklet pane of 10. Engraved, lithographed. BEP.

25c multicolored
2505d   booklet pane of 10, imperf hz   2,250.00
    Quantity: very rare

Panes of No. 2505d are usually split along the fold. Value is for a pane with split. Panes without split are worth more.

Greetings. October 18, 1990. Photogravure. ABN.

25c multicolored
2515a   vrt pair, imperf hz   500.00
    Quantity: 19 sound pairs, 1 faulty pair

Flower. January 22, 1991. Photogravure. Perf. 13. USB.

F (29c) multicolored
2517a   imperf pair   1,000.00
    Quantity: n/a

No. 2517a is usually collected as a vertical pair, though No. 2517 can be distinguished from the other "F" stamp issues.

2517b   hz pair, imperf vrt   1,000.00
    Quantity: 5 pairs reported

Flower. January 22, 1991. Coil. Photogravure. BEP.

F (29c) multicolored

2518a	imperf pair	25.00
	imperf strip with plate No. 1111	225.00
	imperf strip with plate No. 1222	*600.00*
	imperf strip with plate No. 2211	*600.00*
	imperf strip with plate No. 2222	225.00
	imperf pair on first day cover	—
	spliced pair or strip, imperf	—
	Quantity: 1,000+; at least 20 first day covers	

Catalogue values are for plate strips of 5 or 6. Exists miscut. Transition multiples exist and sell for a premium. Refer to the note following No. 2265a regarding first day covers. First day covers exist postmarked either with a "Washington, DC" circular date cancel or a "Glendale, AZ, Sta. No. 7" circular date cancel.

Flower. January 22, 1991. Booklet pane of 10. Photogravure. KCS.

F (29c) multicolored

2520b	booklet pane, imperf hz	—
	Quantity: n/a	

2520c	hz pair, imperf btwn, in error	
	booklet pane of 12	
	Quantity: 1 reported	

No. 2520c is from a paper foldover before perforating

2520d	pair, imperf vrt	—
	Quantity: n/a	

Makeup Rate Stamp. January 22, 1991. Lithographed. ABN.

(4c) bister & carmine

2521a	vrt pair, imperf hz	70.00
	plate block of 4, imperf hz	—
	Quantity: 400+ pairs	

2521b	imperf pair	60.00
	plate block of 4, imperf	—
	Quantity: 300+ pairs	

No. 2521b is likely printer's waste.

Flag & Mt. Rushmore. March 29, 1991. Coil. Engraved. BEP.

29c blue, red & claret

2523b	imperf pair	20.00
	imperf strip with plate No. 1	*350.00*
	imperf strip with plate No. 2	*200.00*
	imperf strip with plate No. 3	*400.00*
	imperf strip with plate No. 4	350.00
	imperf strip with plate No. 6	*250.00*
	imperf strip with plate No. 7	250.00
	imperf strip with plate No. 9	*350.00*
	spliced pair or strip, imperf	—
	Quantity: 1,000+ pairs	

Exists miscut, some with EE bars at top. Catalogue values are for plate strips of 6. Transition multiples exist and sell for a premium.

Flower. April 5, 1991. Booklet pane of 10. Photogravure. KCS.

29c multicolored

| 2527b | hz pair, imperf between | — |
| | Quantity: 3-5 pairs reported | |

No. 2527b results from a foldover.

2527c	hz pair, imperf vrt	*150.00*
	Quantity: included with	
	No. 2527e	

No. 2527c contains a natural straight edge on right and left sides.

| 2527d | booklet pane, imperf hz | *750.00* |
| | Quantity: at least several panes | |

Panes are known with either plate No. K1111 or plate No. K2222.

2527e   booklet pane, imperf vrt   *500.00*
        Quantity: at least 15 panes

U.S. Flag & Olympic Rings. April 21, 1991. Booklet pane of 10. Photogravure. KCS.

29c multicolored
2528c   vrt pair, imperf between   *225.00*
        booklet pane of 10, imperf between   *1,750.00*
        Quantity: 9-10+ panes reported

Vertical strips of 3 are known containing a pair imperf between plus an additional perforated stamp, raising the possibility that they originate from unsevered press sheets. At least one pane is known containing two full pairs as a result of a foldover and is worth more.

2528e   vrt pair, imperf hz   *650.00*
        booklet pane of 10, imperf hz   *2,750.00*
        Quantity: n/a

Hand & Torch. June 25, 1991. Booklet pane of 18. Photogravure. Self-adhesive. Straight die cut. AVR.

29c black, gold & green
2531Ac   pair, die cutting omitted   *1,000.00*
        Quantity: n/a

Switzerland. February 22, 1991. Photogravure. ABN.

50c multicolored
2532a   vrt pair, imperf hz   *1,400.00*
        Quantity: 20 pairs

Imperforate examples are from printer's waste. Refer to the Printer's Waste section.

Love. May 9, 1991. Photogravure. USB.

29c multicolored
2535b   imperf pair   *1,650.00*
        Quantity: 25 pairs reported

Eagle & Olympic Rings. July 7, 1991. Engraved, lithographed. ABN.

$2.90 multicolored

2540a   vrt pair, imperf hz   *900.00*
         Quantity: 4 pairs, 4 strips of 3

Imperforate examples with various colors omitted are proofs. Refer to the Error-Like Imperforates section.

Express Mail. June 16, 1991. Engraved, lithographed. ABN.

$9.95 multicolored

2541a   imperf pair   —
         Quantity: n/a

Imperforate examples with black engraved omitted are printer's waste. Refer to the Printer's Waste section.

Challenger. June 22, 1995. Engraved, lithographed. APU.

$3 multicolored

2544c   hz pair, imperf between   1,000.00
         Quantity: at least 6-10 pairs

▶ Caution. Beware of pairs with deceptive blind perfs between stamps. Expert certificate strongly recommended.

2544d   imperf pair   *800.00*
         plate block of 4, imperf   —
         Quantity: n/a

▶ Caution. Beware of pairs with blind perfs. Expert certificate recommended.

Fishing Flies. May 5, 1991. Se-tenant booklet pane of 5. Photogravure. ABN.

29c multicolored

a) Royal Wulff
b) Jock Scott
c) Apte Tarpon Fly
d) Lefty's Deceiver
e) Muddler Minnow

2545b   hz pair, imperf between   2,400.00
        Quantity: unique

No. 2545b is the result of a foldover. Refer to the Printer's Waste section for other imperforates of this issue.

Cole Porter. June 8, 1991. Photogravure. ABN.

29c multicolored

2550a   vrt pair, imperf hz   400.00
        plate block of 4, imperf hz   —
        Quantity: 50-60 pairs reported

Desert Storm. July 2, 1991. Photogravure. SVS.

29c multicolored

2551a   vrt pair, imperf hz   600.00
        plate block of 4, imperf hz   —
        Quantity: 20-30 pairs reported

Don't confuse No. 2551a with vertical pairs imperforate horizontally of No. 2552, which are printer's waste. Refer to the Printer's Waste section.

Jan E. Matzeliger. September 15, 1991. Photogravure. ABN.

29c multicolored
2567a hz pair, imperf vrt   *600.00*
Quantity: 50 pairs

2567b vrt pair, imperf hz   *550.00*
Quantity: 40-60 pairs

2567c imperf pair   *275.00*
Quantity: 150+ pairs

Christmas. October 17, 1991. Photogravure. ABN.

29c multicolored
2579a hz pair, imperf vrt   175.00
Quantity: 80-100 pairs

Exists with rows of misplaced horizontal perforations.

2579b vrt pair, imperf hz   *350.00*
Quantity: 50-80 pairs reported

Imperforates are from printer's waste. Refer to the Printer's Waste section.

Flag & Pledge. September 8, 1992. Booklet pane of 10. Photogravure. BEP.

29c multicolored; black denomination
2593d imperf pair   *500.00*
Quantity: 10 pairs, including 4
with destruction marks

Eagle & Shield. September 6, 1992. Pane of 17 plus label. Photogravure. Self-adhesive. Straight die cut. BCA.

29c multicolored, brown numeral

2595b	pair, die cutting omitted	*90.00*
	Quantity: included below	

2595d	pane of 17, die cutting omitted	*725.00*
	Quantity: 30-40 panes	

No. 2595d is often encountered with a fold or minor faults. Value is for a sound example.

Eagle & Shield, Bulk Rate-USA. December 13, 1991. Coil. Photogravure. ABN.

(10c) multicolored

2602a	imperf pair	*3,500.00*
	imperf strip with plate No. A43335	*5,250.00*
	Quantity: 10-25 reported	

Examples of No. 2602a are contained in three transition strips. One of the strips is defective, and on it the plate number appears on a perforated stamp.

Eagle & Shield, USA-Bulk Rate. May 29, 1993. Coil. Untagged. Photogravure. BEP.

(10c) multicolored

2603a	imperf pair	20.00
	imperf strip with plate No. 11111	125.00
	imperf strip with plate No. 22221	250.00
	imperf strip with plate No. 22222	175.00
	spliced pair or strip, imperf	—
	Quantity: several thousand pairs	

Exists miscut. Transition multiples exist and sell for a premium. Exists tagged.

Flag & Presorted First-Class. September 27, 1991. Coil. Photogravure. ABN.

23c multicolored

2605a	imperf pair	—
	Quantity: see note	

The unique discovery strip contains 11 stamps of which the 6 stamps at right are misperforated. The 5 stamps at left are imperforate except that perforations exist along the exterior edge of the leftmost stamp.

Chrome USA. October 9, 1992. Coil. Photogravure. BEP.

23c multicolored, deep blue background

2607c	imperf pair	65.00
	imperf strip with plate No. 1111	250.00
	Quantity: 300-500 pairs	

Flag & White House. April 23, 1992. Coil. Engraved. BEP.

29c blue & red

2609a	imperf pair	15.00
	used pair, imperf	*25.00*
	imperf strip with plate No. 1	*300.00*
	imperf strip with plate No. 2	*200.00*
	imperf strip with plate No. 3	*300.00*
	imperf strip with plate No. 4	100.00
	imperf strip with plate No. 5	*300.00*
	imperf strip with plate No. 6	*200.00*
	imperf strip with plate No. 7	250.00
	imperf strip with plate No. 8	250.00
	imperf strip with plate No. 9	*350.00*
	imperf strip with plate No. 10	*725.00*
	imperf strip with plate No. 11	*650.00*
	imperf strip with plate No. 12	*775.00*
	imperf strip with plate No. 13	*650.00*
	spliced strip or pair, imperf	—
	Quantity: 1,000+ pairs	

▶ Caution. Beware of blind perfs.

Exists miscut. Imperforate strips from the edge of the printing web (plate No. 6) exist. They contain various printed elements: production bars, markings and/or plate numbers. At press time, 3 strips the length of a coil of 100 stamps were known, all from plate No. 6. Transition strips exist and sell for a premium.

2609b   pair, imperf between   75.00
         Quantity: 250+ pairs reported

▶ Exercise extreme caution. Rolls from which this error arises contain imperf pairs, imperf between pairs, and many ostensibly imperf between pairs with blind perfs. Check carefully to make sure that imperf between pairs are completely free of blind perfs between stamps.

Exists with plate Nos. 3 or 4.

Love. February 6, 1992. Photogravure. ABN.

29c multicolored
2618a   hz pair, imperf vrt   *300.00*
         Quantity: 50 pairs

2618b   hz pair or strip, imperf vrt &
           green omitted on right stamp   *1,250.00*
         Quantity: 5 pairs or strips

Often encountered as a horizontal transition strip of 4 with green partially omitted on the 3rd stamp and entirely omitted on the 4th stamp.

K1 11

Giraffe
Giant Panda
Flamingo
King Penguins
White Bengal Tiger

Wild Animals. October 1, 1992. Booklet pane of 5. Photogravure. SVS.

29c multicolored

a) Giraffe
b) Giant Panda
c) Flamingo
d) King Penguins
e) White Bengal Tiger

2709b   booklet pane, imperf   *2,000.00*
         Quantity: 8 panes reported

Panes contain normal booklet bend between stamps b & c and gum disturbance on tab from removal from booklet.

Elvis Presley. January 8, 1993. Pane of 40. Photogravure. BEP.

29c multicolored
2721a   imperf pair   —
         Quantity: n/a

Often with fingerprints on gum. Likely printer's waste.

**Garden Flowers. May 15, 1993. Booklet pane of 5.
Engraved, lithographed. BEP.**

29c multicolored
a) Hyacinth
b) Daffodil
c) Tulip
d) Iris
e) Lilac

2764c   booklet pane, imperf   *700.00*
         Quantity: 12-16 panes reported

Value is for pane with usual booklet bend between stamps b & c.
A transition pane exists.

**National Postal Museum. July 30, 1993. Engraved,
lithographed. ABN.**

29c multicolored
a) Ben Franklin   b) Pony Express
c) Charles Lindbergh   d) Stamps & Barcode

2782c   block of 4, imperf   *2,500.00*
         strip of 4, imperf   —
         plate block of 4, imperf   —
         Quantity: 8 blocks of 4; 2 strips reported

The plate block recorded above has a fingerprint on its gum.

**Madonna. October 21, 1993. Booklet pane of 4. Engraved,
lithographed. KCS.**

29c multicolored
2790b   imperf pair   —
         Quantity: included below

2790c   booklet pane, imperf   —
         Quantity: 4 panes reported

**Love. February 14, 1994. Booklet pane of 10.
Photogravure. ABN.**

29c multicolored
2814b   imperf pair   —
         Quantity: n/a

2814d   booklet pane, imperf   —
         Quantity: n/a

Horizontal pairs, imperf between are from printer's waste. Refer to
the Printer's Waste section.

**Garden Flowers. April 28, 1994. Booklet pane of 5.
Engraved, lithographed. BEP.**

29c multicolored

a) Lily
b) Zinnia
c) Gladiola
d) Marigold
e) Rose

2833b   booklet pane of 5, imperf   *400.00*
         Quantity: 20-30 panes reported

Panes contain the normal booklet bend between stamps b & c, as
well as tab faults from removal from booklet, and are valued as
such. Some panes exist attached to cover backing. Panes are also
known without tagging.

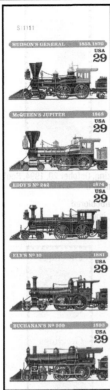

Locomotives. July 28, 1994. Booklet pane of 5. Photogravure. SVS.

29c multicolored

a) Hudson's General
b) McQueen's Jupiter
c) Eddy's No. 242
d) Ely's No. 10
e) Buchanan's No. 999

2847b	pane of 5, imperf	*2,500.00*
	Quantity: 3 panes reported	

Panes contain normal booklet bend between stamps b and c.

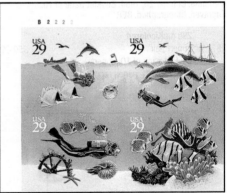

Popular Singers. September 1, 1994. Se-tenant. Photogravure. SVA.

29c multicolored

a) Al Jolson
b) Bing Crosby
c) Ethel Waters
d) Nat "King" Cole
e) Ethel Merman

2853b	pane of 20, imperf	*10,000.00*
	Quantity: one pane reported	

Wonders of the Sea. October 3, 1994. Se-tenant block of 4. Lithographed. BCA.

29c multicolored

a) Motorboat & Buoy   b) Sailing Ship
c) Wheel on Sea Floor   d) Coral Outcropping

2866b	block of 4, imperf	*450.00*
	plate block of 4, imperf	—
	Quantity: 60+ blocks of 4	

Legends of the West. October 18, 1994. Se-tenant pane of 20. Photogravure. SVS.

29c multicolored

2869u   pane of 20, partially imperf   —
     Quantity: reportedly unique

Madonna. October 20, 1994. Booklet pane of 10. Engraved, lithographed. BEP.

29c multicolored

2871Ac   imperf pair   *350.00*
     booklet pane of 10, imperf   —
     Quantity: 10+ panes reported

Transition panes exist.

Christmas Stocking. October 20, 1994. Booklet pane of 20. Lithographed. APU.

29c multicolored

2872b   imperf pair   —
     Quantity: at least 10 pairs

Christmas Stocking. October 20, 1994. Booklet pane of 20. Lithographed. APU.

29c multicolored

2872c   vrt pair, imperf hz   —
     Quantity: at least 8 panes

2872e   vrt pair, imperf between   *125.00*
     Quantity: at least 40 pairs

2872f   booklet pane, imperf   —
     Quantity: n/a

Dove, G Make-Up Rate. December 13, 1994. Lithographed. ABN.

(3c) tan, bright blue & red

2877a   imperf pair   *115.00*
     plate block of 4, imperf   —
     Quantity: few hundred

▶ No. 2877a with bright blue completely or partially omitted are printer's waste. Refer to the Printer's Waste section.

Flag & G. December 13, 1994. Photogravure. BEP.

G (20c) yellow background, black G

2879a   imperf pair   —
         Quantity: 35 stamps

▶ Caution. The discovery pane of 100 contained 35 imperforate examples plus many others with blind perfs. Expert certificate advised.

Flag & G. December 13, 1994. Booklet pane of 10. Photogravure. ABN.

G (32c) multicolored; blue G

2884b   imperf pair   —
         booklet pane, imperf   4,500.00
         Quantity: 2 panes reported

Flag & G. December 13, 1994. Booklet pane of 10. Photogravure. KCS.

G (32c) multicolored; red G

2885b   hz pair, imperf vrt   750.00
         Quantity: n/a

2885c   hz pair, imperf between   —
         Quantity: 2-3 pairs reported

No. 2885c occurs in a booklet pane as the result of a foldover. At least two of the pairs have a natural straight edge at the bottom. A booklet containing two panes, each with an error pair, exists.

Flag & G. December 13, 1994. Coil. Photogravure. BEP.

G (32c) multicolored; black G

2889a   imperf pair   250.00
         imperf strip with plate No. 1111   675.00
         Quantity: 100-150 pairs reported

Flag & Porch. May 19, 1995. Pane of 100. Photogravure. Water activated. Blue 1995 date. SVS.

32c multicolored

2897a   imperf pair   55.00
         plate block, plate No. S22222   —
         Quantity: 500+ pairs

Often collected in vertical pairs to distinguish it from coil imperforates of similar design. Transition multiples exist.

Western Butte. March 10, 1995. Coil. Photogravure. SVS.

(5c) multicolored

2902a	imperf pair	350.00
	imperf strip with plate No. S111	*2,500.00*
	Quantity: 58-80 pairs reported	

Some pairs have counting numbers on the back.

Mountain. March 16, 1996. Coil. Photogravure. SVS.

(5c) multicolored; blue-gray mountains

2904c	imperf pair	225.00
	imperf strip with plate No. S111	*1,500.00*
	spliced pair or strip, imperf	—
	Quantity: 109 pairs,	
	10 plate No. strips	

Transition multiples exist. Some pairs have counting numbers on the back.

Juke Box. March 17, 1995. Coil. Photogravure. Serpentine die cut. BEP.

(25c) multicolored

2911a	imperf pair	*400.00*
	die cutting omitted strip, plate No.	—
	Quantity: n/a	

Flag & Porch. May 19, 1995. Coil. Photogravure. Water activated. Red 1995 date. BEP.

32c multicolored

2913a	imperf pair	30.00
	imperf strip with plate No. 11111	*425.00*
	imperf strip with plate No. 22222	*300.00*
	imperf strip with plate No. 33333	300.00
	imperf strip with plate No. 34333	100.00
	imperf strip with plate No. 44444	*350.00*
	imperf strip with plate No. 45444	*300.00*
	imperf strip with plate No. 66646	*750.00*
	imperf strip with plate No. 66666	*750.00*
	imperf strip with plate No. 77767	*450.00*
	imperf strip with plate No. 78767	350.00
	imperf strip with plate No. 91161	*600.00*
	imperf strip with plate No. 99969	*750.00*
	spliced pair or strip, imperf	—
	imperf pair on first day cover	—
	Quantity: 1,000+ pairs, 5 first day covers	

Exists miscut. Transition multiples exist and sell for a premium. Refer to the note following No. 2265a regarding first day covers.

Flag & Porch. May 21, 1996. Coil. Photogravure. Self-adhesive. Serpentine die cut. Red 1996 date. BEP.

32c multicolored

2915Ah	pair, die cutting omitted	32.50
	strip, plate No. 11111	*300.00*
	strip, plate No. 44444	*750.00*
	strip, plate No. 45444	*750.00*
	strip, plate No. 55555	*450.00*
	strip, plate No. 66666	*200.00*
	strip, plate No. 78777	*600.00*
	strip, plate No. 88888	175.00
	strip, plate No. 89898	*300.00*
	strip, plate No. 99999	*650.00*
	strip, plate No. 11111A	*650.00*
	strip, plate No. 13231A	*600.00*
	strip, plate No. 22222A	*500.00*
	strip, plate No. 44444A	*450.00*
	strip, plate No. 55555A	*625.00*
	strip, plate No. 66666A	*625.00*
	strip, plate No. 88888A	*850.00*
	spliced pair or strip, die cutting omitted	—
	Quantity: 1,000+	

Exists miscut.

Flag & Porch. May 19, 1995. Booklet pane of 10. Photogravure. Water activated. Red 1995 date. BEP.

32c multicolored
2916b   booklet pane of 10, imperf   —
         Quantity: n/a

Flag over Field. March 17, 1995. Booklet pane of 18. Self-adhesive. Straight die cut. Photogravure. AVR.

32c multicolored
2919b   vrt pair, die cutting omitted between   —
         Quantity: n/a

Flag & Porch. April 18, 1995. Booklet pane of 20. Photogravure. Self-adhesive. Serpentine die cut. Large blue 1995 date. AVR.

32c multicolored
2920i   pair, die cutting omitted   —
         Quantity: n/a

2920k   vrt pair, die cutting omitted between   —
         Quantity: 3 pairs

Flag & Porch. May 21, 1996. Booklet pane of 10. Photogravure. Self-adhesive. Serpentine die cut. Red 1996 date. BEP.

32c multicolored

2921e   booklet pane of 10, die cutting omitted   200.00
        Quantity: 50+ panes reported

The backing paper of No. 2921e contains the normal roulette for folding. It does not affect the status of the error.

Alice Hamilton. July 11, 1995. Engraved. Dull gum. BCA.

55c green
2940a   imperf pair   —
        Quantity: 20 pairs reported

Often either in a horizontal or vertical transition strip or block.

Cherub. May 12, 1995. Booklet pane of 10. Engraved, lithographed. Water activated. Design measures 19mm by 22½. BEP.

32c multicolored

2959b   imperf pair   100.00
        Quantity: included below

2959c   booklet pane, imperf   500.00
        Quantity: at least 10 panes

Some panes contain a black rejection mark.

Recreational Sports. May 20, 1995. Se-tenant strip of 5. Lithographed. BCA.

32c multicolored

        a) Golf
        b) Volleyball
        c) Softball
        d) Bowling
        e) Tennis

2965b   vertical strip of 5, imperf   1,750.00
        block of 10, plate numbers at top
         and bottom corners, imperf   —
        Quantity: 8-12 strips of 5

The se-tenant designs vary in order of appearance from vertical strip to vertical strip within a pane.

Marilyn Monroe. June 1, 1995. Pane of 20. Photogravure. SVS.

32c multicolored

2967a	imperf pair	*225.00*
	pane of 20, imperf	*3,250.00*
	Quantity: 20+ imperforate panes,	
	3 partially imperforate panes	

Due to the nature of the grinding process used to perforate this issue, perforations on partially perforated panes can appear in odd configurations such as a single row, multiple rows, or in a corner affecting only a few stamps. Because of the possible variety of partially perforated panes, no attempt has been made to list each one individually.

Great Lakes Lighthouses. June 17, 1995. Photogravure. Se-tenant booklet pane of 5. SVS.

32c multicolored

a) Split Rock
b) St. Joseph
c) Spectacle Reef
d) Marblehead
e) Thirty Mile Point

2973b	booklet pane with one vrt pair	
	each of d & e, imperf hz	—
	Quantity: unique	

No. 2973b is the result of a foldover.

Civil War. June 29, 1995. Se-tenant pane of 20. Photogravure. SVS.

32c multicolored

2975w	pane of 20, imperf	*800.00*
	pane of 20, partially imperforate	—
	Quantity: 30-40 imperforate panes,	
	5-6 partially imperforate panes	

Refer to the note following No. 2967a. Often encountered with light fingerprints on gum.

Women's Suffrage. August 26, 1995. Engraved, lithographed. APU.

32c multicolored

2980b	imperf pair	*750.00*
	plate block of 4, imperf	—
	Quantity: 20 pairs reported	

Often in transition strips.

2980c	vrt pair, imperf between & at bottom	*500.00*
	Quantity: n/a	

Louis Armstrong. September 1, 1995. Lithographed. Pane of 20. APU.

32c multicolored

2982a　imperf pair　　　　—
　　　Quantity: 4 pairs

John Coltrane, Erroll Garner. September 16, 1995. Se-tenant pair. Lithographed. APU.

32c multicolored

2992c　se-tenant pair, imperf　　5,000.00
　　　Quantity: *2 pairs*

The error pairs are from the bottom of a se-tenant pane of the American Music series. The upper part of the pane contains perforations.

Garden Flowers. September 19, 1995. Booklet pane of 5. Engraved, lithographed. BEP.

32c multicolored

　　a) Aster
　　b) Chrysanthemum
　　c) Dahlia
　　d) Hydrangea
　　e) Rudbeckia

2997b　booklet pane of 5, imperf　　2,250.00
　　　Quantity: very rare

Comics. October 1, 1995. Se-tenant pane of 20. Photogravure. SVS.

32c multicolored

3000x　pane of 20, imperf　　　　　4,250.00
　　　pane of 20, partially imperf　3,250.00
　　　Quantity: 1-2 imperforate panes,
　　　　3 partially imperforate panes

Refer to the note following No. 2967a.

Santa & Children. September 30, 1995. Se-tenant block of 4. Lithographed. APU.

32c multicolored

　　a) Santa & Chimney　　b) Child & Jumping Jack
　　c) Child & Tree　　　　d) Santa & Sled

3007d　block of 4 (a-d), imperf　　　325.00
　　　strip of 4 (a-d), imperf　　　325.00
　　　plate block of 4, imperf　　　—
　　　Quantity: 75+ blocks of 4,
　　　　15 strips of 4

Midnight Angel. October 19, 1995. Booklet pane of 20. Lithographed. Self-adhesive. Serpentine die cut. BCA.

32c multicolored

3012b   pane of 20, die cutting omitted from
          third horizontal row & from the top
          of the fourth horizontal row   —
          Quantity: 15-20 reported

Also exists as a horizontal pair (one stamp and one reorder label) with die cutting omitted between as the result of a foldover.

Garden Flowers. January 19, 1996. Booklet pane of 5. Engraved, lithographed. BEP.

32c multicolored

    a) Crocus
    b) Winter Aconite
    c) Pansy
    d) Snowdrop
    e) Anemone

3029b   booklet pane of 5, imperf   —
          Quantity: 4 panes initially reported

Cherub. January 20, 1996. Booklet pane of 20. Engraved, lithographed. Self-adhesive. Serpentine die cut. BCA.

32c multicolored

3030f   pair, die cutting omitted   *225.00*
       Quantity: included below

3030i   booklet pane, die cutting omitted   —
       Quantity: several panes

Kestrel. November 19, 1999. Pane of 50. Lithographed. Self-adhesive. Serpentine die cut. BEP.

1c multicolored

3031c   pair, die cutting omitted   —
       Quantity: 2 panes reported

Kestrel. October 2000. Lithographed. Self-adhesive. Serpentine die cut. BCA.

1c multicolored

3031Ab pair, die cutting omitted   *325.00*
       Quantity: 1 pane of 50 reported

Coral Pink Rose. August 13, 1999. Booklet pane of 20. Photogravure. Self-adhesive. Serpentine die cut. SSP.

33c multicolored

3052j   pair, die cutting omitted   —
       Quantity: included below

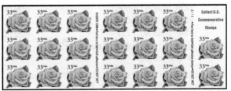

3052k   booklet pane, die cutting omitted   *5,500.00*
       Quantity: at least several panes

Coral Pink Rose. April 7, 2000. Booklet pane of 20. Photogravure. Self-adhesive. Serpentine die cut. SSP.

3052Ei hz pair, die cutting omitted btwn   —
       Quantity: included below

3052Ej   booklet pane, die cutting omitted btwn   —
        Quantity: at least two panes

Some examples are contained in blocks that resulted from miscutting.

Blue Jay. August 2, 1996. Coil. Photogravure. Self-adhesive. Serpentine die cut. SVU.

20c multicolored

3053a	pair, die cutting omitted	*2,100.00*
	strip, plate No. S1111	—
	Quantity: n/a	

▶ Caution. Beware of faintly impressed die cuts.

Yellow Rose. August 1, 1997. Coil. Photogravure. Self-adhesive. Serpentine die cut. Black 1997 date. BEP.

32c yellow, magenta, black & green

3054a	pair, die cutting omitted	85.00
	strip, plate No. 1112	*600.00*
	strip, plate No. 1122	*2,500.00*
	strip, plate No. 2223	*600.00*
	Strip, plate No. 2333	*600.00*
	strip, plate No. 4455	*750.00*
	strip, plate No. 5555	*600.00*
	strip, plate No. 5556	*600.00*
	strip, plate No. 5566	*600.00*
	strip, plate No. 5666	*600.00*
	strip, plate No. 6666	*750.00*
	strip, plate No. 7777	*600.00*
	Quantity: 450+ pairs; plate No. 1122 strip is unique	

Exists miscut. Plate number strips of 5566 and 7777 exist miscut only. Transition multiples exist and sell for a premium.

3054c   pair, die cutting, black, yellow
        & green omitted   —
        strip with magenta plate No. 4   —
        strip with magenta plate No. 7   —
        Quantity: 29+ stamps

3054e   pair, die cutting & black omitted   —
        strip with plate No. 445, black omitted   —
        Quantity: 45 stamps

The quantity known for Nos. 3054c and 3054e consists of three rolls of 100 with die cutting omitted on all stamps and colors omitted on some. The first roll contained 5 normal stamps, 11 black omitted, 15 black, yellow and olive green omitted, and the balance of the roll with all colors omitted. The first roll contained only a single occurrence of plate number, the digit "7" in magenta, the black, yellow and olive green digits being omitted. The second roll contained 68 normal stamps; 1 black partially omitted; 19 black omitted; 1 black, yellow and olive green partially omitted; 6 black, yellow and olive green omitted; and 5 with all colors omitted. The second roll contained three strips with full plate No. 4455 and one strip with plate No. 445, the black digit being omitted. The third roll contained 3 normal stamps; 15 black omitted, 7 black, yellow and green omitted; 23 stamps with various colors omitted to one degree or another; and the balance of the roll with all colors omitted. A fourth roll exists with die cuts, but miscut. It is listed in the Color Omitted section under Nos. 3054b and 3054d. A later find also yields a strip of No. 3054c with a single digit "4."

3054g   pair, die cutting omitted and
        containing one each of 3054c
        and 3054e   —
        Quantity: n/a

Ring-necked Pheasant. July 31, 1998. Coil. Photogravure. Self-adhesive. Serpentine die cut. BEP.

20c multicolored

3055a	pair, die cutting omitted	*125.00*
	strip, plate No. 1111	*1,600.00*
	strip, plate No. 2222	*1,200.00*
	spliced pair or strip	—
	Quantity: 70 pairs reported	

Exists miscut. Fifty pairs are drastically miscut, and 20 pairs are normal. Value is for a miscut pair.

Year of the Rat. February 8, 1996. Pane of 20.
Photogravure. SVS.

32c multicolored

3060a	imperf pair	550.00
	plate block of 4, imperf	—
	Quantity: at least 2 panes	

Transition multiples exist.

▶ Caution. Pairs exist with blind perfs.

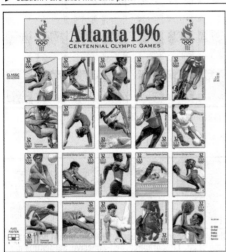

Olympics. May 2, 1996. Se-tenant pane of 20.
Photogravure. SVS.

32c multicolored

3068u	pane of 20, imperf	700.00
	pane of 20, partially imperf	750.00
	Quantity: 60+ panes; partially imperf panes are very rare	

Refer to the note following No. 2967a.

Georgia O'Keeffe. May 23, 1996. Pane of 15. Photogravure. SVS.

32c multicolored

3069a	imperf pair	110.00
	pane of 15, imperf	675.00
	imperf pair on first day cover	—
	Quantity: 75-90 panes, 8 first day covers	

Refer to the note following No. 2967a. Refer to the note following No. 2265a regarding first day covers.

Tennessee. May 31, 1996. Photogravure. Self-adhesive. Serpentine die cut. SVS.

32c multicolored

3071b	hz pair, die cutting omitted between	300.00
	used pair, on cover	—
	Quantity: n/a	

3071c	pair, die cutting omitted	—
	Quantity: n/a	

3071d	hz pair, die cutting omitted vrt	—
	pair, on cover	—
	Quantity: n/a	

▶ Caution. Beware of faintly impressed die cuts.

James Dean. June 24, 1996. Pane of 20. Photogravure. SVS.

32c multicolored

3082a	imperf pair	100.00
	pane of 20, imperf	1,250.00
	pane of 20, partially imperf	1,750.00
	Quantity: 90+ imperf panes; partially imperf panes are scarcer	

Refer to note following No. 2967a.

3082c   imperforate, tan omitted   —
          Quantity: 15 stamps
3082d   imperforate, tan & red omitted   —
          Quantity: 5 stamps

No. 3082c and 3082d occur in a single imperforate pane. The top row of 5 contains the tan and red omitted examples. The bottom 3 rows contain the tan omitted examples. Five combination pairs containing one each of Nos. 3082c and 3082d are possible.

Christmas Scenes. October 8, 1996. Se-tenant pane of 20. Lithographed. Water activated. Perforated. APU.

32c multicolored

          a) Family at Fireplace
          b) Decorating Tree
          c) Dreaming of Santa
          d) Holiday Shopping

3111b   strip of 4, right stamp imperf   *1,000.00*
          block of 8, 2 right stamps imperf   —
          plate block of 8, 2 right stamps
            imperf   —
          Quantity: 1 strip, 1 block
            & 1 plate block

Perforations appear between the left 3 stamps. In addition, perforations appear at top and bottom of the left 3 stamps. The right stamp lacks perforations on all sides.

Madonna. November 1, 1996. Booklet pane of 20. Engraved, lithographed. Self-adhesive. Serpentine die cut. BEP.

32c multicolored
3112b   pair, die cutting omitted   40.00
          Quantity: included below

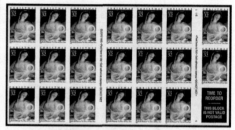

3112c   booklet pane, die cutting
            omitted   *400.00*
          Quantity: 50-75 panes

Christmas Scenes. October 6, 1996. Se-tenant booklet pane of 20. Lithographed. Self-adhesive. Serpentine die cut. APU.

32c multicolored
          a) Family at Fireplace
          b) Decorating Tree
          c) Dreaming of Santa
          d) Holiday Shopping

3116c   booklet pane, die cutting omitted   *1,250.00*
          Quantity: 6-7 panes reported

3116d   strip of 4, die cutting omitted   *500.00*
          Quantity: included below

3116e   block of 6, die cutting omitted   *700.00*
          Quantity: included below

Designs are staggered, so the order of appearance in strips or blocks may vary. The illustration is cropped from the upper left corner of a pane. Strips of 4 contain each of the designs. However, due to the layout, blocks of 6 are necessary to obtain all 4 designs in block form. Blocks may contain gutters. The backing of the self-adhesive error booklet pane contains the normal roulette for fold. It does not affect the status of the error. Value is for an unfolded pane.

Statue of Liberty. February 1, 1997. Booklet pane of 20. Self-adhesive. Serpentine die cut. AVR.

32c multicolored

3122h pane of 20, die cutting omitted —
Quantity: n/a

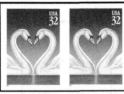

Swans. February 4, 1997. Booklet pane of 20. Lithographed. Self-adhesive. Serpentine die cut. BCA.

32c multicolored

3123b pair, die cutting omitted 100.00
Quantity: included below

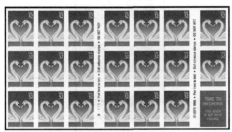

3123c booklet pane, die cutting omitted 1,000.00
Quantity: 15-20 panes reported

Botanical Prints. March 3, 1997. Se-tenant booklet pane of 20. Photogravure. Self-adhesive. Serpentine die cut. SVS.

a) Citron   b) Flowering Pineapple

32c multicolored

3127c vrt pair, die cutting omitted btwn 350.00
Quantity: 28 pairs reported

Error pairs in the initial discovery panes result from die cuts shifted downward one row from the top.

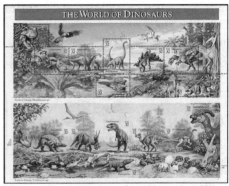

Dinosaurs. May 1, 1997. Pane of 15. Lithographed. APU.

32c multicolored

3136p pane, bottom half imperf 2,500.00
Quantity: 1 pane reported
3136q pane, top half imperf 2,500.00
Quantity: 2 panes reported

Celebrate the Century 1910s. February 3, 1998. Se-tenant pane of 15. Engraved, lithographed. APU.

32c multicolored

3183p   pane of 15, five stamps imperf   *7,000.00*
        Quantity: 2 reported

The error is the result of a perforation shift upward leaving 5 stamps without perforations. They are: Jim Thorpe, First Crossword Puzzle, Jack Dempsey, Construction Toys, and Child Labor Reform.

Flowering Trees. March 19, 1998. Se-tenant strip of 5. Lithographed. Self-adhesive. Serpentine die cut. BCA.

32c multicolored

a) Southern Magnolia
b) Blue Paloverde
c) Yellow Poplar
d) Prairie Crab Apple
e) Pacific Dogwood

3197b   strip of 5, die cutting omitted   —
        pane of 20, die cutting omitted   —
        Quantity: one pane reported

The five designs are arranged in horizontal strips of 5.

Madonna & Child. October 15, 1998. Booklet pane of 20. Self-adhesive. Serpentine die cut. Lithographed. BEP.

32c multicolored

3244b   pair, die cutting omitted   —
        Quantity: n/a

Holiday Wreaths. October 15, 1998. Se-tenant booklet pane of 20. Lithographed. Self-adhesive. Serpentine die cut. Design measures 22 mm by 25 mm. BCA.

32c multicolored

a) Evergreen Wreath   b) Chili Wreath
c) Colonial Wreath   d) Tropical Wreath

3248d   pane of 4, die cutting omitted   —
        Quantity: n/a

3248e   pane of 5, die cutting omitted   —
        Quantity: n/a

3248f   pane of 6, die cutting omitted   —
        Quantity: n/a

Holiday Wreaths. October 15, 1998. Se-tenant pane of 20. Lithographed. Self-adhesive. Serpentine die cut. Design measures 23 mm by 30 mm. BCA.

32c multicolored

a) Evergreen Wreath   b) Chili Wreath
c) Colonial Wreath   d) Tropical Wreath

3252h   block or strip of 4, die cutting omitted   —
        Quantity: n/a

3252i   booklet pane, die cutting omitted   *4,500.00*
        Quantity: n/a

Weather Vane. November 9, 1998. Lithographed. Water activated. AP.

(1c) multicolored
3257b   hz pair, imperf vrt and at top   —
        Quantity: n/a

Uncle Sam. November 9, 1998. Coil. Photogravure. Self-adhesive. Serpentine die cut. BEP.

22c multicolored
3263a   pair, die cutting omitted   *750.00*
        strip, plate No. 1111   *5,500.00*
        Quantity: n/a

Plate No. 1111 strip is unique.

Hat & H. November 9, 1998. Coil. Photogravure. Water activated. BEP.

(33c) multicolored
3264a   imperf pair   *325.00*
        strip, plate No. 1111   *1,800.00*
        Quantity: 105 stamps

Hat & H. November 9, 1998. Coil. Photogravure. Self-adhesive. Serpentine die cut. BEP.

(33c) multicolored
3265a   pair, die cutting omitted   65.00
        strip, plate No. 1111   *250.00*
        strip, plate No. 1131   *250.00*
        strip, plate No. 2222   *250.00*
        strip, plate No. 3333   *250.00*
        used pair, die cutting omitted   —
        Quantity: 200+ pairs

3265d   pair, die cutting & black omitted   *675.00*
        strip, plate No. 111   —
        Quantity: 20 stamps reported

Red, blue and gray digits appear on the plate strip, which is unique.

3265e	pair, die cutting & red omitted	500.00
	strip of 6, plate No. 111	1,750.00
	Quantity: 114 stamps	

Love. January 28, 1999. Booklet pane of 20. Lithographed. Self-adhesive. Serpentine die cut. AVR.

33c multicolored

| 3274b | pair, die cutting omitted | 100.00 |
| | Quantity: n/a | |

| 3274c | booklet pane, die cutting omitted | 1,000.00 |
| | Quantity: n/a | |

Hospice Care. Feb. 9, 1999. Lithographed. Self-adhesive. Serpentine die cut. BCA.

33c multicolored

| 3276a | hz pair, vrt die cutting omitted | — |
| | Quantity: n/a | |

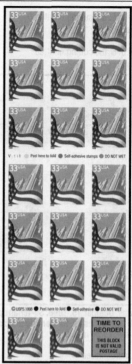

Flag Over City. February 25, 1999. Booklet pane of 20. Photogravure. Self-adhesive. Serpentine die cut. AVR.

33c multicolored

| 3278h | booklet pane, die cutting omitted | — |
| | Quantity: n/a | |

Flag Over City. February 25, 1999. Coil. Water activated. Small 1999 date. BEP.

33c multicolored

3280b	imperf pair	200.00
	as above, used	150.00
	imperf strip with plate No. 1111	—
	imperf strip with plate No. 2222	—
	Quantity: 55-60 pairs	

TYPES OF No. 3281

Type I. The long vertical feature at left and right of tallest building consists of 3 separate lines.
Type II. The same feature consists of solid color.

Flag Over City. February 25, 1999. Coil. Photogravure. Self-adhesive. Serpentine die cut. Type I. Large 1999 date. BEP.

33c multicolored

3281a	pair, die cutting omitted	30.00
	strip, plate No. 6666	250.00
	strip, plate No. 7777	250.00
	strip, plate No. 8888	250.00
	strip, plate No. 9999	250.00
	strip, plate No. 1111A	250.00
	strip, plate No. 2222A	250.00
	strip, plate No. 4444A	250.00
	strip, plate No. 5555A	250.00
	Quantity: several hundred pairs	

Exists miscut.

Flag Over City. February 25, 1999. Coil. Photogravure. Self-adhesive. Serpentine die cut. Type II. Small 1999 date. BEP.

33c multicolored

3281e	pair, die cutting omitted	—
	strip, plate No. 2222	—
	strip, plate No. 3433	*2,250.00*
	Quantity: 55-60 pairs; 2 plate strips with No. 3433	

Flag and Chalkboard. March 13, 1999. Photogravure. Self-adhesive. Serpentine die cut. AVR.

33c multicolored

3283b	pair, die cutting omitted	—
	Quantity: 1 block of 9 reported	

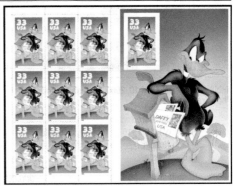

Daffy Duck. April 16, 1999. Pane of 10. Photogravure. Self-adhesive. Serpentine die cut. AVR.

33c multicolored

3307d	vrt pair, die cutting omitted between	*4,250.00*
	Quantity: *1 pair reported*	

The omission of die cutting occurs between positions 6 and 9 on the error pane.

Holiday Deer. October 20, 1999. Se-tenant booklet pane of 20. Lithographed. Self-adhesive. Serpentine die cut. BCA.

33c gold (deer); red, blue, purple or green (background)

3363c	block of 4, die cutting omitted	*100.00*
	Quantity: included below	

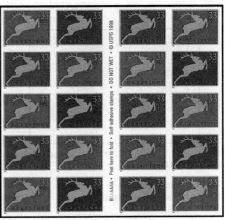

3363d	booklet pane, die cutting omitted	*500.00*
	Quantity: several panes reported	

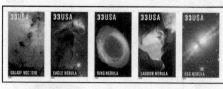

Hubble Telescope. April 10, 2000. Se-tenant pane of 20. Photogravure. SSP.

33c multicolored
a) Galaxy NGC 1316   b) Eagle Nebula
c) Ring Nebula   d) Lagoon Nebula
e) Egg Nebula

3388b   hz strip of 5, imperf   *900.00*
         pane of 20, imperf   *4,500.00*
         Quantity: at least 2 panes

Designs are staggered, so their order of appearance in strips may vary.

Coyote & Roadrunner. April 26, 2000. Pane of 10. Photogravure. Self-adhesive. Serpentine die cut. BCA.

33c multicolored
3391d   pane of 10, die cutting omitted   *2,250.00*
         Quantity: 3 panes reported

Single stamps lacking die cutting exist on the right panel of one variety of the booklet. They were regularly issued and are not errors.

Adoption. May 10, 2000. Lithographed. Self-adhesive. Serpentine die cut. BCA.

33c multicolored
3398a   pair, die cutting omitted   *2,500.00*
         Quantity: n/a

NOTE. Quantities for listings appearing for the first time in this edition are marked "new." They are tentative and subject to change.

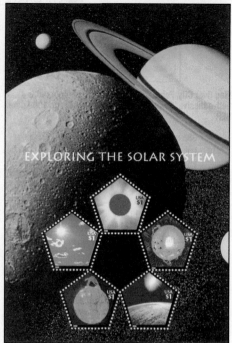

Exploring the Solar System. July 11, 2000. Pane of 5. Photogravure. SSP.

$1 multicolored

a) Solar Corona
b) Solar Core
c) Sun over Earth
d) Solar Flare
e) Sun in Sky

3410f   pane of 5, imperf   *2,000.00*
         Quantity: very rare

Joseph W. Stillwell. August 24, 2000. Engraved, lithographed. BCA.

10c red & black
3420a   imperf pair   *200.00*
         plate block of 4, imperf   —
         Quantity: at least 2 panes of 20 stamps

Transition items exist.

Wilma Rudolph. July 14, 2004. Pane of 20. Engraved, lithographed. Self-adhesive. Serpentine die cut. APU.

23c red & black
3422a   pair, die cutting omitted   —
Quantity: 2 panes reported

Wilma Rudolph. July 14, 2004. Booklet pane of 10. Lithographed. Self adhesive. Serpentine die cut. APU.

23c red and black
3436c   booklet pane, die cutting omitted, peel strip intact, plate No. P44   —
Quantity: n/a

No. 3436c occurs on a folded booklet pane, which can be distinguished by the plate number P44. Flat booklet panes were printed from plates P11 and P22.

3436e   booklet pane, die cutting omitted   —
Quantity: n/a

Flag over Farm. December 15, 2000. Booklet pane of 18. Photogravure. Self-adhesive. Serpentine die cut. AVR.

(34c) multicolored
3450b   pair, die cutting omitted   —
Quantity: one half pane with 9 stamps

Statue of Liberty. December 15, 2000. Booklet pane of 20. Photogravure. Self-adhesive. Serpentine die cut. AVR.

(34c) multicolored
3451d   pair, die cutting omitted   —
Quantity: n/a

Statue of Liberty. December 15, 2000. Coil. Photogravure. Self-adhesive. Serpentine die cut. BEP.

(34c) multicolored
3453a   pair, die cutting omitted   *300.00*
strip, plate No. 1111   *4,000.00*
Quantity: n/a

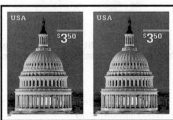

Capitol Dome. January 29, 2001. Lithographed. Self-adhesive. Serpentine die cut. BCA.

$3.50 multicolored
3472a   pair, die cutting omitted   *500.00*
Quantity: 20 pairs reported

Statue of Liberty. February 7, 2001. Coil. Photogravure. Self-adhesive. Serpentine die cut. BEP.

34c multicolored

3477a	pair, die cutting omitted	65.00
	strip, plate No. 1111	*700.00*
	strip, plate No. 3333	*700.00*
	strip, plate No. 4444	*700.00*
	strip, plate No. 5555	*700.00*
	strip, plate No. 6666	*700.00*
	strip, plate No. 7777	*700.00*
	Quantity: few hundred	

Plate strips of plate No. 1111 are 50% miscut.

Statue of Liberty. February 7, 2001. Booklet pane of 20. Photogravure. Self-adhesive. Serpentine die cut. AVR.

34c multicolored

3485e	pair, die cutting omitted	—
	Quantity: n/a	
3485f	booklet pane, die cutting omitted	—
	Quantity: n/a	

▶ Caution. Beware of pairs with traces of die cutting between stamps.

Apple & Orange. March 6, 2001. Se-tenant booklet pane of 20. Photogravure. Self-adhesive. Serpentine die cut. BCA.

34c multicolored

3492d	pair, die cutting omitted	*1,100.00*
	Quantity: included below	
3492e	booklet pane, die cutting omitted	*5,500.00*
	Quantity:15-20 panes	

Love. January 19, 2001. Booklet pane of 20. Lithographed. Self-adhesive. Serpentine die cut. BCA.

(34c) multicolored

3496b	vertical pair, die cutting omitted between	—
	Quantity: 5 pairs	

The discovery pane is miscut and contains five error pairs. Margin pairs at left and right contain a natural vertical straight edge on the margin side.

Love. February 14, 2001. Booklet pane of 20. Lithographed. Self-adhesive. Serpentine die cut. BCA.

34c multicolored

3497b	vertical pair, die cutting omitted between	—
	Quantity: 5 pairs	

The discovery pane is miscut and contains five error pairs that comprise rows two and three. Margin pairs at left and right contain a natural vertical straight edge on the margin side.

Nobel Prize. March 22, 2001. Engraved, lithographed. DLR.

34c multicolored

3504a	imperf pair	—
	plate block of 4, imperf	—
	Quantity: one pane of 20 reported	

The discovery pane was broken up into four plate blocks of 4 and two horizontal pairs.

Lucille Ball. August 6, 2001. Lithographed. Self-adhesive. Serpentine die cut. BCA.

34c multicolored

3523a	pair, die cutting omitted	*700.00*
	pane of 20, die cutting omitted	—
	Quantity: at least 7 panes	

Winter Olympics. January 8, 2002. Se-tenant pane of 20. Photogravure. Self-adhesive. Serpentine die cut. SSP.

34c multicolored

a) Ski Jumping   b) Snowboarding
c) Ice Hockey   d) Figure Skating

3555c   block of 4, die cutting omitted   *825.00*
         Quantity: 2 panes reported

Langston Hughes. February 1, 2002. Lithographed.Self-adhesive. Serpentine die cut. BCA.

34c multicolored
3557a   pair, die cutting omitted   *850.00*
         plate block, die cutting omitted   —
         Quantity: at least 1 pane

▶ Caution. Examples exist with deceptively faint die cuts. Expert certificate recommended.

Longleaf Pine Forest. April 26, 2002. Se-tenant pane of 10. Photogravure. Self-adhesive. Serpentine die cut. SSP.

34c multicolored
3611k   pane of 10, die cutting omitted   *2,500.00*
         Quantity: very rare, possibly unique

Toleware Coffeepot. May 31, 2002. Coil. Photogravure. SSP.

5c multicolored
3612a   imperf pair   —
         Quantity

The discovery examples exist as a single and a strip of five on an unused DAV reply envelope.

Star. June 7, 2002. Lithographed. Self-adhesive. Serpentine die cut. BCA.

3c red, blue & black
3613a   pair, die cutting omitted   —
         Quantity: 25 pairs reported

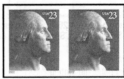

George Washington. June 7, 2002. Coil. Photogravure. Self-adhesive. Serpentine die cut. 2002 date AVR.

23c gray green
3617a   pair, die cutting omitted   —
         strip, plate No. V11   —
         strip, plate No. V35   —
         Quantity: n/a

George Washington. June 7, 2002. Booklet pane of 10.
Lithographed. Self-adhesive. Serpentine die cut. APU.

23c green
3619i   booklet pane, die cutting
           omitted vrt btwn   —
           Quantity: possibly unique

U.S. Flag. June 7, 2002. Coil. Photogravure. Self-adhesive.
Serpentine die cut. BEP.

(37c) multicolored
3622a   pair, die cutting omitted   —
          strip, plate No. 1111   —
          Quantity: 88 stamps in the initial discovery

U.S. Flag. November 24, 2003. Sheet stamp. Lithographed.
Water activated. APU.

37c multicolored
3629Fg imperf pair   *100.00*
          Quantity: n/a

U.S. Flag. June 7, 2002. Coil. Photogravure. Self-adhesive.
Serpentine die cut. 2002 date. BEP.

37c multicolored
3632b   pair, die cutting omitted   55.00
          strip, plate No. 1111   *1,500.00*
          strip, plate No. 2222   *750.00*
          strip, plate No. 3333   —
          strip, plate No. 6666   *750.00*
          strip, plate No. 7777   —
          strip, plate No. 1111A   —
          strip, plate No. 3333A   —
          Quantity: 200+pairs

Exists miscut and miscut with EE bars at top. Plate strips of No.
1111A exist 50% miscut. Plate strips of No. 7777 exist only miscut.

U.S. Flag. August 7, 2003. Coil. Photogravure. Self-
adhesive. Serpentine die cut. 2003 date. SSP.

37c multicolored
3632Af pair, die cutting omitted   *250.00*
          strip, plate No. S2222   —
          strip, plate No. S3333   *1,500.00*
          spliced pair or strip   —
          Quantity: 2 rolls of 100 reported

The roll of 100 with plate No. S2222 possesses solid tagging.
The roll of 100 with plate No. S3333 possesses uneven tagging.

Counterfeits exist that resemble die-cutting omitted errors Nos.
3632a and 3632Af. They were created to defraud the Postal
Service. They were printed on self-adhesive stock, lack tagging,
and lack the microprinted "USPS."

3632Ag vrt pair, hz die-cut slits omitted   *750.00*
           Quantity: n/a

U.S. Flag. June 7, 2002. Double-sided booklet pane of 20. Photogravure. Self-adhesive. Serpentine die cut. SSP.

37c multicolored
3636f   pane, die cutting omitted on the
     side with 8 stamps   —
     Quantity: unique

The 12-stamp side of the pane lacks most stamp paper; 11 stamps and part of 12th stamp are printed on the backing liner.

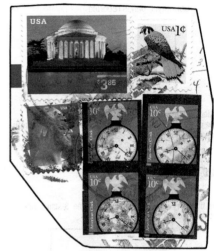

Masters of Photography. June 13, 2002. Photogravure. Se-tenant pane of 20. Self-adhesive. Serpentine die cut. SSP.

37c multicolored
3649u   pane, die cutting omitted   —
     Quantity: 1-2 reported

Toleware Coffeepot. August 2008. Date "2007." Lithographed. Self-adhesive. Serpentine die cut. BCA. 5c multicolored
3756Ab pair (dated 2007), die cutting omitted   *400.00*
     Quantity: several panes reported.

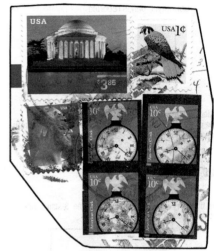

American Clock. January 24, 2003. Pane of 20. Lithographed. Self-adhesive. Serpentine die cut. APU.

10c multicolored
3757a used pair, die cutting omitted   —
    Quantity: 2 pairs

The two discovery pairs are used on piece together with three additional normal stamps of various denominations.

Purple Heart. May 30, 2003. Pane of 20. Lithographed. Self-adhesive. Serpentine die cut. BCU.

37c multicolored
3784d booklet pane, die cutting omitted   —
    Quantity: 1 pane reported

Purple Heart. August 1, 2003. Pane of 20. Lithographed. Self-adhesive. Serpentine die cut. APU.

37c multicolored

3784Ae	pair, die cutting omitted	*150.00*
	pane, die cutting omitted	*1,600.00*
	Quantity: 3 panes reported	

Madonna. October 23, 2003. Double-sided booklet pane of 20. Self-adhesive. Serpentine die cut. Design measures 19½ by 28mm. APU.

37c multicolored

3820b	pair, die cutting omitted	—
	Quantity: 4 pairs reported	

The discovery pairs are contained on the 8-stamp side of a booklet pane of 20.

Snowy Egret. January 30, 2004. Booklet pane of 20. Photogravure. Self-adhesive. Serpentine die cut. Without microprinting on bird's breast. APU.

37c multicolored

3830b	booklet pane, die cutting omitted	—
	Quantity: n/a	

Snowy Egret. January 30, 2004. Booklet pane of 20. Lithographed. Self-adhesive. Serpentine die cut. With "USPS" microprinting on bird's breast. APU.

37c multicolored

3830Df	pair, die cutting omitted	*150.00*
	Quantity: included below	

3830Dg	booklet pane, die cutting omitted	*1,200.00*
	Quantity: several panes	

Dr. Seuss. March 2, 2004. Self-adhesive. Photogravure. Serpentine die cut. SSP.

37c multicolored

3835a	pair, die cutting omitted	*1,400.00*
	Quantity: 2 panes reported	

Choreographers. May 4, 2004. Se-tenant pane of 20. Self-adhesive. Serpentine die cut. APU.

37c multicolored

a) Martha Graham
b) Alvin Ailey
c) Agnes de Mille
d) George Ballanchine

3843b	strip of 4, die cutting omitted	*300.00*
	pane of 20, die cutting omitted	*1,750.00*
	Quantity: at least 3 panes	

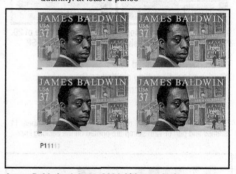

James Baldwin. July 23, 2004. Lithographed. Self-adhesive. Serpentine die cut. APU.

37c multicolored

3871a	pair, die cutting omitted	*750.00*
	plate block of 4, No. P11111	
	die cutting omitted	—
	Quantity: new, 1 pane of 20	

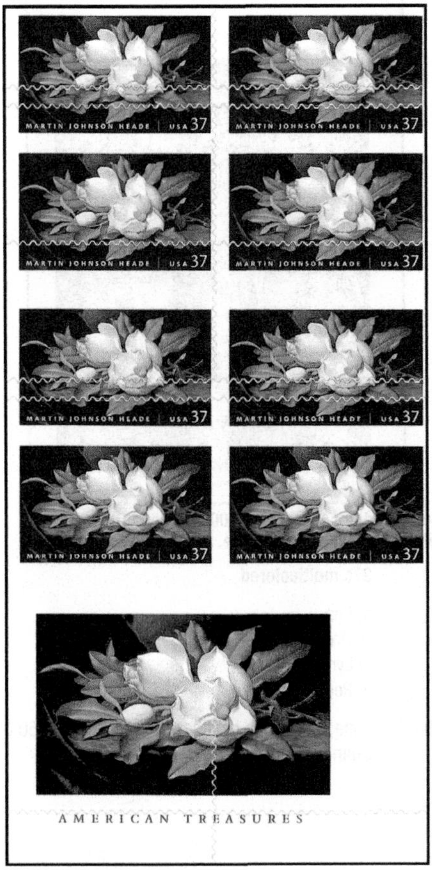

Giant Magnolias. August 12, 2004. Double-sided booklet pane of 20. Self-adhesive. Serpentine die cut. SSP.

37c multicolored

3872b pair, die cutting omitted —
Quantity: unique

The unique error pair occurred as a result of a shift in die cutting on the side of the booklet pane containing 8 stamps and a label.

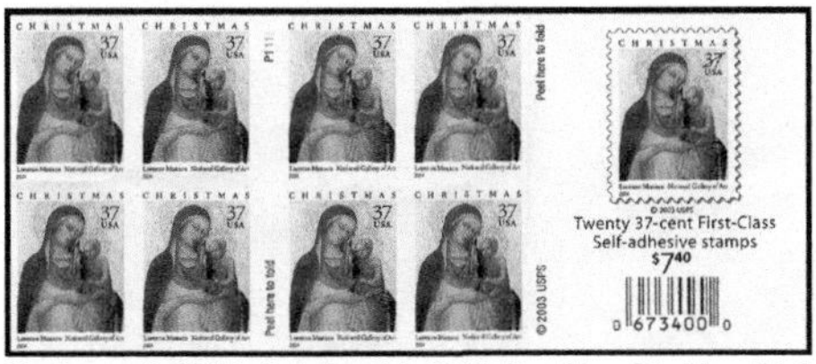

Madonna & Child. October 14, 2004. Double-sided booklet of 20. Lithographed. Self-adhesive. Serpentine die cut. APU.

37c multicolored

3879b pane, die cutting omitted —
Quantity: n/a

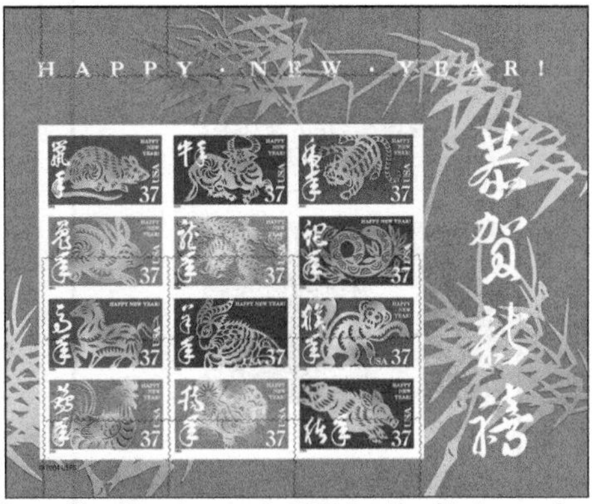

Lunar New Year. January 6, 2005. Double-sided pane of 12 se-tenant designs. Photogravure. SSP.

37c multicolored

a) Rat	b) Ox
c) Tiger	d) Rabbit
e) Dragon	f) Snake
g) Horse	h) Ram
i) Monkey	j) Rooster
k) Dog	l) Boar

3895m pane, a, b & c with die cutting omitted *1,100.00*
Quantity: at least 5 panes

No. 3895m was caused by a perforation shift on the reverse side of the two-sided pane.

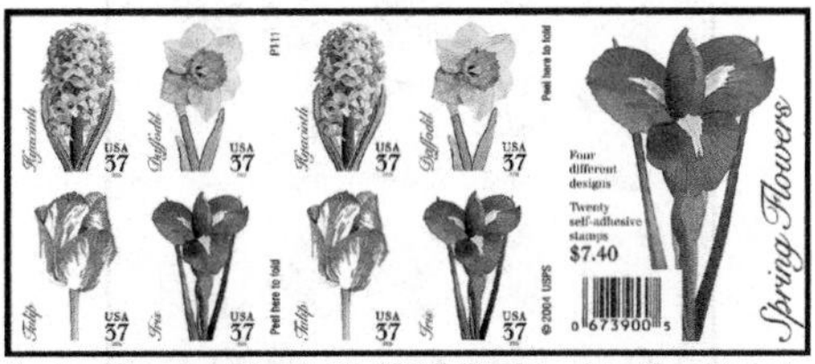

Spring Flowers. March 15, 2005. Double-sided booklet of 20. Lithographed. Self-adhesive. Serpentine die cut. APU.

37c multicolored

a) Hyacinth
b) Daffodil
c) Tulip
d) Iris

3903c pane, die cutting omitted on the side with 8 stamps —
Quantity: n/a

American Scientists. May 4, 2005. Se-tenant pane of 20. Lithographed. Self-adhesive. Serpentine die cut. BCA.

37c multicolored

a) Barbara McClintock   b) Josiah Willard Gibbs
c) John von Neumann   d) Richard Feynman

3908a vrt pair (a & c), die cutting omitted   —
       Quantity: n/a

3909d vrt pair (b & d), die cutting omitted   —
       Quantity: n/a

Disney Characters. June 30, 2005. Se-tenant pane of 20. Offset. Self-adhesive. Serpentine die cut. SSP.

37c multicolored

a) Mickey Mouse   b) Alice & Mad Hatter
c) Flounder, Ariel   d) Snow White & Dopey

3915b pane of 20, die cutting omitted   *5,500.00*
       used pane, die cutting omitted   *1,400.00*
       Quantity: n/a

The used pane is postmarked Cape Neddick, ME, March 19, 2008.

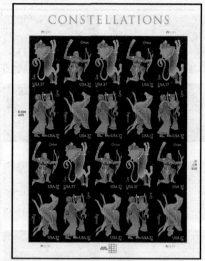

Constellations. October 3, 2005. Se-tenant pane of 20. Lithographed. Self-adhesive. Serpentine die cut. APU.

37c multicolored

a) Leo
b) Orion
c) Lyra
d) Pegasus

3948b pane, die cutting omitted   750.00
       Quantity: at least 3 panes

U.S. Flag. December 8, 2005. Double-sided booklet pane of 20. Lithographed. Self-adhesive. Serpentine die cut. APU.

(39c) multicolored

3966b pane, die cutting omitted   —
     Quantity: 1 pane reported

Flag & Liberty. April 8, 2006. Double-sided booklet pane of 20. Lithographed. Self-adhesive. Serpentine die cut. APU.

39c multicolored

3978c pane, die cutting omitted on the
     side with 8 stamps   —
     Quantity: 1 pane

Stamps on the 12-stamp side of the booklet were removed and used.

Flag & Liberty. April 8, 2006. Coil. Lithographed. Self-adhesive. Serpentine die cut. APU.

39c multicolored

3981a	pair, die cutting omitted	*150.00*
	strip, plate No. P1111	*1,000.00*
	Quantity: at least 2 rolls of 100.	

Flag & Liberty. April 8, 2006. Coil. Photogravure. Self-adhesive. Serpentine die cut. SSP.

39c multicolored

3982a	vrt pair, unslit between	*500.00*
	Quantity: 100 pairs	

Error pairs result from coil rolls produced in "stick" form. Postal clerks broke off rolls from a stick for individual sale.

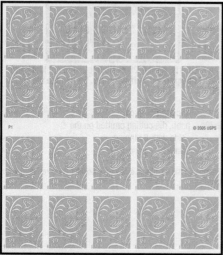

Wedding Doves. March 1, 2006. Booklet pane of 20. Lithographed. Self-adhesive. Serpentine die cut. APU.

39c pale lilac & bluish lilac

3998b	pane, die cutting omitted	—
	Quantity: 1 pane reported	

Judy Garland. June 6, 2006. Pane of 20. Lithographed. Self-adhesive. Serpentine die cut. BCA.

39c multicolored

4077a	pair, die cutting omitted	—
	Quantity: 1 pane reported	

Hanukkah. October 6, 2006. Lithographed. Self-adhesive. Serpentine die cut. BCA.

39c multicolored

4118a	pair, die cutting omitted	—
	Quantity: 1 pane of 20	

Liberty Bell. April 18, 2007. Booklet pane of 20. Large microprinting. Photogravure. Self-adhesive. Serpentine die cut. AVR.

Forever (41c) multicolored

4125i	hz pair (dated 2007), die cutting omitted	—
	Quantity: unique	

No. 4125i results from a die cutting shift on the 8-stamp side of the booklet pane. The stamps on the 12-stamp side were normal and had been removed and used.

Liberty Bell. August 22, 2008. Booklet pane of 20. Small microprinting. Lithographed. Self-adhesive. Serpentine die cut. APU.

Forever (42c) multicolored

4126g	pane (dated 2008), die cutting omitted	—
	Quantity: n/a	

Liberty Bell. May 12, 2008. Booklet pane of 20. Medium microprinting. Photogravure. Self-adhesive. Serpentine die cut. SSP.

Forever (42c) multicolored

4127k	pair (dated 2009), die cutting omitted	—
	Quantity: n/a	
4127m	booklet pane (dated 2008), die cutting omitted	*500.00*
	Quantity: several	

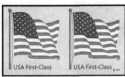

U.S. Flag. April 12, 2007. Coil. Lithographed. Self-adhesive. Serpentine die cut. BCA.

(41c) multicolored

4133a	pair, die cutting omitted	*1,250.00*
	strip, plate No. S1111	*3,400.00*
	Quantity: 100 reported	

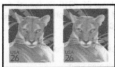

Florida Panther. May 12, 2007. Coil. Photogravure. Self-adhesive. Serpentine die cut. BCA.

26c multicolored

4141a	pair, die cutting omitted	*500.00*
	strip, plate No. S1111	*1,000.00*
	Quantity: 700+ pairs	

Flowers. August 10, 2007. Double-sided booklet of 20. Photogravure. Self-adhesive. Serpentine die cut. AVR.

41c multicolored

a) Iris
b) Dahlia
c) Magnolia
d) Red Gerbera Daisy
e) Coneflower
f) Tulip
g) Water Lily
h) Poppy
i) Chrysanthemum
j) Orange Gerbera Daisy

4185b	pane, die cutting omitted on "a" & "h" on the side with 8 stamps	*1,000.00*
	Quantity: at least 2 panes	

Madonna & Child. October 23, 2008. Double-sided booklet of 20. Lithographed. Self-adhesive. Serpentine die cut. APU.

42c multicolored

4359b	booklet, die cutting omitted on the side with 8 stamps	—
	Quantity: 1 reported	

The discovery example is damaged from a postal patron's careless handling and attempt to remove error stamps.

Polar Bear. April 16, 2009. Lithographed. Self-adhesive. Serpentine die cut. SSP.

28c multicolored

4387a	pane of 20, die cutting omitted	*7,250.00*
	Quantity: 1 pane reported	

American Flag. May 8, 2009. Coil. Lithographed. Self-adhesive. Serpentine die cut. SSP.

44c multicolored

4392a   pair, die cutting omitted   —
         strip, plate No. S111   —
         Quantity: 2 rolls reported

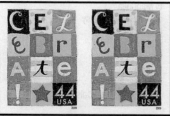

Celebrate. June 10, 2009. Lithographed. Self-adhesive. Serpentine die cut. BCA.

44c multicolored

4407a   pair, die cutting omitted   —
         Quantity: 1 pane of 20

Christmas. October 8, 2009. Se-tenant, double-sided booklet pane of 20. Lithographed. Self-adhesive. Serpentine die cut. BCA.

Forever (44c) multicolored

    a) Reindeer
    b) Snowman
    c) Gingerbread Man
    d) Toy Soldier

4428c   booklet pane, die cutting omitted   —
             on side with 12 stamps
Quantity: n/a

4428d   booklet pane, die cutting omitted   —
             on side with 8 stamps
Quantity: n/a

4428e   block of 4, die cutting omitted   375.00
         Quantity: n/a

Evergreens. October 21, 2010. Se-tenant, double-sided booklet pane of 20. Lithographed. Self-adhesive. Serpentine die cut. BCA.

Forever (44c) multicolored

    a) Ponderosa Pine
    b) Eastern Red Cedar
    c) Balsam Fir
    d) Blue Spruce
4481c   block of 4, die cutting omitted   —
         as above, used   500.00
         Quantity: at least several

4481d   booklet pane, die cutting omitted   700.00
             on side with 12 stamps
         Quantity: several

4481e   booklet pane, die cutting omitted
         on side with 8 stamps   *700.00*
         Quantity: several

4481f   booklet pane, die cutting omitted
         on bottom row of 4 stamps on
         side with 8 stamps   —
         Quantity: unique

**Statue of Liberty, U.S. Flag. December 1, 2010. Coil.
Lithographed. Self-adhesive. Serpentine die cut. BCA.**

Forever (44c) multicolored

a) Statue of Liberty
b) U.S. Flag

4488a   vrt pair (a), hz unslit between   —
         Quantity: new, 1 used pair on cover

4489b   block of 4, one vrt pair each of
         (a & b), unslit between hz   —
         Quantity: n/a

No. 4488a and No. 4489b are the result of the omission of slitting
between coils of stamps produced in "stick" form. Postal clerks
broke off rolls from a stick for individual sale.

**George Washington. April 11, 2011. Coil. Lithographed.
Self-adhesive. Serpentine die cut. APU.**

20c multicolored

4512a   imperf, on cover   —
         Quantity: one cover reported

No. 4512a is recorded only on a single cover bearing a strip of
9 and three strips of 10. The editors would welcome reports of
unused examples.

**Aloha Shirts. January 19, 2012. Se-tenant coil.
Lithographed. Self-adhesive. Serpentine die cut. BCA.**

32c multicolored

a) Surfers & Palm Trees
b) Surfers
c) Bird of Paradise Flowers
d) Kilauea Volcano
e) Fossil Fish & Shells

4601b   strip of 5, die cutting omitted   —
         strip, plate No. S1111111   *2,500.00*
         Quantity: 2 rolls of 100

**Love. February 12, 2012. Lithographed. Self-adhesive.
Serpentine die cut. BCA.**

Forever (45c) red

4626a   pair, die cutting omitted   *450.00*
         Quantity: n/a

Four Flags. February 22, 2012. Se-tenant coil. Lithographed. Self-adhesive. Serpentine die cut. BCA.

Forever (45c) multicolored
a) Equality
b) Justice
c) Freedom
d) Liberty

4640b	strip of 4, die cutting omitted	350.00
	strip, plate No. S22222	800.00
	Quantity: *at least 95 stamps*	

Girl Scouting. June 9, 2012. Lithographed. Self-adhesive. Serpentine die cut. BCA.

Forever (45c) multicolored
4691a   pair, die cutting omitted —
Quantity: 1 pane of 20

Die cutting is completely omitted between stamps, however, roulette die cutting used to facilitate the separation of individual stamps is present on the liner.

OSTENSIBLE ERROR STAMPS

For some modern issues, the Postal Service sold uncut press sheets. Certain configurations taken from uncut press sheets mimic error stamps, such as the illustrated example (ostensibly a vertical pair, imperforate between). In addition, the Postal Service sold during 2012-16 press sheets without die cutting. Pairs and multiples trimmed from such sheets are not errors, although they appear from time to time on online auctions in the Errors, Freaks and Oddities category, giving the impression that they are die cutting omitted errors.

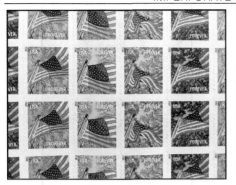

Four Flags. May 3, 2013. Se-tenant coil. Lithographed. Self-adhesive. Serpentine die cut. BCA.

Forever (46c) multicolored

a) Flag in Autumn
b) Flag in Winter
c) Flag in Spring
d) Flag in Summer

4777b   block of 28 (4x7), Nos. 4774-4777,
hz. die-cut slits omitted   —
Quantity: unique
strip of 5, plate No. S1111, block of
seven strips (5x7), hz die-cut slits omitted   —
Quantity: n/a
strip of 9, plate No. S1111, block of
seven strips (9x7), hz die-cut slits omitted   —
Quantity: n/a

No. 4777b has no horizontal slits and therefore is an error that can be collected as pairs or larger units of strips "imperf." horizontally.

Four Flags. March 17, 2014. Se-tenant, double-sided booklet pane of 20. Lithographed. Self-adhesive. Serpentine die cut. BCA.

Forever (46c) multicolored

a) Flag in Autumn
b) Flag in Winter
c) Flag in Spring
d) Flag in Summer

4785i   booklet pane, die cutting omitted
on side with 8 stamps and 3 pairs
on side with 12 stamps   —
Quantity: unique

Fort McHenry Flag and Fireworks. January 28, 2014. Coil. Lithographed. Self-adhesive. Serpentine die cut. APU.

Forever (49c) multicolored

4854a   pair, die cutting omitted   200.00
Quantity: At least 91 stamps reported

Hummingbird. February 7, 2014. Coil. Lithographed. Self-adhesive. Serpentine die cut. APU.

34c multicolored

4858b   pair, die cutting omitted   —
Quantity: n/a

No. 4858b has overall tagging.

Fort McHenry Flag and Fireworks. March 3, 2014. Coil. Lithographed. Self-adhesive. Serpentine die cut. BCA.

    Forever (49c) multicolored
4868a   vrt strip of three, hz die-cut
    slits omitted   60.00
    Quantity: 3 rolls of 100 reported

No. 4868a contains one single each from three different coil rolls.

4868b   pair, die cutting omitted   —
    Quantity: n/a

Love. January 12, 2016. Lithographed. Self-adhesive. Serpentine die cut. BCA.

    Forever (49c) multicolored
5036b   block of 4 (plate No. B11111),
    die cutting omitted   *100.00*
    Quantity: n/a

No. 5036b was printed from P#B11111 only and may also be collected in plate blocks of 6, half panes of 10 and full panes of 20. Pairs or other multiples without P#B11111 selvage attached cannot be distinguished from No. 5036a, the imperforate from press sheets without die cuts, which was printed only from P#S11111.

Flag. January 29, 2016. Coil. Lithographed. Self-adhesive. Serpentine die cut. BCA.

    Forever (49c) multicolored
5052a   pair, die cutting omitted   —
    Quantity: n/a

Flag. January 29, 2016. Double-sided booklet pane of 20. Lithographed. Self-adhesive. Serpentine die cut. BCA.

    Forever (49c) multicolored
5054c   booklet pane, hz die cutting omitted
    on side with 12 stamps   —
    Quantity: n/a

Flag. January 27, 2017. Coil. Lithographed. Self-adhesive. Serpentine die cut. BCA.

    Forever (49c) multicolored
5158a pair, die cutting omitted   —
       Quantity: n/a

The Art of Magic. August 7, 2018. Typographed with lenticular lens affixed. Self-adhesive. Serpentine die cut. BCA.

    Forever (50c) multicolored
5306b sheet of 3, die cutting omitted   —
       Quantity: 70 reported

Dragons. August 9, 2018. Lithographed with foil application. Self-adhesive. Serpentine die cut. BCA.

    Forever (50c) multicolored
5310b hz strip of 4, die cutting missing   —
       Quantity: 13 reported

No. 5310b results from an upward shift of the die cuts that left the bottom strip of 4 stamps in a pane imperforate.

AIR MAIL STAMPS

Beacon on Sherman Hill. July 25, 1928. Engraved.

5c carmine & blue

C11a   vrt pair, imperf between in a vrt strip
       of 3   *7,000.00*
       Quantity: very rare, likely unique

Winged Globe. February 10, 1930. Engraved. Flat plate press. BEP.

5c violet

C12a   hz pair, imperf between   *4,500.00*
       bottom strip of 5 with plate No.,
          left pair imperf between   *6,000.00*
       Quantity: very rare

Eagle & Shield. May 14, 1938. Engraved. BEP.

6c dark blue & carmine

C23a   vrt pair, imperf hz   *300.00*
       as above, used   *300.00*
       plate block of 4, imperf hz   *1,750.00*
       top plate block of 10   *2,500.00*
       center line block of 4   *1,000.00*
       vrt line pair, imperf hz   *450.00*
       pair on cover postmarked 5/15/38   —
       pair on cover postmarked
          1/18/39   —
Quantity: 1,000 pairs

C23b   hz pair, imperf vrt   *12,500.00*
       hz strip of 5, left pair imperf vrt   *12,500.00*
       top plate block of 10, left 6
          stamps imperf vrt   *37,500.00*
       Quantity: 8 pairs

Three error pairs resulting from a perforation shift are contained in an intact pane of 50 stamps.

Transport Plane. June 25, 1941. Engraved. BEP.

6c carmine

C25b   hz pair, imperf between   *2,250.00*
       plate strip of 10, containing
          two error pairs   —
       Quantity: 20 pairs

Often sold in strips of 5 containing one error pair and three normal stamps. Usually with inspector's blue crayon mark, which is often lightened due to attempted erasure. Value is for pair or strip without crayon mark. Value for strip with crayon mark: $1,500.00.

HINGING. Prices for stamps from No. C35a onward are for never hinged examples. Hinged examples sell for less.

Statue of Liberty at New York. August 20, 1947. Engraved. BEP.

15c bright blue green
C35a hz pair, imperf between   1,500.00
       as above, block of 4   —
       Quantity: 20 pairs

All known pairs are poorly centered.

Jet & Numeral. July 31, 1959. Booklet pane. Engraved. BEP.

7c blue
C51b vrt pair, imperf between   4,000.00
       Quantity: 2 recorded

No. C51b occurs as the result of a foldover.

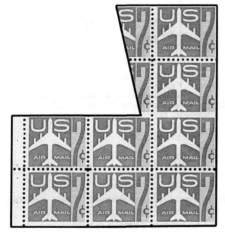

Jet & Numeral. August 19, 1960. Booklet pane. Engraved. BEP.

7c carmine
C60b vrt pair, imperf between   5,500.00
       Quantity: 2 recorded

No. C60b occurs as the result of a foldover.

Statue of Liberty. June 28, 1961. Engraved, lithographed. BEP.

15c black & orange
C63b hz pair, imperf vrt   15,000.00
       strip of 5, 3 stamps & margin at
         left imperf vrt   —
       strip of 5, 3 stamps at left
         imperf vrt   —
       Quantity: 3 as listed above

C63c hz pair, imperf between &
       at left   2,750.00
       Quantity: unique

No. C63c is the bottom left pair in a block of 6.

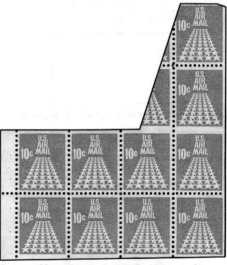

Runway of Stars. January 5, 1968. Booklet pane of 8. Engraved. BEP.

10c carmine
C72d vrt pair, imperf between   5,250.00
       Quantity: 2 recorded

No. C72d occurs as the result of a foldover.

Runway of Stars. January 5, 1968. Coil. Engraved. BEP.

10c carmine

C73a	imperf pair	*450.00*
	line pair, imperf	*750.00*
	spliced pair, imperf	—
	Quantity: 100+ pairs	

Jet Aircraft. May 7, 1971. Coil. Engraved. BEP.

11c carmine

C82a	imperf pair	*200.00*
	line pair, imperf	*375.00*
	spliced pair, imperf	—
	Quantity: fewer than 200 pairs reported	

Exists miscut. Slightly miscut pairs usually sell for less than listed pairs; dramatically miscut pairs often sell for more than listed pairs. Transition multiples exist.

Winged Envelope. December 27, 1973. Coil. Engraved. BEP.

13c carmine

C83a	imperf pair	65.00
	line pair, imperf	150.00
	Quantity: 500+ pairs	

Philip Mazzei. October 13, 1980. Photogravure. BEP.

40c multicolored

C98b	imperf pair	*2,250.00*
	plate strip of 20, imperf at right (see note)	—
	Quantity: 15 pairs	

The plate strip contains ten imperforate stamps at right and ten stamps with blind perfs at left.

C98Ac	hz pair, imperf vrt	*3,250.00*
	Quantity: very rare	

No. C98Ac is from the perf 10½x11¼ version issued in 1982.

Blanche Stuart Scott. December 30, 1980. Photogravure. BEP.

28c multicolored

C99a	imperf pair	*2,000.00*
	Quantity: at least 10 pairs	

Olympics. Se-tenant block of 4. June 17, 1983. Photogravure. BEP.

28c multicolored

a) Gymnastics	b) Hurdles
c) Basketball	d) Soccer

C104b	block of 4 (a-d), imperf vrt	*5,000.00*
	as above, plate block of 4	—
	Quantity: the 2 blocks as listed	

Olympics. Se-tenant block of 4. April 8, 1983.
Photogravure. BEP.

40c multicolored

a) Shot Put   b) Gymnastics
c) Swimming   d) Weight Lifting

C108d   block of 4 (a-d), imperf   650.00
        plate block of 4, imperf   —
        copyright block of 4, imperf   —
        vrt pair (a & c) or (b & d), imperf   —
        Quantity: 30-40 blocks of 4,
          20-30 pairs reported

Alfred V. Verville. February 13, 1985. Photogravure. BEP.

33c multicolored

C113a   imperf pair   600.00
        plate block of 4, imperf   —
        Quantity: 75-100 pairs

Lawrence & Elmer Sperry. February 13, 1985.
Photogravure. BEP.

39c multicolored

C114a   imperf pair   1,250.00
        plate block of 4, imperf   —
        Quantity: 25 pairs reported; plate block unique

Reportedly, 14 of the 25 pairs are sound. Value is for a sound example; those with faults sell for 50% or less depending on the degree of the fault.

Transpacific Airmail 1935. February 15, 1985.
Photogravure. BEP.

44c multicolored

C115a   imperf pair   600.00
        plate block of 4, imperf   —
        Quantity: 75 pairs reported

Vertical pairs exist with perforations at bottom between stamp and selvage.

Junipero Serra. August 22, 1985. Photogravure. BEP.

44c multicolored

C116a   imperf pair   900.00
        plate block of 8, imperf   —
        Quantity: 19-25 pairs

Often encountered with disturbed gum or small faults. Value is for a sound example. Those with faults sell for about 50% less.

Pre-Columbian America. October 12, 1990.
Photogravure. ABN.

45c multicolored

C127a   vrt pair, imperf btwn and at top   —
        Quantity: 1 reported

No. C127a is the upper left pair in a pane of 50 with a paper foldover before perforating. The pair has diagonal perforations from rows other than the top and between perforations.

Harriet Quimby. April 27, 1991. Photogravure. BEP.

50c multicolored

C128a   vrt pair, imperf hz   *850.00*
       plate block of 4, imperf hz   —
       Quantity: 50 pairs

Many pairs contain a light, cyan wiper-blade mark. Value is for an example without wiper mark. Those with wiper mark sell for slightly less.

Grand Canyon. January 20, 2000. Lithographed. Self-adhesive. Serpentine die cut. BCA.

60c multicolored

C135a   pair, die cutting omitted   *1,250.00*
       Quantity: 15-20 pairs reported

C135b   vrt pair, die cutting omitted hz   —
       Quantity: 2 pairs reported

C135c   vrt pair, die cutting omitted between   —
       Quantity: 2 pairs reported

C135d   hz pair, die cutting omitted vrt   —
       Quantity: 6 pairs

Bryce Canyon. February 24, 2006. Pane of 20. Lithographed. Self-adhesive. Serpentine die cut. BCA.

63c multicolored

C139a   pair, die cutting omitted   *450.00*
       Quantity: 1-2 panes reported

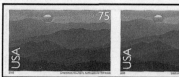

Great Smoky Mountains. February 24, 2006. Pane of 20. Lithographed. Self-adhesive. Serpentine die cut. APU.

75c multicolored

C140a   pair, die cutting omitted   *500.00*
       Quantity: 2-3 sound pairs;
         3-4 faulty pairs

Lancaster County. January 20, 2012. Lithographed. Self-adhesive. Serpentine die cut. BCA.

$1.05 multicolored

C150a   pair, die cutting omitted   *700.00*
       plate block, die cutting omitted   *1,400.00*
       Quantity: 6 to 8 panes of 20 reported

Die cutting is completely omitted between stamps, however, roulette die cutting used to facilitate the separation of individual stamps is present on the liner.

AIR MAIL SPECIAL DELIVERY

Great Seal of the United States. February 10, 1936. Engraved.

16c red & blue

CE2a   hz pair, imperf vrt   *4,250.00*
       block of 6, 2 plate Nos. and
         red & blue "TOP" markings   *60,000.00*
       arrow block of 6   —
       center line block of 4,
         imperf vrt   —
       Quantity: 10 pairs

SPECIAL DELIVERY

Motorcycle Messenger. November 29, 1927. Engraved. Rotary press.

10c gray violet
E15c   hz pair, imperf between   *350.00*
       plate block of 4, imperf vrt between   *1,100.00*
       Quantity: 80-100 pairs

Many pairs are poorly centered. Value is for a poorly centered pair. Well-centered pairs sell for more.

POSTAGE DUE

Numeral. September 9, 1879. Engraved.

10c light brown
J5a   imperf pair   *2,500.00*
     Quantity: rare

Numeral. August 14, 1894. Engraved.

1c deep claret
J31b   vrt pair, imperf hz   —
      Quantity: n/a

OFFICIAL STAMPS

War Department. George Washington. 1879. Engraved.

3c rose red
O116a   imperf pair   *5,000.00*
       Quantity: rare

Official Mail. January 12, 1983. Coil. Engraved. BEP.

20c red, blue & black
O135a   imperf pair   *1,000.00*
       imperf strip with plate No. 1   —
       spliced strip, imperf   —
       Quantity: fewer than 25 pairs reported

Official Mail. June 11, 1988. Coil. Engraved. BEP.

25c red, blue & black
O141a   imperf pair   *1,000.00*
       Quantity: 40-50 pairs, 1 used pair

BIRD HUNTING STAMPS

Snow Geese. June 30, 2003. Water activated gum. APU.

$15 multicolored
RW70b   imperf pair   *5,000.00*
       plate block 4, imperf   —
       plate block of 6, imperf   —
       Quantity: 2 panes of 20

ERROR-LIKE IMPERFORATES

Traditionally, to be regarded as an error, an imperforate of an issue that normally contained perforations must have found its way into public hands by being inadvertently sold across a post office counter. Over the years, several kinds of imperforates have found their way into philatelic domain by other means. While not errors in the traditional sense, they are similar in appearance and are included here for reference and identification. Refer to the Introduction for more information.

George Washington. 1860. Engraved.

	24c lilac	
37P5	imperf pair	*10,000.00*
	single, imperf	*1,500.00*
	Quantity: 2 pairs reported; singles very rare	

In his book *Postage Stamps of the United States*, John Luff claims to "have seen 2 copies used on original envelopes." He thinks perhaps a pane got out. Lester Brookman claims these (24c-30c-90c) were trial printings submitted by Toppan, Carpenter & Co. to the Postmaster General and, therefore, not regularly issued.

Benjamin Franklin. 1860. Engraved.

	30c orange	
38P5	imperf pair	*7,750.00*
	single, imperf	*1,500.00*
	imperf pair, used	—
	Quantity: 3 unused pairs and 1 used pair reported; singles very rare	

Refer to note following No. 37P5. Luff states that a used single, printed in the brown orange shade peculiar to imperfs, exists on cover to France.

George Washington. August 1860. Engraved.

	90c blue	
39P5	imperf pair	*37,500.00*
	single, imperf	*4,500.00*
	Quantity: 1 pair reported; singles very rare	

According to Lester Brookman, a used single, with "good margins," appeared in the Pelander sale of February 1943. A set of Nos. 37P5-39P5, including the unique 90c pair, sold at auction for $55,000 in May 2000.

SERIES OF 1857/1860
SPECIAL PRINTING OF 1875

Engraved. Printed by the Continental Bank Note Co. on white paper without gum. Imperforates are varieties of the perforated stamps issued for the Centennial Exposition of 1876. The 24c, 30c and 90c values vary in color from Nos. 37P5, 38P5 and 39P5 and thus can be distinguished.

40	1c Franklin, bright blue
41	3c Washington, scarlet
42	5c Jefferson, orange brown
43	10c Washington, blue green
44	12c Washington, greenish black
45	24c Washington, blackish violet
46	30c Franklin, yellow orange
47	90c Washington, deep blue

set of 8 pairs, imperf	*110,000.00*
set of 8 imperf margin singles	—

Quantity: singles very rare; one set of pairs reported; plus two pairs of the 1c, one pair of the 10c, and one pair of the 12c

Infrequent sales of individual pairs and singles make it impossible to establish values for them at this time.

George Washington. August 17, 1861. Engraved.

3c rose

65P5	imperf pair, without gum	1,000.00
	block of 4, imperf	—
	block of 6, imprint & plate	
	No. 11, imperf	—
	block of 8, imprint & plate	
	No. 11, imperf	—
Quantity: scarce		

No. 65P5 typically occurs with mottled paper.

3c lake

66TC6a	imperf pair	1,850.00
	block of 4, imperf	—
	strip of 4, imprint & plate	
	No. 52, imperf	—
	bottom block of 8, imprint & plate	
	No. 52, imperf	—
	Quantity: scarce; 3 imprint blocks,	
	1 imprint strip, and 1 full pane	

Regular trial color proofs were printed from Plate No. 34. Imprint blocks or strips if the 3c lake on gummed paper are from Plate No. 52.

George Washington. 1867. Engraved.

3c rose, A grill

79P5	imperf pair	1,500.00
	bottom imprint block of 8,	
	imperf	10,000.00
	Quantity: rare	

3c rose, C grill

83P5	imperf pair	1,750.00
	imperf margin single with selvage	1,000.00
	Quantity: n/a	

3c red, F grill

94P5	imperf pair	1,500.00
	Quantity: very rare	

SERIES OF 1869

A unique partial set of imperforate singles of the 1869 issue exists printed on gummed stamp paper that, unlike the regularly issued stamps of the series, lacks grills. The center of the 24c denomination is inverted. They were not regularly issued. The set includes the 1c, 3c, 12c, 15c (type I), 24c, 30c and 90c denominations. This group of seven sold for $94,600 in 1989.

SERIES OF 1870/1871

George Washington. April 1870. Engraved.

3c green, with grill

136P5	imperf pair	1,000.00
	block of 16 with plate No. 44, imperf	—
	Quantity: very scarce	

3c green, without grill

147-	imperf pair	500.00
E13e	block of 10 with bottom imprint & plate No. 11, imperf	—
	Quantity: rare	

Andrew Jackson. 1873. Engraved. Secret mark. White wove paper.

2c brown

157P5	imperf pair	—
	Quantity: very rare	

See No. 178P5 for 2c vermilion.

George Washington. 1873. Engraved. Secret mark.

3c green

158P5	imperf pair	150.00
	Quantity: n/a	

3c green, with grill

158P5a	imperf pair	650.00
	Quantity: n/a	

Andrew Jackson. June 21, 1875. Engraved. Secret mark. Yellowish wove paper.

2c vermilion

178P5	imperf pair	600.00
	block of 4, imperf	—
	imperf block of 16 with inscription & plate No. 161	12,000
	imperf pair, used	1,750.00
	Quantity: scarce; 2 plate blocks	

George Washington. 1879. Engraved.

3c green

184P6	imperf pair	500.00
	plate block of 12, imperf	—
	Quantity: rare	

Commodore O.H. Perry. 1879. Engraved.

90c carmine

191P5	imperf pair	2,250.00
	block of four, imperf	—
	plate No. strip of 5, imperf	—
	Quantity: scarce	

Often contains faults. Value is for a sound example.

George Washington. 1883. Engraved.

2c red brown

210P5	imperf pair	—
	Quantity: rare	

SPECIAL PRINTING OF 1883

George Washington. 1883. Engraved. Soft porous paper.

2c pale red brown

211Bc	hz pair, imperf between	2,000.00
	top margin inscription strip of 6, center	
	pair imperf between	35,000.00
	part sheet of 66 with right six pairs	
	imperf between - affixed to	
	cardboard	—

Quantity: at least 20 pairs and
     likely more

Value is for a sound, hinged example. Never hinged examples are rare and command a premium of 50%-100%.

No. 211Bc is from a special trial printing by a new steam-powered American Bank Note Company press. Approximately 1,000 of these stamps (in sheets of 200 with an imperforate gutter between the panes of 100, from which the imperforate between examples arise) were delivered as samples to the Third Assistant Postmaster General and subsequently made their way into the philatelic market.

Andrew Jackson. October 1, 1883. Engraved.

4c blue green

211P5	imperf pair	—
	Quantity: scarce	

Benjamin Franklin. June 11, 1887. Engraved.

1c ultramarine

212P5	imperf pair	—
	imperf pair, used	—
	strip of 3, used on piece	—
	Quantity: rare	

A horizontal strip of 3 on piece postmarked Hoboken, New Jersey, March 25, 1890 (with toning on the left pair) and a horizontal strip on cover postmarked Hoboken, New Jersey, have been reported.

George Washington. September 10, 1887. Engraved.

2c green

213P5	imperf pair	2,000.00
	imperf pair, used	—
	imperf strip of 3, used	—
	imperf pair, used on cover	—
	block of 6, used on piece	—
	Quantity: rare unused; two used pairs,	
	one used block of 6, and one used	
	strip of 3 reported.	

James A. Garfield. February 10, 1888. Engraved.

5c indigo

216P5	imperf pair	1,400.00
	hz plate strip of 5, No. 539	
	and letter "K," imperf	—
	Quantity: rare, plate strip unique	

Alexander Hamilton. January 3, 1888. Engraved.

30c orange brown

217P5	imperf pair	1,500.00
	Quantity: rare	

Often contains faults. Value is for a sound example.

Commodore O.H. Perry. February 28, 1888. Engraved.

90c purple

218P5	imperf pair	—
	Quantity: rare	

Usually contains faults.

ISSUES OF THE
AMERICAN BANKNOTE COMPANY
SMALL FORMAT 1890/1893

In order to acquire rare stamps for the official collection at the National Museum, imperforate stamps, gummed and identical to their perforated counterparts, were exchanged for acquisitions, such as the 1869 inverts. A total of 56 imperforate sets, mostly in pairs or blocks of four, were released. Imperforate postage due stamps, series of 1891, were simultaneously released and appear toward the end of this section.

Some difference of opinion exists as to whether these stamps are proofs or imperforate stamps that were not regularly issued. For purposes of this catalogue, examples archived by the Postal Service that subsequently found their way into private hands are treated as proofs and so numbered.

In addition to the above, proofs of the 2c, 4c, and 5c denominations in various shades similar to the issued colors exist on gummed stamp paper. The 2c denomination reportedly exists in 5 shades; the 4c, in 11 shades; and the 5c, in 13 shades. They should not be confused with the imperforates listed below.

Valuing Note: Most examples of this series are heavily hinged, contain disturbed or partial original gum, and often contain faults. Values are for such examples. Sound, lightly hinged examples sell for a premium of 50% to 100% more. Never hinged examples are rare and worth a premium of 100% to 150% more.

Benjamin Franklin. February 22, 1890. Engraved.

1c ultramarine
219P5	imperf pair	190.00
	block of 4, imperf	380.00
	plate block of 12 (No. 14), imperf	1,400.00
	Quantity: 56 stamps	

George Washington. February 22, 1890. Engraved.

2c lake (issued without gum)
219DP5	imperf pair	80.00
	block of 4, imperf	160.00
	plate block of 8, imperf	800.00
	Quantity: 150+ pairs	

2c carmine (May 12, 1890)
220P5	imperf pair	125.00
	block of 4, imperf	275.00
	plate block of 12 (No. 18), imperf	—
	Quantity: 56 stamps	

Andrew Jackson. February 22, 1890. Engraved.

3c purple
221P5	imperf pair	225.00
	block of 4, imperf	450.00
	top plate block of 12 (No. 21), imperf	—
	Quantity: 56 stamps	

Abraham Lincoln. June 2, 1890. Engraved.

4c dark brown
222P5	imperf pair	210.00
	block of 4, imperf	420.00
	Quantity: 56 stamps	

Ulysses S. Grant. June 2, 1890. Engraved.

5c yellow brown
223P5	imperf pair	225.00
	block of 4, imperf	450.00
	top plate block of 12, imperf	—
	Quantity: 56 stamps	

James A. Garfield. February 22, 1890. Engraved.

6c brown red
224P5	imperf pair	225.00
	block of 4, imperf	450.00
	top plate block of 12, plate No. 23, imperf	1,200.00
	bottom strip of 6 with imprint & plate No. 23	900.00
	Quantity: 56 stamps	

William T. Sherman. March 21, 1893. Engraved.

8c lilac
225P5   imperf pair   *1,000.00*
        block of 4, imperf   —
        Quantity: n/a

Daniel Webster. February 22, 1890. Engraved.

10c green
226P5   imperf pair   *325.00*
        block of 4, imperf   —
        Quantity: 56 stamps

Henry Clay. February 22, 1890. Engraved.

15c indigo
227P5   imperf pair   *625.00*
        block of 4, imperf   *1,200.00*
        plate block of 12 (No. 22), imperf   *5,000.00*
        Quantity: 56 stamps

Thomas Jefferson. February 22, 1890. Engraved.

30c black
228P5   imperf pair   *1,000.00*
        block of 4, imperf   *2,100.00*
        Quantity: 56 stamps

Commodore O.H. Perry. February 22, 1890. Engraved.

90c orange
229P5   imperf pair   *1,450.00*
        block of 4, imperf   —
        Quantity: 56 stamps

COLUMBIAN SERIES OF 1893

The B.K. Miller Collection at the New York Public Library Collection contains a complete set of imperforate horizontal pairs, 1c-$5 (Nos. 231-245). They were originally the property of John Wanamaker, Postmaster General 1889-1893.

Columbus Landing. January 2, 1893. Engraved.

2c brown violet
231P5   imperf pair, without gum   *2,000.00*
        imperf block of 4   —
        Quantity: 50-100 stamps

These stamps are from a crumpled sheet. All known examples are without gum and defective to one degree or another.

SERIES OF 1894

Similar to the Series of 1890 except with triangles added to the upper corners. Printed on unwatermarked paper. They were issued without gum. Those with gum had it added later.

Andrew Jackson. September 24, 1894. Engraved.

3c purple
253P5   imperf pair   *300.00*
        block of 4, imperf   *625.00*
        imperf plate block of 6   *7,500.00*
        Quantity: 400 stamps

Abraham Lincoln. September 11, 1894. Engraved.

4c dark brown
254P5   imperf pair   *275.00*
        block of 4, imperf   *575.00*
        plate block of 6 (No. 50), imperf   *7,500.00*
        Quantity: 400 stamps

Ulysses S. Grant. September 28, 1894. Engraved.

5c chocolate

255P5	imperf pair	300.00
	block of 4, imperf	625.00
	plate block of 6, imperf	9,500.00
	Quantity: 300-400 stamps	

Daniel Webster. September 17, 1894. Engraved.

10c green

258P5	imperf pair	500.00
	block of 4, imperf	1,100.00
	plate block of 6, imperf	9,500.00
	used pair, imperf	—
	Quantity: 400 stamps	

Lester Brookman mentions that the 50c denomination was reported as a single on cover. Brookman also describes a bottom margin pair with no perforations between the bottoms of the stamps and the selvage. He also mentions that the $1 denomination (type I, broken circle around the $1) exists imperforate, but he does not mention its form, i.e., imperforate horizontally, vertically, or between.

SERIES OF 1895

Similar to the Series of 1894 except with double-line watermark USPS horizontally or vertically.

Imperforates of this series reached public hands via Gilbert Jones, owner of the *New York Times*, who accepted them in exchange for services rendered to the Bureau of Engraving and Printing. They are gummed and identical to regular stamps of the series except for the lack of perforations. It is reported that the 1c, 2c, 3c, 4c and 8c denominations exist used philatelically on cover.

Valuing Note: Most examples of this series are heavily hinged, contain disturbed or partial original gum, and often contain faults. Values are for such examples. Sound, lightly hinged examples sell for a premium of 50% to 100% more. Never hinged examples are rare and worth a premium of 100% to 150% more.

Benjamin Franklin. January 17, 1898. Engraved. Double-line watermark.

1c blue

264P5	imperf pair	275.00
	block of 4, imperf	700.00
	plate block of 6, imperf	1,150.00
	imperf pair, used on cover	—
	Quantity: 900 stamps	
264P5a	hz plate strip of 3, imperf vrt	19,000.00
	Quantity: unique	

George Washington. 1895. Engraved. Double-line watermark.

2c carmine, type III

267P5	imperf pair	200.00
	block of 4, imperf	550.00
	plate strip of 3, (No. 319), imperf	650.00
	plate block of 6 (No. 319), imperf	1,100.00
	used pair, imperf	—
	Quantity: 500 stamps	

Andrew Jackson. October 31, 1895. Engraved. Double-line watermark.

3c purple

268P5	imperf pair	250.00
	block of 4, imperf	700.00
	plate strip of 3, imperf	950.00
	plate block of 6, imperf	2,000.00
	imperf pair, used on cover	—
	Quantity: 300 stamps	

Abraham Lincoln. June 5, 1895. Engraved. Double-line watermark.

4c dark brown

269P5	imperf pair	250.00
	block of 4, imperf	700.00
	plate strip of 3, imperf	1,250.00
	plate block of 6, imperf	3,250.00
	imperf pair, used on cover	—
	Quantity: 300 stamps	

Ulysses S. Grant. June 11, 1895. Engraved. Double-line watermark.

5c chocolate

270P5	imperf pair	250.00
	block of 4, imperf	700.00
	plate strip of 3, imperf	950.00
	plate block of 6, imperf	—
	Quantity: 300 stamps	

James A. Garfield. August 31, 1895. Engraved. Double-line watermark.

6c dull brown

271P5	imperf pair	275.00
	block of 4, imperf	825.00
	plate strip of 3, imperf	1,150.00
	plate block of 6, imperf	—
	Quantity: 300 stamps	

William T. Sherman. July 22, 1895. Engraved. Double-line watermark.

8c violet brown

272P5	imperf pair	400.00
	block of 4, imperf	1,100.00
	plate strip of 3, imperf	1,500.00
	plate block of 6, imperf	3,100.00
	imperf pair, used on cover	—
	Quantity: 300 stamps	

Daniel Webster. June 7, 1895. Engraved. Double-line watermark.

10c dark green

273P5	imperf pair	325.00
	block of 4, imperf	900.00
	plate strip of 3, imperf	1,250.00
	plate block of 6, imperf	—
	Quantity: 400 stamps	

Henry Clay. September 10, 1895. Engraved. Double-line watermark.

15c dark blue

274P5	imperf pair	1,000.00
	block of 4, imperf	2,750.00
	plate strip of 3, imperf	3,750.00
	plate block of 6, imperf	—
	Quantity: 100 stamps	

Thomas Jefferson. November 9, 1895. Engraved. Double-line watermark.

50c orange

275P5	imperf pair	1,100.00
	block of 4, imperf	3,250.00
	plate strip of 3, imperf	4,500.00
	Quantity: 100 stamps	

Commodore O.H. Perry. August 12, 1895. Engraved. Double-line watermark.

$1 black, type I

276P5	imperf pair	1,450.00
	block of 4, imperf	3,750.00
	plate strip of 3, imperf	5,250.00
	Quantity: 100 stamps	

James Madison. August 13, 1895. Engraved. Double-line watermark.

$2 bright blue
277P5	imperf pair	3,250.00
	block of 4, imperf	7,500.00
	plate strip of 3, imperf	10,500.00
	Quantity: 100 stamps	

John Marshall. August 16, 1895. Engraved. Double-line watermark.

$5 dark green
278P5	imperf pair	3,250.00
	block of 4, imperf	7,500.00
	plate strip of 3, imperf	10,500.00
	Quantity: 100 stamps	

Benjamin Franklin. 1908. Booklet pane. Engraved. Double-line watermark.

1c green
331	hz pair, imperf between	3,750.00
	Quantity: n/a	

From a booklet pane experiment.

George Washington. 1919. Engraved. Rotary press. Unwatermarked. Design measures 19½ to 20mm by 22 to 22¼mm. Perf 11x10.

1c green
538a	vrt pair, imperf hz	60.00
	vrt pair, imperf hz, used	125.00
	block of 4, imperf hz	130.00
	block of 4, imperf hz, used	300.00
	plate block of 4, imperf hz	900.00
	Quantity: 1,000+	

Never hinged examples sell for 75%-100% more.

George Washington. 1919. Engraved. Rotary press. Unwatermarked. Design measures 19½ to 20mm by 22 to 22¼mm. Perf 11x10.

2c carmine rose, type III
540a	vrt pair, imperf hz	60.00
	vrt pair, imperf hz, used	140.00
	block of 4, imperf hz	130.00
	block of 4, imperf hz, used	350.00
	plate block of 4, imperf hz	1,000.00
	plate block of 4, star, imperf hz	1,050.00
	Quantity: 1,000+	

Never hinged examples sell for 75%-100% more.

SERIES OF 1922/26

Stamps of 1922/26 series (Nos. 551-573 and Nos. 622-623) exist in a unique set of imperforate blocks of 4 without gum. The set was not regularly issued and is, as far as is known, unique. It sold at auction in 1968 for $12,200.

NATIONAL PARKS SERIES OF 1934

Imperforate, gummed examples of the National Parks Series (Nos. 740-749) exist in various forms, including pairs, strips, and blocks. They are from the original issue of 1934 and possess the gum and coloration of the original issue. They reached public hands via public auction of various items from President Franklin D. Roosevelt's collection conducted by H.R. Harmer in February 1946. They are marked on the back with a Franklin D. Roosevelt collection rubber stamp. The items include: No. 740, plate block of 6 (unique); No. 741, horizontal sheet margin pair (2 pairs) and left arrow block of 4 (unique); No. 742, horizontal sheet margin pair (2 pairs) and left arrow block of 4 (unique); No. 743, horizontal margin pair (unique), and block of 4 with plate number (unique); No. 744, vertical margin pair (2 pairs) and bottom arrow block of 4 (unique); No. 745, horizontal strip of 3 (unique) and top plate block of 6 (unique); No. 746, horizontal strip of 3 (unique) and top plate block of 6 (unique); No. 747, vertical pair (unique) and top arrow block of 4 (unique); No. 748, horizontal strip of 3 (unique) and top plate block of 6 (unique); and No. 749, top plate block of 6 (unique). In addition, a set of 10 covers exists, each bearing an imperforate block of 4 with plate number (except the 2c and 3c denominations, which are plate blocks of 6), each cover addressed to President Roosevelt, and each with the return card and signature of Secretary of the Interior Harold L. Ickes. The covers, which measure 7¼ x 3¾ inches, are variously postmarked between November 24, 1934 and January 3, 1935, thus predating the 1935 special printing. A second similar set exists on larger envelopes postmarked December 25, 1936.

Nos. 1789P through 2788aP are all from proof files of the American Bank Note Co. archives that were sold and are available to collectors. Nos. 3261P through 3262P were printed by the Banknote Corporation of America. They are listed first despite appearing to be out of numerical sequence. All items listed here are on gummed paper and imperforate unless otherwise noted, and they, therefore, have the appearance of imperforate or part-perforate stamps, though their source makes clear that they are, in fact, proofs. The group includes progressive proofs in various colors, plus one variety of No. 2624P and three varieties of No. 2770aP that differ slightly from the issued designs, and therefore, are actually essays. Where single proofs are listed, pairs are worth double the values shown.

3261P

$3.20 Space Shuttle

3261P	magenta color only	—
3261Pa	magenta color only, on coated paper	—
3261Pb	magenta color only, on uncoated paper	—

3262P

3262Pc

$11.75 Piggyback Space Shuttle

3262P	cyan color only	—
3262Pa	cyan color only, on coated paper	—
3262Pb	cyan color only, on uncoated paper	—
3262Pc	as No. 3262Pa, vrt pair, Nos. 3261P and 3262P, with full hz gutter between	1,150.00
3262Pd	as No. 3262Pb, vrt pair, Nos. 3261P and 3262P, with full hz gutter between	—

1789Pg finished design as issued, pair

1789Pd blue color only, pair

1789P	15c John Paul Jones	
1789Pa	single, red color ("John Paul Jones") only	50.00
	pair with vrt gutter between	—
	pair with hz gutter between	—
	cross gutter block of four	—
1789Pb	single, yellow color only	50.00
	pair with vrt gutter between	—
	pair with hz gutter between	—
	cross gutter block of four	—
1789Pc	single, magenta color only	50.00
	pair with vrt gutter between	—
	pair with hz gutter between	—
	cross gutter block of four	—
1789Pd	single, blue color only	50.00
	pair with vrt gutter between	—
	pair with hz gutter between	—
	cross gutter block of four	—
1789Pe	single, black color only	50.00
	pair with vrt gutter between	—
	pair with hz gutter between	—
	cross gutter block of four	—
1789Pg	single, finished design as issued	25.00
	pair	50.00
	pair with vrt gutter between	700.00
	pair with hz gutter between	600.00
	cross gutter block of four	3,000.00

2418P 25c Ernest Hemingway

2418P	pair	2,000.00
	pair with vrt gutter between	—
	pair with hz gutter between	—
	cross gutter block of four	

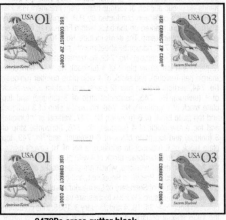

2478Pa cross gutter block

1c Kestrel

2476P	pair	150.00
	pair with vrt gutter between	200.00
	pair with hz gutter between	200.00
	cross gutter block of four	—

3c Bluebird

2478P	pair	150.00
	pair with vrt gutter between	200.00
	pair with hz gutter between	200.00
	cross gutter block of four	—
2478Pa	se-tenant pair, No. 2476P and No. 2478P, with vert. gutter between	—
	cross gutter block of four, two No. 2476P at left and two No. 2478P at right	—

25c Olympics

2500aP	hz strip of five	1,500.00
	two strips of five with vrt gutter between	—
	two strips of five with hz gutter between	—
	cross gutter block of four strips of five	—

25c Dwight D. Eisenhower

2513P	pair	875.00

2540Pi with all litho. colors

2540Pf magenta, yellow and blue colors only

2540P	**$2.90 Eagle**	
2540Pa	single, magenta color only	175.00
	pair with vrt gutter between	—
	pair with hz gutter between	—
	cross gutter block of four	—
2540b	single, yellow color only	175.00
	pair with vrt gutter between	—
	pair with hz gutter between	—
	cross gutter block of four	—
2540c	single, blue color only	175.00
	pair with vrt gutter between	—
	pair with hz gutter between	—
	cross gutter block of four	—
2540d	single, magenta & yellow colors only	175.00
	pair with vrt gutter between	—
	pair with hz gutter between	—
	cross gutter block of four	—
2540e	single, yellow & blue colors only	175.00
	pair with vrt gutter between	—
	pair with hz gutter between	—
	cross gutter block of four	—
2540f	single, magenta, yellow & blue colors only	175.00
	pair with vrt gutter between	—
	pair with hz gutter between	—
	cross gutter block of four	—
2540g	single, black (litho.) color only	175.00
	pair with vrt gutter between	—
	pair with hz gutter between	—
	cross gutter block of four	—
2540h	single, black (litho.) & yellow colors only	175.00
	pair with vrt gutter between	—
	pair with hz gutter between	—
	cross gutter block of four	—
2540i	single, all litho. colors, w/o engr. black	175.00
	pair with vrt gutter between	—
	pair with hz gutter between	—
	cross gutter block of four	—

2540j	single, finished design as issued	500.00
	pair	1,000.00
	pair with vrt gutter between	—
	pair with hz gutter between	—
	cross gutter block of four	—

For perforated varieties of modern proofs refer to the Scott Specialized Catalogue.

2605P, with plate numbers

23c Flag

2605P	vrt pair, uncut between	250.00
	vrt pair, uncut between, with P#A111	—

1992 Columbian souvenir sheets

2624P	1c, 4c and $1 Columbian souvenir sheet	*750.00*
	pair of sheets	—
2624Pa	As No. 2624P, but with background of No. 2627P (essay)	—
2625P	2c, 3c and $4 Columbian souvenir sheet	*750.00*
	pair of sheets	—
2626P	5c, 30c and 50c Columbian souvenir sheet	*750.00*
	pair of sheets	—
2627P	6c, 8c and $3 Columbian souvenir sheet	*750.00*
	pair of sheets	—
2628P	10c, 15c and $2 Columbian souvenir sheet	*750.00*
	pair of sheets	—
2629P	$5 Columbian souvenir sheet	*750.00*
	pair of sheets	—

2646aPi finished design as issued

2646aPe brown color only

2646aP **29c Hummingbirds**

2646aPb	pane of five, yellow color only	450.00
	two panes of five with vrt gutter between	—
	two panes of five with hz gutter between	—
	cross gutter block of four panes of five	—
2646aPc	pane of five, magenta color only	450.00
	two panes of five with vrt gutter between	—
	two panes of five with hz gutter between	—
	cross gutter block of four panes of five	—
2646aPd	pane of five, blue color only	450.00
	two panes of five with vrt gutter between	—
	two panes of five with hz gutter between	—
	cross gutter block of four panes of five	—
2646aPe	pane of five, brown color (birds) only	450.00
	two panes of five with vrt gutter between	—
	two panes of five with hz gutter between	—
	cross gutter block of four panes of five	—
2646aPf	pane of five, brown color ("USA/29") only	450.00
	two panes of five with vrt gutter between	—
	two panes of five with hz gutter between	—
	cross gutter block of four panes of five	—
2646aPg	pane of five, green color (frames) only	450.00
	two panes of five with vrt gutter between	—
	two panes of five with hz gutter between	—
	cross gutter block of four panes of five	—
2646aPh	pane of five, orange color (frames) only	450.00
	two panes of five with vrt gutter between	—
	two panes of five with hz gutter between	—
	cross gutter block of four panes of five	—
2646aPi	pane of five, finished design as issued	450.00
	two panes of five with vrt gutter between	—
	two panes of five with hz gutter between	—
	cross gutter block of four panes of five	—

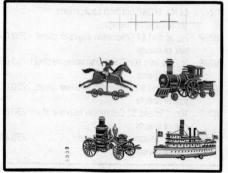

2718aPe

29c Christmas Toys

2718aP	booklet pane of four	600.00
	hz pair of panes of four	1,500.00
	vrt pair of panes of four	1,500.00
2718aPb	as No. 2718aP, pane of four with two stamps at top from bottom row of normal pane and two stamps at bottom from top row of normal pane	1,000.00
2718aPc	as No. 2718aP, perf pair of panes, uncut hz	2,000.00
2718aPe	pane of four without red "Greetings" or green denominations	1,200.00

2718aPf	as No. 2718aPe, two stamps at top from bottom row of "normal" pane and two stamps at bottom from top row of "normal" pane	1,500.00
2718aPg	pane of four without green denominations	1,200.00
2718aPh	as No. 2718aPg, two stamps at top from bottom row of "normal" pane and two stamps at bottom from top row of "normal" pane	1,500.00

29c American Music

2737aP	booklet pane of eight	—
	pair of panes of eight	—
2737aPc	as No. 2737aP, perf hz, uncut vrt, pair of panes of eight	—
2737bP	booklet pane of four	2,000.00
2737bPd	as No. 2737bP, perf hz, uncut vrt, pair of panes of four	—
2737bPe	pair of panes, one No. 2737aP and one No. 2737bP	—
2737bPf	pair of panes, one No. 2737aPc and one No. 2737bPd	—

2754Pb

29c Cherokee Strip Land Run

2754P	pair	350.00
	pair with vrt gutter between	400.00
	pair with hz gutter between	—
	cross gutter block of four	1,500.00
2754Pb	as No. 2754P, pair without purple inscriptions and black inscriptions	—
	pair with vrt gutter between	—
	pair with hz gutter between	—
	cross gutter block of four	—
2754Pc	die proof, signed 11/25/92 for color and/or engraving	—

29c American Musicals

2770aP	booklet pane of four	1,250.00
	pair of panes	—
2770aPa	perf hz, uncut vrt, pair of panes of four	—
2770aPb	pane of four, blue color only,	

with designs slightly different
from issued designs (essay) —

2770aPc pane of four, blue and magenta
colors only, with designs slightly
different from issued designs (essay) —

2770aPd pane of four, blue, magenta and
yellow colors only, with designs slightly
different from issued designs (essay) —

2778aP 29c American Music

2778aPa pane of four, yellow color only *300.00*
on approval card (unique) —

2778aPb pane of four, pink color only *300.00*
on approval card (unique) —

2778aPc pane of four, red color only *300.00*
on approval card (unique) —

2778aPd pane of four, blue color only *300.00*
on approval card (unique) —

2778aPe pane of four, black color (frames
and wording) only *300.00*
on approval card (unique) —

2778aPf pane of four, black color (Musicians) only *300.00*
on approval card (unique) —

2778aPg pane of four, finished design as issued *1,500.00*
on approval card (unique) —

2778aPh pane of four, finished design as issued,
on cromalin paper, taped to approval
card (unique) —

2778aPi booklet cover, finished design as issued,
on card stock, pair of covers —

2778aPj booklet cover, finished design as issued,
on cromalin paper, taped to approval
card (unique) —

2778aPk perf hz, uncut vrt, pair of panes of four *1,500.00*

Some of the sets of progressive proofs are in panes that are 2½ to
3½ stamps tall. These sell for somewhat less than the full panes.

About 20 percent of the examples of No. 2778aPk are split into
two pieces. From these pieces come horizontal pairs or blocks of
booklet stamps imperf vertically.

29c Classic Books

2788aP block of four *400.00*
pair of blocks with vrt gutter between —
pair of blocks with hz gutter between —
cross gutter block of four blocks —

AIR MAIL STAMPS

Nos. C13Pb-C15Pb are on gummed stamp paper and, except
for the lack of perforations, are identical to the regularly issued
stamps.

Zeppelin Above Atlantic Ocean. April 19, 1930. Engraved.
BEP.

65c green
C13P2b imperf single —
Quantity: unique

Zeppelin Above Map. April 19, 1930. Engraved. BEP.

$1.30 brown
C14P2b imperf single —
Quantity: unique

Zeppelin and Globe. April 19, 1930. Engraved. BEP.

$2.60 blue
C15P2b imperf single —
Quantity: unique

SPECIAL DELIVERY

Messenger & Tablet. October 10, 1894. Engraved.

10c blue
E4P5 hz pair, imperf *6,500.00*
vrt block of 6, without gum,
imperf —
Quantity: very rare

Messenger & Tablet. October 16, 1895. Engraved. Double line watermark.

10c blue

E5P5	imperf pair	4,500.00
	block of 4, imperf	—
	sheet margin single, imperf	2,000.00
	Quantity: very rare	

POSTAGE DUE

See the note preceding issues of the American Banknote Company, 1890/1893.

Numeral. 1891. Engraved.

1c bright claret

J22P5	imperf pair	425.00
	Quantity: 46 stamps	

Numeral. 1891. Engraved.

2c bright claret

J23P5	imperf pair	425.00
	Quantity: 46 stamps	

Numeral. 1891. Engraved.

3c bright claret

J24P5	imperf pair	425.00
	Quantity: 46 stamps	

Numeral. 1891. Engraved.

5c bright claret

J25P5	imperf pair	425.00
	Quantity: 46 stamps	

Numeral. 1891. Engraved.

10c bright claret

J26P5	imperf pair	425.00
	Quantity: 46 stamps	

Numeral. 1891. Engraved.

30c bright claret

J27P5	imperf pair	500.00
	Quantity: 46 stamps	

Numeral. 1891. Engraved.

50c bright claret

J28P5	imperf pair	500.00
	Quantity: 46 stamps	

Numeral. August 14, 1894. Engraved.

1c deep claret

J31P5	imperf pair	225.00
	block of 4, imperf	500.00
	Quantity: n/a	

Usually encountered without gum. Value is for an example without gum.

COLOR-OMITTED ERRORS

Red Cross. May 21, 1931. Engraved. BEP.

2c black & red

702a   red omitted   *40,000.00*
       Quantity: 1 example documented

No. 702a results from a paper fold that prevented the application of the red cross. Examples with red partially omitted may exist but do not qualify as the error.

HINGING. Prices for stamps from No. 1137a forward are for never hinged examples. Hinged examples sell for less.

Ernst Reuter. December 29, 1959. Engraved. BEP.

8c carmine, ultramarine & ocher

1137a   ocher omitted   *3,000.00*
       Quantity: 3

1137b   ultramarine omitted   *3,750.00*
       Quantity: 3

1137c   ocher & ultramarine omitted   *4,000.00*
       Quantity: 2

Nos. 1137a-1137c all result from a single pane that passed through the printing press with a sizable piece of extraneous paper adhering to the top of it. When overlaying flap of paper was removed, certain stamps were left with only a partial impression, including those listed above with colors omitted. No. 1137a occurs in positions 10, 20 and 30; No. 1137b occurs in positions 17, 36 and 46; and No. 1137c occurs in positions 27 and 37.

Water Conservation. April 18, 1960. Engraved. BEP.

4c dark blue, brown orange & green

1150a   brown orange omitted   *2,750.00*
       Quantity: 4

New York World's Fair. April 22, 1964. Engraved. BEP.

5c blue green

1244a   All color omitted   —
       Quantity: 1 reported

On No. 1244a, a clear albino impression of the design is present.

American Music. October 15, 1964. Engraved. BEP.

5c red, black & red (gray paper)

1252a   blue omitted   *650.00*
       Quantity: 20-40 reported

Transition multiples exist and sell for a premium.

▶ Caution. Should contain no traces of blue. Beware of examples with traces of blue.

Christmas. November 9, 1964. Engraved. BEP.

5c green, carmine & black

1254c   All color missing   *2,000.00*
       Quantity: unique

No. 1254c resulted from a foldover. It is unique and is in a block of four with the other three stamps missing parts of the designs.

Florida Settlement. August 28, 1965. Engraved. BEP.

5c red, yellow & black

1271a   yellow omitted   *200.00*
         Zip block of 4, yellow omitted   —
         Quantity: 300-400

▶ Caution. A shift in yellow can give the stamp the appearance of
having the color omitted. Examine carefully.

Ten vertical transition pairs exist, each with an error stamp at top
and a normal stamp at bottom.

**Marine Corps Reserve. August 29, 1966. Engraved,
lithographed. BEP.**

**5c black & bister (engraved); red &
ultramarine (lithographed)**

1315b   black & bister omitted   *16,000.00*
         Quantity: unique

**Savings Bonds. October 26, 1966. Engraved, lithographed.
BEP.**

**5c red, dark blue & black (engraved);
light blue (lithographed)**

1320b   red, dark blue & black (engraved)
         omitted   *3,750.00*
         Quantity: 6 reported

Transition multiples exist and sell for a premium.

1320c   dark blue (engraved) omitted   *5,000.00*
         Quantity: at least 2

Davy Crockett. August 17, 1967. Engraved, lithographed. BEP.

**5c black & gray green (engraved);
yellow & green (lithographed)**

1330b   gray green (engraved) omitted   —
         Quantity: unique

1330c   black & gray green (engraved) omitted   —
         Quantity: unique

An example of No. 1330 exists with lithographed yellow and green
omitted; however, part of the upper right corner of the stamp is
missing.

Pairs of No. 1331-1332 are known with the red flag omitted from
the space capsule. However, red litho dots are present elsewhere
on the stamp, so it is not considered to be a 100% color-omitted
error. Nevertheless, it is still a collectible variety, most often
encountered as a block of nine with flag omitted from the center
stamp: value $195.00

U.S. Flag. January 28, 1968. Engraved. BEP.

6c dark blue, red & green
1338v   All color omitted   —

On No. 1338v, an albino impression of the engraved plate is present.

U.S. Flag. May 10, 1971. Engraved. BEP.

8c dark blue, red & slate green
1338Fp   slate green omitted   *300.00*
          Quantity: 100

Hemisfair '68. March 30, 1968. Engraved, lithographed. BEP.

6c white (engraved); blue & rose red (lithographed)
1340a   white omitted   *650.00*
         Quantity: 100

Walt Disney. September 11, 1968. Photogravure. UCC.

6c black, yellow, magenta, blue & ocher
1355a   ocher omitted   *350.00*
         as above, plate block of 4   —
         Quantity: 400-500

1355d   black omitted   *1,750.00*
         as above, plate block of 4   —
         Quantity: 35 reported

1355f   blue omitted   *1,500.00*
         as above, plate block of 4   —
         Quantity: 35 reported

Transition multiples exist for Nos. 1355a, 1355d and 1355f. They sell for a premium.

John Trumball. October 18, 1968. Engraved, lithographed. BEP.

6c black (engraved); magenta & ocher (litho)
1361b   black (engraved) omitted   *11,000.00*
         Quantity: 2

The 2 error stamps resulted from a foldover on the lower right corner of a pane of 50. Two stamps above and 2 stamps to the left of the color-omitted pair contain partial omission of engraved black in varying degrees.

Waterfowl Conservation. October 24, 1968. Engraved, lithographed. BEP.

    6c black (engraved); yellow, red, blue & blue green (lithographed)

1362b   red & blue omitted   *350.00*
        as above, plate block of 4   —
        used, red & blue omitted   —
        Quantity: 150

▶ Caution. Fakes exist. Expert certificate recommended for both unused and used examples.

1362c   used, red omitted   *1,750.00*
        Quantity: 1 recorded

The existing unique example has been expertized by 3 different expertizing services.

Christmas Angel. November 1, 1968. Engraved, lithographed. BEP.

    6c black, red, blue & brown (engraved); yellow (lithographed)

1363c   yellow omitted   *50.00*
        as above, plate block of 10 —
        Quantity: 1,000+

▶ Caution. Beware of examples with yellow partially omitted.

Grandma Moses. May 1, 1969. Engraved, lithographed. BEP.

    6c black & Prussian blue (engraved); yellow, red, blue & blue green (lithographed)

1370b   black & Prussian blue omitted   *400.00*
        as above, plate block of 4   —
        Quantity: 150

Usually with mottled gum. Value is for an example with good gum. Deduct 33% for an example with mottled gum.

California. July 16, 1969. Engraved, lithographed. BEP.

    6c red & black brown (engraved); orange & light blue (lithographed)

1373b   red (engraved) omitted   *400.00*
        Quantity: n/a

Professional Baseball. September 24, 1969. Engraved, lithographed. BEP.

    6c black (engraved); yellow, red & green (lithographed)

1381a   black omitted   *500.00*
        Quantity: 300+

Value is for a well-centered example; poorly centered examples sell for less. Exists with tagging ghosts. Transition multiples exist and sell for a premium.

Christmas. November 3, 1969. Engraved, lithographed. BEP.

6c dark green & dark brown (engraved);
yellow, red, & light green (lithographed)

1384c light green omitted   30.00
       plate block of 10, light green omitted   —
       Quantity: 1,000+

1384d light green, red & yellow omitted   *600.00*
       as above, used   —
       Quantity: 50-60 unused, 6 examples
       used reported

1384e yellow omitted   *1,500.00*
       Quantity: very rare

1384g yellow & red omitted   *2,250.00*
       Quantity: very rare

▶ Caution. Specks of red are often present on Nos. 1384d and 1384g. Expert certificate advised. Transition multiples exist for Nos. 1384d and 1384e and sell for a premium.

1384h yellow & light green omitted   *500.00*
       Quantity: n/a

1384i light green & red omitted   —
       Quantity: n/a

Nearly all the yellow is omitted; therefore, it resembles No. 1384d, except with traces of yellow.

Eisenhower. May 10, 1971. Engraved. BEP.

8c black, red & gray blue

1394c red omitted   *1,250.00*
       Quantity: 4

1394e red & gray blue omitted   *1,000.00*
       Quantity: 1

No. 1394e id the result of a foldover at the lower right on a pane of 100 stamps. The top portion of the pane is precancelled AKRON, OH. This error should not be confused with color missing item that results from a perforation shift.

Christmas Nativity Scene. November 5, 1970.
Photogravure. GGI.

6c black, magenta, blue & ocher

1414b black omitted   *400.00*
       Quantity: 50 reported

▶ Caution. Many examples similar to the error exist with partial black. However, in order to qualify as the listed error, no trace of black should be visible under 30-power magnification. Expert certificate advised. Transition multiples exist and sell for a premium.

Christmas Precancel. November 5, 1970. Photogravure.

**6c black, magenta, blue & ocher,
precanceled with black bars**

1414c	blue omitted	*1,100.00*
	plate block, blue omitted	—
	transition multiple, blue omitted	—
	Quantity: 15 reported; plate block unique	

The unique plate block contains 4 error stamps, 2 transitional stamps, and 2 normal stamps.

Christmas Toys. November 5, 1970. Se-tenant block of 4. Photogravure. GGI.

6c black, magenta, blue & ocher

a) Locomotive　　　　b) Toy Horse
c) Tricycle　　　　　　d) Doll carriage

1418e	block of 4, black omitted	*8,000.00*
	block of 4, black omitted on	
	c & d (Scott 1418f)	*4,000.00*
	upper right plate block of 8,	
	black omitted on a & b (Scott 1418g)	—
	any single (1415-1418), black omitted	*1,750.00*
	Quantity: 2 blocks, 5-6 of each	
	single reported	

Some singles exist unused on piece and, due to the rarity of the issue, sell for nearly as much as mint examples.

Landing of Pilgrims. November 21, 1970. Engraved, lithographed. BEP.

6c black (engraved); yellow, red & blue (lithographed)

1420a	yellow omitted	*525.00*
	Quantity: 200	

Beware of used examples of No. 1420 with magenta purportedly omitted.

Wool. January 19, 1971. Engraved, lithographed. BEP.

6c greenish blue, dark brown, olive green (engraved); yellow, cyan, orange, olive green (lithographed)

1423b	greenish blue (engraved) omitted	*400.00*
	Quantity: 6-8 reported	

No. 1423b results from an upward shift of the engraved greenish blue portion of the design (the words "United States"). On some examples, the color is not completely shifted off the stamp and, therefore, they do not qualify as the error. Expert certificate advised. Transition multiples exist.

Wildlife Conservation. June 12, 1971. Se-tenant block of 4. Engraved, lithographed. BEP.

8c black, dark brown & dark green (engraved); red, blue, buff, olive green & bluish green (lithographed)

a) Trout	b) Alligator
c) Polar Bear	d) California Condor

1430b block of 4, olive & bluish green
   omitted from a & b   *3,250.00*
   as above, plate block of 4   —
   Quantity: 8 blocks including unique
   plate block

1430c block of 4, red omitted
   from a, c & d   *3,000.00*
   used single (a)   —
   Quantity: block of 4 very rare, possibly
   unique; used single unique

Due to color schemes used in the four designs, some colors are normally not present on every stamp. For example, lithographic red was not used in the alligator design and, therefore, cannot be considered to have been omitted.

On the polar bear stamp, red dots are printed in the green background and at lower left, and are not readily apparent except under magnification.

▶ Caution. The red head of the condor may appear to be omitted if shifted to the lower left. Expert certificate advised.

American Revolution Bicentennial. July 4, 1971. Engraved, lithographed.

8c black & gray (engraved); red & blue (lithographed)

1432a gray & black omitted   *325.00*
   Quantity: 100-150

1432b gray omitted   *650.00*
   Quantity: rare

No. 1432b often occurs in pairs or larger multiples with gray completely omitted from one stamp, and gray and black partially omitted from others. They sell for a premium.

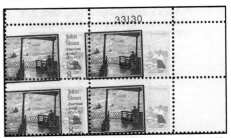

John Sloan. August 2, 1971. Engraved, lithographed. BEP.

8c red & black (engraved); yellow, red & light blue (lithographed)

1433b red (engraved) omitted   *950.00*
   Quantity: rare

No. 1433b results from a shift of the engraved red portion of the design (the words "John Sloan" and the numeral "8"). It is usually encountered in a transition pair or multiple.

Space Achievement. August 2, 1971. Se-tenant pair. Engraved, lithographed. BEP.

8c black (engraved); yellow, red, blue & gray (lithographed)

a) Earth & Sun   b) Lunar Vehicle

1435d	pair, blue & red omitted	950.00
	single (b), blue & red omitted	450.00
	plate block of 4, blue & red omitted	—
	Quantity: 40 pairs, 10 singles reported	

▶ Caution. The flag on the lunar lander is often shifted into the lander and not visible. Examine carefully.

Emily Dickinson. August 28, 1971. Engraved, lithographed. BEP.

8c black & light olive green (engraved); dark olive green, red & pale rose (lithographed); (greenish paper)

1436a	black & light olive green omitted	500.00
	as above, plate block of 4	—
	Quantity: 150	

| 1436b | pair, pale rose omitted on one | 5,000.00 |
| | Quantity: 4 | |

Some examples of No. 1436b appear to have light olive green omitted, but traces are visible under magnification.

| 1436c | red omitted | — |
| | Quantity: n/a | |

San Juan. September 12, 1971. Engraved, lithographed. BEP.

8c black, red brown & dark brown (engraved); pale brown & yellow (lithographed)

1437b	dark brown (engraved) omitted	1,500.00
	used on cover	—
	Quantity: 2 reported	

CARE. October 27, 1971. Photogravure. BEP.

8c black, blue, purple & violet
| 1439a | black omitted | 1,100.00 |
| | Quantity: 10 | |

Transition multiples exist.

Normal Block

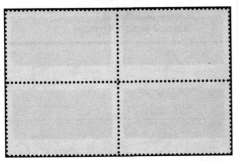

Historic Preservation. October 29, 1971. Se-tenant block of 4. Engraved, lithographed. BEP.

8c black brown (engraved); ocher (lithographed); (buff paper)

a) Decatur House   b) The Charles W. Morgan
c) Cable Car   d) San Xavier Mission

1443b block of 4, black brown omitted   *800.00*
       plate block of 4, black brown omitted   —
       Quantity: 24 blocks of 4 reported

Eleven blocks contain damage or separations. Value is for an undamaged, intact block.

1443c block of 4, ocher omitted   *2,500.00*
       Quantity: 8 blocks of 4

Two blocks of No. 1443c are damaged and one is reportedly broken.

Christmas. November 10, 1971. Photogravure. BEP.

8c black, magenta, blue, ocher, light bister & metallic gold

1444a gold omitted   *350.00*
       as above, plate block   —
       Quantity: 150-200

Transition multiples exist and sell for a premium.

National Parks Centennial. April 5, 1972. Se-tenant block of 4. Engraved, lithographed. BEP.

2c black & dark blue (engraved); black, yellow, red, blue & tan (lithographed)

a) Wrecked Hull   b) Lighthouse
c) Shorebirds   d) Shorebirds & Grass

1451b block of 4, black (litho) omitted   *1,000.00*
       plate block, black omitted   —
       Quantity: 50 blocks of 4 reported,
       including 2 plate blocks

Mt. McKinley. July 28, 1972. Engraved, lithographed. BEP.

15c black, light blue & dark brown (engraved); yellow, magenta, gray, gray green & brown (lithographed)

1454b yellow omitted   *3,000.00*
       Quantity: 1 reported

▶ Caution. Beware of fakes. Expert certificate essential.

Family Planning. March 18, 1972. Engraved, lithographed. BEP.

8c black (engraved); dark brown, yellow,
magenta & olive green (lithographed)

1455a	yellow omitted		*300.00*
	Quantity: 100		

▶ Caution. Expert certificate essential.

1455c	dark brown omitted		*9,500.00*
	Quantity: unique		

No. 1455c results from a foldover and occupies the lower left corner position in a block of 15.

Wildlife Conservation. September 20, 1972. Se-tenant block of 4. Engraved, lithographed. BEP.

8c black (engraved); yellow, red, blue,
green & brown (lithographed)

a) Fur Seal	b) Cardinal
c) Brown Pelican	d) Bighorn Sheep

1467b	block of 4, brown omitted	*2,750.00*
	as above, plate block of 4	—
	single (c or d), brown omitted	—
	Quantity: 8-16 blocks of 4 reported	

1467c	block of 4, green & blue omitted	*2,750.00*
	as above, plate block of 4	—
	Quantity: 8 blocks of 4 reported	

1467d	block of 4, red & brown omitted	*3,250.00*
	plate block of 4, red & brown omitted	—
	Quantity: 16 blocks of 4 reported	

Tom Sawyer. October 13, 1972. Engraved, lithographed. BEP.

8c black & deep red (engraved); yellow, red,
blue, & gray (lithographed)

1470b	black & deep red (engraved) omitted	*800.00*
	as above, plate block of 4 (plate No. also omitted)	—
	Quantity: 150	

1470c yellow & tan (litho) omitted   *1,100.00*
as above, plate block of 4   —
Quantity: 50, including unique plate block

Christmas Angels. November 9, 1972. Photogravure. BEP.

8c black, yellow, magenta, blue, gray & pink
1471a pink omitted   *100.00*
pair, one with pink omitted   —
plate block of 12, pink omitted   —
Quantity: several hundred

1471b black omitted   *2,500.00*
multiple, black omitted on one   *3,000.00*
Quantity: 10 reported

Transition multiples exist and sell for a premium.

Pharmacy. November 10, 1972. Engraved, lithographed. BEP.

8c black (engraved); yellow, blue, purplish red & orange (lithographed)
1473a blue & orange omitted   *600.00*
as above, plate block of 4   —
Quantity: 150 reported

1473b blue omitted   *1,250.00*
Quantity: rare

1473c orange omitted   *1,250.00*
plate block of 4, 2 stamps with
orange omitted   *4,000.00*
Quantity: rare

▶ Caution. Expert certificate necessary for No. 1473c. Transition pairs exist and sell for a premium.

Stamp Collecting. November 17, 1972. Engraved, lithographed. BEP.

8c brown & black (engraved); black & greenish blue (lithographed)
1474a black (litho) omitted   *325.00*
as above, plate block of 4   —
Quantity: 80-100

The lithographed black part of the design consists of a pattern of dots printed on the greenish blue field. They are visible under magnification on the normal stamp.

Boston Tea Party. July 4, 1973. Se-tenant block of 4. Engraved, lithographed. BEP.

8c black (engraved); black, yellow red, light blue & dark blue (lithographed)

a) Tea Cast Overboard   b) Ship
c) Boat & Keel   d) Pier

1483b block of 4, black (engraved) omitted   *950.00*
hz pair (a & c) or (b & d),
black (engraved) omitted   *450.00*
Quantity: 32 blocks of 4 including
one without gum; sets of horizontal
pairs also exist

1483c   block of 4, black (litho) omitted   *900.00*
        as above, Zip block   —
        Quantity: 32 blocks of 4
1483e   block of 4, dark blue omitted   *1,500.00*
        as above, used   *750.00*
        Quantity: rare
        block of 4 on first day cover
          with Artcraft cachet,
          dark blue omitted   —
        Quantity: at least 26

Copernicus. April 23, 1973. Engraved, lithographed. BEP.

8c black (engraved); orange (lithographed)
1488a   orange omitted   *400.00*
        as above, plate block of 4   —
        as above, Zip block of 4   —
        Quantity: 100

▶ Caution. Extremely dangerous fakes, including color changelings, exist. Genuine examples of this error each have an APS certificate. Expert certificate absolutely essential. Examples without certificates should be avoided.

1488b   black omitted   *600.00*
        Quantity: 100

Progress in Electronics. July 10, 1973. Engraved, lithographed. BEP.

8c black (engraved); orange, dark brown, tan, green & lilac (lithographed)
1501a   black omitted   *300.00*
        plate block of 4, black omitted   —
        Quantity: 300-400

1501b   tan & lilac omitted   *600.00*
        as above, plate block 4   —
        Quantity: 50

Progress in Electronics. July 10, 1973. Engraved, lithographed. BEP.

15c black (engraved); yellow, brown, gray & gray green (lithographed)
1502a   black omitted   *850.00*
        Quantity: 50

Rural America. October 5, 1973. Engraved, lithographed. BEP.

8c black, brown red & dark blue (engraved); yellow, green, red brown & brown (lithographed)
1504a   green & red brown (litho) omitted   *600.00*
        Quantity: 100

Rural America. August 16, 1974. Engraved, lithographed. BEP.

10c black & blue (engraved); yellow, red, gray blue & brown (lithographed)
1506a black & blue (engraved) omitted   *450.00*
       Quantity: 100

Crossed Flags. December 8, 1973. Engraved. BEP.

10c red & blue
1509b blue omitted   *150.00*
       pair, one normal & one with
         blue omitted   *200.00*
       single used on cover, blue omitted   —
       Quantity: 100-125 singles or pairs
         with one normal attached; 2-3 used

Often with tagging ghosts.

Zip Code. January 24, 1974. Photogravure. BEP.

10c black, yellow, magenta & blue
1511a yellow omitted   40.00
       as above, plate block of 8   —
       Quantity: 1,000+

▶ Caution. Extremely dangerous fakes, including color changelings, exist. Beware of used examples. Expert certificate essential.

Horse Racing. May 4, 1974. Photogravure. BEP.

10c black, yellow, magenta, blue, red & ultramarine
1528a ultramarine ("Horse Racing") omitted   *650.00*
       as above, Zip block of 4   —
       Quantity: 75-100

1528b red omitted   *1,750.00*
       Quantity: 1-4 reported

▶ Caution. To be considered the error, all traces of red must be absent under 30-power magnification. Many examples containing traces of red exist; therefore, expert certificate is advised.

Mineral Heritage. June 13, 1974. Se-tenant block of 4. Engraved, lithographed. BEP.

10c black, red, purple (engraved); yellow, light blue, gray, brown & green (lithographed)

a) Petrified Wood   b) Tourmaline
c) Amethyst   d) Rhodochrosite

1538a single a, light blue & yellow (litho) omitted   —
       Quantity: 24-28 (including those in blocks)

Light blue (the lithographed background color) was printed on all four stamps. Lithographic yellow was printed only on stamps a and c; therefore, its absence on stamps b and d is not the result of an error. No. 1538a is usually collected in a block of four, which also includes Nos. 1539a, 1540a, and 1541b, and which is listed below as No. 1541b.

▶ Caution. Dangerous fakes of Nos. 1538a, 1539a, 1540a, and 1541c exist. Expert certificate essential.

1539a   single b, light blue (litho) omitted   —
    Quantity: 24-28 (including those in blocks)

1539b   single b, black & purple (engraved) omitted   —
    Quantity: 4 (including those in blocks)

1540a   single c, light blue & yellow (litho) omitted   —
    Quantity: 24-28 (including those in blocks)

1541b   block of 4, light blue (litho) omitted on
    a-d, yellow (litho) omitted on a & c   *900.00*
    Quantity: 24-28

1541c   single d, light blue (litho) omitted   —
    Quantity: 24-28 (including those in blocks)

1541d   single d, black & red (engraved) omitted   —
    Quantity: 4 (including those in blocks)

1541e   block of 4, containing Nos.
    1539b & 1541d   *7,000.00*
    Quantity: 4

Nos. 1539b and 1541d result from a single pane in which one se-tenant vertical row, occurring on the right side of the pane and containing the two designs, lack the engraved colors, black (inscription) and red or purple (mineral color) respectively. Nos. 1539b and 1541d are usually collected together in transition blocks of 6 or larger.

Kentucky Settlement. June 15, 1974. Engraved, lithographed. BEP.

    10c black & dark green (engraved); black, light red, blue, light green & tan (lithographed)
1542a   black (litho) omitted   *400.00*
    as above, plate block of 4   —
    used single, black omitted   —
    Quantity: 100-150 including 2 plate blocks

Transition multiples exist and sell for a premium.

1542b   black & dark green (engraved),
    black, green & blue (litho) omitted   *1,750.00*
    Quantity: 29 reported including
    those in strips of 3 or 10

Exists in strips of 3 containing one normal, one with colors partially omitted and one with listed colors completely omitted. Also exists in strips of 10 (with various stages of colors omitted), which tend to sell for a substantial premium.

1542c   dark green (engraved) omitted   *3,000.00*
    Quantity: very rare

1542d   dark green (engraved) &
    black (litho) omitted   —
    Quantity: very rare

1542f   blue (litho) omitted   —
    Quantity: 2 reported

Energy Conservation. September 23, 1974. Engraved, lithographed. BEP.

    10c black (engraved); yellow, blue, purple, orange (lithographed).
1547a   blue & orange omitted   *400.00*
    Quantity: approx 100

1547b   orange & green omitted   *275.00*
    plate block of 4   *1,400.00*
    Quantity: 150-200

One pane of 50 has disturbed gum.

1547c   green omitted   *400.00*
         Quantity: approx 100

Christmas. October 23, 1974. Photogravure. BEP.

**10c black, yellow, magenta, blue, &
very light buff**
1551a   buff omitted   12.50
         pane of 50, buff omitted   *525.00*
         Quantity: 75-100 panes of 50

▶ Caution. The buff color is a very light, transparent shade. Error
stamps are extremely difficult to distinguish from normal stamps.
Expert certificate strongly advised. Many prefer to collect this
error in intact pane form because the omission of buff is more
readily evident due to the absence of the buff plate number in
the selvage.

D. W. Griffith. May 27, 1975. Engraved, lithographed. BEP.

**10c brown (engraved); yellow, magenta,
& cyan (lithographed)**
1555a   brown omitted   *450.00*
         Quantity: 100-150

▶ Caution. Color variations and color shifts on this stamp are
common and can be mistaken for the color-omitted error. Expert
certificate advised.

**Pioneer - Jupiter. February 28, 1975. Engraved,
lithographed. BEP.**

**10c yellow & dark blue (engraved); dark
yellow, red & blue (lithographed)**
1556a   red & dark yellow omitted   *750.00*
         Zip block of 4   —
         Quantity: 50-100 reported

1556b   dark blue omitted   450.00
         Quantity: 200 reported

1556d   dark yellow omitted   —
         Quantity: 2 reported

One of the two reported examples of No. 1556d contains traces of
red visible under magnification. To the naked eye, it is similar in
appearance to No. 1556a.

Mariner 10. April 4, 1975. Engraved, lithographed. BEP.

**10c black (engraved); red, ultramarine
& bister (lithographed)**
1557a   red omitted   *275.00*
         plate block of 4, red omitted   —
         used, red omitted   —
         Quantity: 300-400

▶ Caution. The red star may be shifted downward and hidden in
the spacecraft giving the appearance of being the error stamp.
Examine carefully. Expert certificate essential for used examples.

1557b ultramarine & bister omitted   *850.00*
       Quantity: 100

Apollo-Soyuz. July 15, 1975. Se-tenant pair. Photogravure. BEP.

10c black, yellow, red, blue, light
gray & dark violet
1570d pair, yellow omitted   *900.00*
       Quantity: 12 pairs

200 Years of Postal Service. September 3, 1975. Se-tenant
block of 4. Photogravure. BEP.

10c black, yellow, red (2 plates), blue
& ultramarine
   a) Stagecoach   b) Locomotive
   c) Biplane   d) Satellite

1575b block of 4, red (10c denomination)
       omitted   —
       as above, pair   —
       any single   —
       single "c" used on piece   —
       Zip block of 4   —
       Quantity: 6-8 blocks of 4,
          2 pairs of each

Two plates were used for red: one for the denomination, the other
for design elements. Only the red denomination is omitted. Red
printed from the second plate appears elsewhere on the stamps.
The arrangement for the se-tenant stamps in error blocks may not
necessarily appear in Scott order.

Banking & Commerce. October 6, 1975. Se-tenant pair.
Engraved, lithographed. BEP.

10c dark brown, green, greenish gray
(engraved); yellow, blue & brown (lithographed)

   a) Banking   b) Commerce

1578b pair, brown & blue omitted   *1,400.00*
       single a or b, blue & brown omitted   *425.00*
       Quantity: 16-32 pairs; 8-16 singles

1578c pair, brown, blue & yellow omitted   *1,750.00*
       Quantity: 16 pairs, 8 singles (a)

AMERICANA SERIES OF 1975/81

Eagle & Shield. December 1, 1975. Photogravure. BEP.

13c black, yellow, red, blue, brown & olive green
1596b yellow omitted   *75.00*
       pair, one with yellow omitted   *110.00*
       Quantity: 500

▶ Caution. Dangerous fakes exist. Beware of used stamps
offered as No. 1596b. Expert certificate strongly advised.

Flag. June 30, 1978. Engraved. BEP.

15c gray, dark blue & red

1597b	gray omitted	*300.00*
	pair, one with gray omitted	—
	Quantity: 100-200	

▶ Caution. Stamps with gray partially omitted exist.

Lamp. September 11, 1979. Engraved, lithographed. BEP.

50c black (engraved); tan & orange (lithographed)

1608a	black omitted	*375.00*
	transition pair or strip	*450.00*
	Quantity: 120-150 reported	

Transition multiples exist with some stamps showing partial omission of black. Transition multiples sell for a premium.

Candle Holder. July 2, 1979. Engraved, lithographed. BEP.

$1 brown (engraved); tan, orange & yellow (lithographed)

1610a	brown omitted	*175.00*
	as above, plate block of 4	—
	transition strip, one with dark brown omitted	*400.00*
	Quantity: 1,000+	

Tagging ghosts exist.

1610b	tan, orange & yellow omitted	*175.00*
	Quantity: 300-400	

Flag. June 30, 1978. Coil. Engraved. BEP.

15c gray, dark blue & red

1618Cf	gray omitted	30.00
	pair, one with gray omitted	55.00
	Quantity: 1,000+	

Most show bleed of blue into area of gray.

BICENTENNIAL SOUVENIR SHEETS

A great variety of color-omitted and imperforate varieties exist, many with multiple errors. Those that are imperforate in addition to having colors omitted are listed in the imperforates section. Those normally perforated but lacking one or more colors are listed below.

The Surrender of Lord Cornwallis at Yorktown
From a Painting by John Trumbull

Surrender at Yorktown. May 29, 1976. Souvenir sheet of 5. Lithographed. BEP.

13c multicolored

1686g	yellow (USA 13c) omitted on "a" & "e"	*500.00*
	as above, used, 5/29/76 PHILADELPHIA, PA first day cancellation	*300.00*
	Quantity: rare	
1686i	brown (USA 13c) omitted on "b," orange (USA 13c) omitted on "c" & "d"	*500.00*
	Quantity: very rare	

1686k   orange (USA 13c) omitted on "c" & "d"   750.00
        Quantity: very rare

1686l   yellow (USA 13c) omitted on "e"   475.00
        Quantity: very rare

1686q   yellow (USA 13c) omitted on "a"   750.00
        Quantity: very rare

For imperforate varieties of Bicentennial souvenir sheets with color(s) omitted refer to the Imperforates section of the catalogue.

The Declaration of Independence, 4 July 1776 at Philadelphia
From a Painting by John Trumbull

The Declaration of Independence. May 29, 1976. Souvenir sheet of 5. Lithographed.

18c multicolored

1687f   all process colors omitted, sheet
        blank except for USA 18c,
        tagging & perfs   2,500.00
        Quantity: very rare

The term "process colors" refers to those colors that were reduced to a pattern of dots and printed atop one another to achieve the effect of full color. The denominations and "USA" were added by a separate operation and printed in "solid color" rather than in a pattern of dots. The difference in printing can be seen on a normal sheet by examination under 10-power magnification.

1687g   brown (USA 18c) omitted on "a" & "c"   550.00
        Quantity: rare

1687h   orange (USA 18c) omitted on "b" &
        "e," yellow (USA 18c) omitted on "d"   350.00
        Quantity: rare

1687i   yellow (USA 18c) omitted on "d"   425.00
        as above, used   475.00
        Quantity: rare

1687j   black (screened dots for contrast in
        mural) omitted   1,500.00
        Quantity: very rare

1687m   orange (USA 18c) omitted on "b" & "e"   500.00
        Quantity: rare

1687n   orange (USA 18c) omitted on "b,"
        yellow (USA 18c) omitted on "d"   1,000.00
        Quantity: very rare

1687q   brown (USA 18c) omitted on "c"   —
        Quantity: very rare

1687r   yellow omitted (background color)   5,000.00
        Quantity: very rare, possibly unique

1687u   brown (USA 18c) omitted on "a"   5,000.00
        Quantity: very rare, possibly unique

Washington Crossing the Delaware
From a Painting by Emanuel Leutze / Eastman Johnson

Washington Crossing the Delaware. May 29, 1976. Souvenir sheet of 5. Lithographed. BEP.

24c multicolored

1688g   white (USA 24c) omitted on "d" & "e"   400.00
        as above, used   400.00
        Quantity: very rare

1688h   all process colors omitted, sheet
        blank except for USA 24c, tagging
        & perfs   2,500.00
        Quantity: reportedly unique

Refer to the note following No. 1687f.

1688i   blue (USA 24c) omitted on "a,"
        light blue (USA 24c)
        omitted on "b" & "c"   400.00
        as above, used   400.00
        Quantity: very rare

1688i   blue (USA 24c) omitted on "a,"
        light blue (USA 24c)
        omitted on "b" & "c"   400.00
        as above, with 5/29/76
        PHILADELPHIA, PA
        first day cancellation   400.00
        Quantity: very rare

1688n   perforations inverted and reversed   7,500.00
        Quantity: very rare

1688r   blue (USA 24c) omitted on "a"   400.00
        Quantity: very rare

On the discovery example, light blue on "b" and "c" is partially omitted.

Washington Reviewing His Ragged Army at Valley Forge
From a Painting by William T. Trego

Washington at Valley Forge. May 29, 1976. Souvenir sheet of 5. Lithographed. BEP.

31c multicolored

1689g	gray (USA 31c) omitted on "a" & "c" Quantity: rare	375.00
1689h	brown (USA 31c) omitted on "b" & "d," white omitted on "e" Quantity: rare	450.00
1689i	white (USA 31c) omitted on "e" Quantity: rare	375.00
1689j	black (screened process dots in mural) omitted Quantity: very rare	1,450.00

In process color printing, a printed screen of black dots is often used to intensify contrast and add crispness to the finished image. Refer to the note following No. 1687f.

1689l	brown (USA 31c) omitted on "b" & "d" Quantity: rare	300.00
1689m	gray (USA 31c) omitted on "a" & "c," white (USA 31c) omitted on "e" Quantity: very rare	750.00
1689r	brown (USA 31c) omitted on "d," white (USA 31c) omitted on "e" Quantity: very rare	600.00
1689t	brown (USA 31c) omitted on "d" Quantity: very rare	500.00
1689y	gray (USA 31c) omitted on "a" Quantity: very rare	—

NOTE: Bicentennial souvenir sheets containing both imperforate and color-omitted errors are listed in the Imperforates section.

Benjamin Franklin. June 1, 1976. Engraved, lithographed. BEP.

13c dark blue (engraved); yellow, light blue & brown (lithographed)

1690a	light blue omitted as above, plate block of 4 Quantity: 800-1000 reported	*150.00* —

Christmas. October 27, 1976. Photogravure. BEP.

13c black, yellow, red (magenta) & cyan

1703d	red omitted Quantity: rare	*500.00*

Transition multiples exist.

1703e	yellow omitted Quantity: n/a	—

▶ Caution. Nos. 1703d and 1703e exist with color partially omitted. Expert certificate recommended.

Articles of Confederation. September 30, 1977. Engraved. BEP.

13c red & brown (cream paper)

1726b	red omitted Quantity: n/a	*500.00*
1726c	red and brown omitted	*300.00*

No. 1726b is the middle stamp in the illustrated strip of 3. No. 1726c is the third stamp in the illustrated strip and must be collected as a transition multiple, certainly with No. 1726b and preferably also with No. 1726.

Carl Sandburg. January 6, 1978. Engraved. BEP.

13c black & brown

1731a	brown omitted	*1,750.00*
	Quantity: 10	

Usually in transition pair or strip.

CAPEX. June 10, 1978. Souvenir sheet of 8. Engraved, lithographed. BEP.

13c black & dark green (engraved); black, yellow, red, blue, brown & light green (lithographed)

a) Cardinal   b) Mallard
c) Canada Goose   d) Blue Jay
e) Moose   f) Chipmunk
g) Red Fox   h) Raccoon

1757i	souvenir sheet of 8, all lithographed colors omitted	*6,000.00*
	as above, with plate No.	—
	Quantity: 6 souvenir sheets reported	
1757l	single (d or h), black (engraved) omitted	—
	Quantity: very rare	

1757p	pane of 6 souvenir sheets, yellow, red & brown (litho) omitted	—
	Quantity: *unique*	

Owls. August 26, 1978. Lithographed and Engraved. BEP.

15c brown, blue & black (engraved); yellow, orange, light blue, dark blue & gray (lithographed)

a) Great Gray Owl
b) Saw-whet Owl
c) Barred Owl
d) Great Horned Owl

1763c	block of 4, yellow and orange (litho) omitted	—
	Quantity: 2 panes reported	

One one pane of 1763c, the engraved black is shifted to the left.

Christmas. October 18, 1979. Photogravure. BEP.

15c black, yellow, magenta, green, tan & purple
1800a   green & yellow omitted,
     black misaligned   *400.00*
     Quantity: 150

1800b   green, yellow & tan omitted,
     black misaligned   *400.00*
     Quantity: 250

Misalignment of black color occurs on all examples of Nos. 1800a and 1800b.

1800c   vertical pair containing one each of
     Nos. 1800a and 1800b   *850.00*
     Quantity: 10 pairs

Emily Bissell. May 31, 1980. Engraved. BEP.

15c black & red
1823c   red omitted   —
     Quantity: n/a

No. 1823c results from a foldover.

1823d   red omitted   —
     Quantity: n/a

On No. 1823d, traces of black are present.

General Bernardo Galvez. July 23, 1980. Engraved, lithographed. BEP.

15c dark brown, claret & light gray-blue (engraved); light yellow, red, blue & brown (lithographed)
1826a   dark brown, claret & light gray-
     blue (engraved) omitted   *550.00*
     Quantity: 50

1826b   light yellow, red, blue & brown
     (litho) omitted   *550.00*
     plate block of 4   —
     Quantity: 50

Christmas. October 31, 1980. Photogravure. BEP.

15c black, yellow, red, green & buff
1843b   buff omitted   22.50
     plate block of 20, buff omitted   375.00
     Quantity: several hundred

This error is very subtle and difficult to see. It is much more evident on plate blocks. Certificate recommended.

Flag over Supreme Court. December 17, 1981. Engraved. BEP.

20c black, dark blue & red

1894c   dark blue omitted   *60.00*
        Quantity: few hundred

▶ Caution. Stamps exist with color partially omitted. Transition multiples exist and sell for a premium.

1894d   black omitted   *225.00*
        Quantity: n/a

Transition multiples exist and sell for a premium.

Flag over Supreme Court. Coil. December 17, 1981. Engraved. BEP.

20c black, dark blue & red

1895f   black omitted   *45.00*
        pair, 1 normal, 1 black omitted   *80.00*
        Quantity: 1,000+

1895g   dark blue omitted   *1,000.00*
        Quantity: very rare

Edna St. Vincent Millay. July 10, 1981. Engraved, lithographed. BEP.

18c black (engraved); black, yellow, magenta, blue, gray & buff (lithographed)

1926a   black (engraved) omitted   *200.00*
        as above, plate block of 4   —
        as above, Zip block of 4   —
        used, black omitted   —
        Quantity: 500+

Frederic Remington. October 9, 1981. Engraved, lithographed. BEP

18c brown (engraved); light brown & gray green (lithographed)

1934b   brown (engraved) omitted   *190.00*
        as above, plate block of 4   —
        Quantity: 300-400

Yorktown - Virginia Capes. October 16, 1981. Se-tenant pair. Engraved, lithographed. BEP.

18c black (engraved); red, light blue, dark blue, brown & tan (lithographed)

a) Yorktown   b) Virginia Capes

1938b   pair, black (engraved) omitted   *275.00*
        as above, plate block of 4   —
        as above, Zip block of 4   —
        single a or b, black (engraved) omitted   *90.00*
        Quantity: 80 pairs, 10 of each
          single reported

1938d   pair, black (litho) omitted   —
           Quantity: 2 pairs

The two pairs occur in a plate block of 4.

Cactus. December 11, 1981. Se-tenant block of 4. Engraved, lithographed. BEP.

          20c dark green & dark blue (engraved); yellow, red, deep brown, tan, light green & cyan (lithographed)

          a) Barrel Cactus   b) Agave
          c) Beavertail Cactus d) Saguaro

1945b   block of 4, deep brown
           (litho) omitted   *3,000.00*
           Zip block of 4   —
           Quantity: 20 blocks of 4

1945d   block of 4, dark green & dark blue
           (engraved) omitted   —
           Quantity: 5 blocks

1945e   block of 4, dark green (engraved)
           omitted on "a"   —
           Quantity: 3 blocks

Love. February 1, 1982. Photogravure. BEP.

          20c yellow, magenta, blue, purple & olive green

1951c   blue omitted   *200.00*
           Quantity: 50-100 well centered
                    150-200 poorly centered

Value is for a well-centered example. Examples from some panes are centered high with the design running slightly off at the top; for those deduct 33%.

1951d   yellow omitted   *600.00*
           Quantity: 35 reported

▶ Caution. Expert certificate essential.

1951e   purple omitted   —
           Quantity: 2 reported

The discovery examples of No. 1951e are the right two stamps in a lower right plate block of 4 on which the purple plate number digit is also omitted.

▶ Caution. Expert certificate essential.

State Birds & Flowers. April 14, 1982. Se-tenant pane of 50. Photogravure. BEP.

20c black, yellow, magenta & cyan

1981b	black omitted (New Hampshire)	4,000.00
1991b	black omitted (Rhode Island)	4,000.00
2001b	black omitted (Wisconsin)	4,000.00
	Quantity: each of the above is unique	

Nos. 1981b and 1991b are contained in transition pairs. No. 2001b is a single stamp.

The Barrymores. June 8, 1982. Photogravure. BEP.

20c black, blue, yellow, magenta & cyan

2012a	black omitted	—
	Quantity: unique	

International Peace Garden. June 30, 1982. Engraved, lithographed. BEP.

20c black (engraved); yellow, red, green & gray (lithographed)

2014a	black (engraved) omitted	200.00
	Quantity: 250-400 reported	

Science & Industry. January 19, 1983. Engraved, lithographed. BEP.

20c black (engraved); yellow, magenta & blue (lithographed)

2031a	black (engraved) omitted	750.00
	plate block of 6 containing 2	
	error stamps & 4 normal stamps	—
	Quantity: 40	

Transition multiples exist and sell for a premium.

Medal of Honor. June 7, 1983. Engraved, lithographed. BEP.

20c red (engraved); black, ocher, blue & green (lithographed)

2045a	red omitted	150.00
	plate block of 4, red omitted	—
	Quantity: 320-400	

Inventors. September 21, 1983. Se-tenant block of 4. Engraved, lithographed. BEP.

20c black (engraved); salmon (lithographed)

a) Charles Steinmetz	b) Edwin Armstrong
c) Nikola Tesla	d) Philo T. Farnsworth

2058b	block of 4, black (engraved) omitted	275.00
	as above, plate block of 4	—
	as above, Zip block of 4	—
	any single, black (engraved) omitted	85.00
	Quantity: 200+ blocks of 4 reported	

Streetcars. October 8, 1983. Se-tenant block of 4.
Engraved, lithographed. BEP.

20c black (engraved); black, yellow,
magenta, & blue (lithographed)

a) First Streetcar   b) Early Electric Streetcar
c) Bobtail Streetcar   d) St. Charles Streetcar

2062b block of 4, black (engraved) omitted   *250.00*
as above, plate block of 4   —
any single (a-d), black (engraved) omitted *60.00*
Quantity: 120+ blocks of 4 reported

Jim Thorpe. May 24, 1984. Engraved. BEP.

20c dark brown
2089a All color omitted   —
Quantity: n/a

On No. 2089a, an albino impression of the design is present.

Sea Shells. April 4, 1985. Se-tenant booklet pane of 10.
Engraved, lithographed. BEP.

22c black, reddish brown & violet

a) Frilled Dogwinkle
b) Reticulated Helmet
c) New England Neptune
d) Calico Scallop
e) Lightning Whelk

2121b booklet pane, violet omitted   *400.00*
single "d," violet omitted   *190.00*
Quantity: 75-100+

Violet was used only on stamp "d," the Calico Scallop; therefore, it is the only stamp in the booklet pane on which the color-omitted error occurs. Each booklet pane contains 2 examples of stamp "d."

Tractor. February 6, 1987. Coil. Engraved. BEP.

7.1c lake; black precancel

2127c black precancel omitted   —
Quantity: possibly unique

AMERIPEX. May 25, 1985. Engraved, lithographed. BEP.

22c black, red & blue (engraved); gray & beige (lithographed)

2145a	red, black & blue (engraved) omitted	110.00
	plate block of 4	—
	Quantity: 700-800	

| 2145b | red & black (engraved) omitted | 1,250.00 |
| | Quantity: 4-5 reported | |

| 2145c | red (engraved) omitted | 1,750.00 |
| | Quantity: 2-3 reported | |

No. 2145b shows traces of blue. No 2145c shows traces of blue and black.

Stamp Collecting. January 23, 1986. Booklet pane of 4. Engraved, lithographed. BEP.

22c black, bright green, purple, & dark blue (engraved); yellow, red, blue & buff (lithographed)

a) American Philatelic Association
b) Youngster with Album
c) Magnifying Glass
d) Ameripex 86

2201b	booklet pane of 4, black omitted	50.00
	unexploded booklet of 2 panes,	
	black omitted	100.00
	booklet pane on first day cover	150.00
	Quantity: several thousand	

Engraved black was used only on stamps a & d; therefore, absence of black on stamps b & c is not the result of an error.

First day covers exist containing any of the following postmarks: "State College, PA - First Day of Issue" slogan cancel; "Dayton, OH, M.O. Box Section" circular date stamp; or "Dayton, OH, MOWS" circular date stamp. A variety of cachets exist on FDCs containing either error singles, error panes, or error panes broken into pairs. Refer to note following No. 2265a in the Imperforates section regarding first day covers.

2201c	booklet pane of 4, blue	
	(litho) omitted	1,500.00
	Quantity: 4 booklets reported	

| 2201d | booklet pane of 4, buff (litho) omitted | — |
| | Quantity: 3-5 reported | |

Texas. March 2, 1986. Photogravure. ABN.

22c black, dark red & dark blue

| 2204b | dark red omitted | 1,750.00 |
| | Quantity: 20 reported | |

2204c	dark blue omitted	5,000.00
	Quantity: 2 stamps, which appear as the right	
	stamps in two different transition strips	

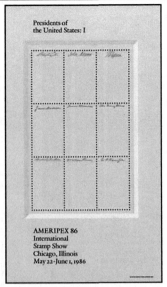

Presidents I. May 22, 1986. Souvenir sheet of 9. Engraved, lithographed. BEP.

22c blue (engraved); black, red & beige (lithographed)

2216j   sheet of 9, blue omitted   *1,800.00*
       Quantity: 5-6 reported

2216k   sheet of 9, black marginal
          inscription omitted   *1,000.00*
          Quantity: 6-10 reported

2216m   sheet of 9, black marginal inscription
          omitted, double impression of red   —
          Quantity: very rare

2216n   sheet of 9, blue omitted on all
          except stamps 4 & 7   —
          Quantity: n/a

Presidents II. May 22, 1986. Souvenir sheet of 9. Engraved, lithographed. BEP.

22c dark green (engraved); black, red & beige (lithographed)

2217j   sheet of 9, black marginal
          inscription omitted   *1,500.00*
          Quantity: very rare

Presidents III. May 22, 1986. Souvenir sheet of 9.
Engraved, lithographed. BEP

      **22c brown (engraved); black,
      red & beige (lithographed)**

2218j   sheet of 9, brown omitted   —
         Quantity: very rare

2218k   sheet of 9, black marginal
         inscription omitted   *1,500.00*
         Quantity: rare

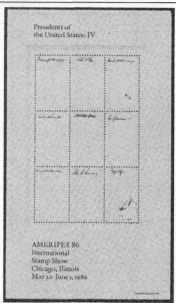

Presidents IV. May 22, 1986. Souvenir sheet of 9.
Engraved, lithographed. BEP.

      **22c blackish blue (engraved); black,
      red & beige (lithographed)**

2219j   sheet of 9, blackish blue omitted
         from left 6 stamps   *2,250.00*
         Quantity: unique

Presidents of
the United States: IV

AMERIPEX 86
International
Stamp Show
Chicago, Illinois
May 22-June 1, 1986

2219l   sheet of 9, blackish blue omitted
         from all stamps   —
         Quantity: unique

Arctic Explorers. May 28, 1986. Se-tenant block of 4. Photogravure. ABN.

22c black, gray black, yellow, red, blue & gray

a) Kane	b) Greely
c) Stefansson	d) Peary, Henson

2223b	block of 4, black omitted	*4,500.00*
	plate block of 4, black omitted	—
	Quantity: 4 blocks	

2223c	block of 4, black omitted on	*1,000.00*
	a & b; c & d normal	
	Quantity: 4 blocks & 4 pairs	—

2223d	block of 4, black omitted on	*1,000.00*
	c & d; a & b normal	
	Quantity: 4 blocks & 4 pairs	

Navajo Art. September 4, 1986. Se-tenant block of 4. Engraved, lithographed. BEP.

22c black (engraved); black, yellow, magenta & blue (lithographed)

a) Navajo Blanket	b) Navajo Blanket
c) Navajo Blanket	d) Navajo Blanket

2238c	block of 4, black (engraved) omitted	*275.00*
	any single (a-d), black omitted	65.00
	Quantity: 150-200 blocks of 4	

Pan American Games. January 29, 1987. Photogravure. BEP.

22c black, yellow, red, blue & silver

2247a	silver omitted	*550.00*
	Quantity: 30 reported	

All known examples are poorly centered. Transition multiples exist and sell for a premium.

Enrico Caruso. February 27, 1987. Photogravure. ABN.

22c black, yellow, magenta & gray

2250a	black omitted	*3,500.00*
	Quantity: 10	

Transition multiples exist and sell for a premium.

Girl Scouts. March 12, 1987. Engraved, lithographed. BEP.

22c red & black (engraved); black, yellow, magenta, cyan & green (lithographed)

2251a   black, yellow, magenta, cyan & green (litho) omitted   *1,600.00*
     plate block   —
     Quantity: 46, including unique plate block

Many contain stray flecks of lithographed color in places where they would not normally occur, such flecks believed to have been deposited by the tagging roller. Price is for stamp with such flecks.

2251b   red & black (engraved) omitted   *1,500.00*
     Quantity: 50

The error is very subtle. The omission of color occurs in only a few merit badges. It can be easily overlooked. Expert certificate recommended.

Honeybee. September 2, 1988. Coil. Engraved, lithographed. BEP.

25c black (engraved); black, yellow, magenta, blue, & beige (lithographed)

2281b   single, black (engraved) omitted   45.00
     as above, used   —
     as above, used on cover   *100.00*
     Quantity: several hundred unused;
       20-50 used on cover

Often collected in pairs. Cover listing is for contemporaneous use on commercial cover. Covers are known postmarked Pensacola, Florida, during September 1989 and Midland, Texas, during January and April 1990.

▶ Blocks and vertical pairs with engraved black omitted were purloined by employees at a paper recycling firm. They are printer's waste and are untagged. It is estimated that 150 may have been used on mail, but no examples are known in collector's hands at this time.

2281c   single, black (litho) omitted   *500.00*
     strip of 5, plate No. 2   —
     Quantity: 100+ reported

▶ Caution. Many examples exist with a few black litho dots, which, although invisible to the naked eye, are visible under magnification. In order to qualify as a color-omitted error, a stamp must contain no trace of lithographic black. Examples with traces of lithographed black sell for a small fraction of the price of true 100% black omitted examples.

2281e   single, yellow (litho) omitted   *700.00*
     line strip of 6   —
     Quantity: 50-60 reported

▶ Caution. Certificate necessary. Examples often exist with a few yellow litho dots, which, although difficult to see with the naked eye, are visible under 30-power magnification. In order to be considered a yellow omitted error, a stamp must contain no trace of lithographic yellow. Often found with tagging ghosts.

Wildlife. June 13, 1987. Se-tenant pane of 50. Photogravure. BEP.

22c black (2 plates), yellow, magenta & cyan

2286b-2335b
     any single, magenta omitted   *2,000.00*
     Quantity: unique pane of 50, see note

The discovery pane (No. 2286b-2335b) has been broken up and sold as individual stamps. Expert certificate recommended.

New Jersey. August 26, 1987. Photogravure. BEP.

22c black, yellow, red, cyan & tan
2338a   black omitted   *2,750.00*
      transition pair, black omitted   —
      Quantity: 4 reported

Transition multiples exist.

Friendship With Morocco. July 17, 1987. Engraved, lithographed. BEP.

22c black (engraved); dark rose (litho)
2349a   black omitted   *180.00*
      plate block of 4, black omitted   —
      Quantity: 175-200 reported

Lacemaking. August 14, 1987. Se-tenant block of 4. Engraved, lithographed. BEP.

22c white (engraved); ultramarine (lithographed)
2354b   block of 4, white omitted   *350.00*
      single stamp, white omitted   *90.00*
      Quantity: 80 blocks of 4;
       80 singles reported

When separated from se-tenant blocks, single stamps of this error are indistinguishable from one another.

Constitution Bicentennial. August 28, 1987. Booklet pane of 5. Photogravure. BEP.

22c black, yellow, red & grayish green

a) The Bicentennial
b) We The People
c) Establish Justice
d) And Secure
e) Do Ordain

2355a-2359b
      any single, grayish green omitted   *400.00*
      Quantity: 1-3 singles of each reported

▶ Caution. Expert certificate necessary. The greenish gray is the background color on the stamps. No intact booklet pane is known at this time. Pairs and strips of 3 exist.

CPA. September 21, 1987. Engraved, lithographed. BEP.

22c black (engraved); black, red, green & tan (lithographed)
2361a   black (engraved) omitted   *425.00*
      Quantity: 300-400 reported

Locomotives. October 1, 1987. Se-tenant booklet pane of 5. Engraved, lithographed. BEP.

    22c black (engraved); black, yellow, red, blue & dark green (lithographed)

    a) Stourbridge Lion
    b) Best Friend of Charleston
    c) John Bull
    d) Brother Jonathan
    e) Gowan & Marx

2362a   used single (a), red (litho) omitted   —
      Quantity: n/a

2363a   used single (b), red (litho) omitted   —
      Quantity: n/a

2364a   used single (c), red (litho) omitted   —
      Quantity: n/a

2365a   stamp d, red omitted   1,000.00
      used single (d), red omitted   250.00
      Quantity: 1 unused & 1 used reported

2366b   black (engr.) omitted on e   —
      Quantity: very rare, possibly unique

2366c   used single (e), blue omitted   —
      Quantity: n/a

Antarctic Explorers. September 14, 1988. Se-tenant block of 4. Photogravure. ABN.

    25c black, gray black, yellow, magenta, cyan, brown & Prussian green

    a) Nathaniel Palmer   b) Lt. Charles Wilkes
    c) Richard E. Byrd   d) Lincoln Ellsworth

2389b   black omitted   750.00
      single stamp, black omitted   —
      plate block of 4, black omitted   —
      Quantity: 2 panes (20 blocks and
         20 singles)

Madonna & Child. October 20, 1988. Engraved, lithographed. BEP.

    25c black & red (engraved); yellow, red, blue, pale rose & gold (lithographed)

2399a   gold omitted   25.00
      plate block of 4, gold omitted   —
      Quantity: few thousand

Astronauts. July 20, 1989. Engraved, lithographed. BEP.

$2.40 black (engraved); black, yellow, red, blue & dark blue (lithographed)

2419a	black (engraved) omitted	1,350.00
	plate block of 4	—
	Quantity: 60-80	

▶ Caution. No black engraved cross hatching should be visible on the white area of the space suits.

2419c	black (litho) omitted	1,500.00
	plate block of 4	—
	Quantity: 20-30 reported, including 2 plate blocks	

No. 2419 also exists with a gray background instead of the normal dark blue. Some of these may have been caused by a chemical wiping of the blue plate at the Bureau of Engraving and Printing. Be aware, however, that the same or extremely similar effect can be produced by exposing normal stamps to sunlight or fluorescent light for varying lengths of time.

Bill of Rights. September 25, 1989. Photogravure. BEP.

25c black (engraved); black, red & blue (lithographed)

2421a	black (engraved) omitted	225.00
	Quantity: 200	

Dinosaurs. October 1, 1989. Se-tenant block of 4. Engraved, lithographed. BEP.

25c black (engraved); black, yellow, magenta & cyan (lithographed)

a) Tyrannosaurus   b) Pteranodon
c) Stegosaurus   d) Brontosaurus

2425c	block of 4, black (engraved) omitted	
	well-centered block of 4	325.00
	poorly centered block of 4	225.00
	any single, a-d	50.00
	any single, used	—
	Quantity: 75-100 blocks of 4 reported	

Some examples of this error were discovered in postal vending machine packets in which the blocks had been folded along one row of perforations and are, therefore, prone to separation. Value is for sound block with perforations that have not been folded. Folded blocks sell for less. Most blocks are poorly centered.

Christmas Madonna. October 19, 1989. Engraved, lithographed. BEP.

25c black & red (engraved); pink, yellow, magenta & pale gray blue (lithographed)

2427b	magenta (litho) omitted	400.00
	Quantity: 50	

Christmas. October 19, 1989. Booklet pane of 10. Photogravure. ABN.

25c black, yellow, magenta, red & cyan

2429d	booklet pane of 10, red omitted	3,250.00
	Quantity: 10 stamps	

20th UPU Congress. November 19, 1989. Se-tenant block of 4. Perf 11. Engraved, lithographed. BEP.

25c dark blue (engraved); black, yellow, magenta & cyan (lithographed)

a) Stagecoach b) Riverboat
c) Biplane   d) Delivery Truck

2437b	block of 4, dark blue (engraved) omitted	
	well-centered block of 4	*300.00*
	poorly centered block of 4	*200.00*
	any single (a-d), dark blue omitted	*55.00*
	plate block of 4, dark blue omitted	*275.00*
	Quantity: 75-100 blocks reported	

Most examples of No. 2437b are poorly centered.

A review of historical methods of delivering the mail in the United States is the theme of these four stamps issued in commemoration of the convening of the 20th Universal Postal Congress in Washington, D.C. from November 13 through December 14, 1989. The United States, as host nation to the Congress for the first time in ninety-two years, welcomed more than 1,000 delegates from most of the member nations of the Universal Postal Union to the major international event.
©USPS 1989

20th UPU Congress. November 27, 1989. Souvenir sheet of 4. Imperforate. Engraved, lithographed. BEP.

25c dark blue & gray (engraved); black, yellow, magenta & cyan (lithographed)

a) Stagecoach b) Riverboat
c) Biplane   d) Delivery Truck

2438e	souvenir sheet, dark blue & gray (engraved) omitted	*4,000.00*
	Quantity: 2 reported	

Love. January 18, 1990. Booklet pane of 10. Photogravure. BEP.

25c black, ultramarine, bright pink & dark green

2441b	single, bright pink omitted	*80.00*
	Quantity: included below	
2441c	booklet pane, bright pink omitted	*950.00*
	Quantity: 20 panes	

Umbrella. February 3, 1990. Booklet pane of 10. Photogravure. BEP.

15c yellow, magenta, cyan, blue, green & buff

2443b	single, blue omitted	*100.00*
	Quantity: included below	

2443c	booklet pane, blue omitted	*900.00*
	Quantity: 75 panes reported	

Wyoming. February 23, 1990. Engraved, lithographed. BEP.

25c black (engraved); black, yellow, magenta & cyan (lithographed)

2444a	black (engraved) omitted	900.00
	as above, affixed to 4x5 card	375.00
	used, black (engraved) omitted	—
	Quantity: 80 mint examples, 10 of which are affixed to 4x5 cards; 1 used example	

Canoe. May 21, 1991. Coil. Engraved. BEP.

5c brown & gray

2453b	gray (service inscription) omitted	—
	Quantity: 1 reported	

The only known example is unused on piece.

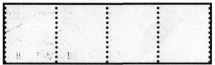

Tractor Trailer. May 25, 1991. Coil. Engraved. BEP.

10c green (gray service inscription)

2457b	All color omitted	—
	Quantity: n/a	

No. 2457b must be accompanied by a 2012 certificate of authentication confirming that stamps are from the discovery coil roll that also contained normal and partially printed stamps.

Lighthouses. April 25, 1990. Booklet pane of 5. Engraved, lithographed. BEP.

25c white (engraved); black, yellow, magenta & cyan (lithographed)

2474b	booklet pane of 5, white omitted	85.00
	unexploded booklet with 4 panes	350.00
	any single used	—
	any single, used on cover	—
	Quantity: 500+ booklets	

Value is for pane with usual tab disturbance, which is not considered a fault. Cover listing is for contemporaneous use on commercial cover.

▶ Caution. Examples exist with white ink lightly applied or with white shifted to the bottom of the design. White ink must be 100% omitted in order to qualify as a color-omitted error.

Fawn. March 11, 1991. Photogravure. BEP.

19c black, yellow, red, cyan & dark gray green

2479b	red omitted	425.00
	Quantity: 100 reported	

The non-omitted colors on No. 2479b are misregistered.

Sunfish. December 2, 1992. Engraved, lithographed. SVS.

45c black (engraved); black, yellow, magenta & cyan (lithographed)

2481a	black (engraved) omitted	300.00
	used, black (engraved) omitted	—
	Quantity: 100-200 reported; 2 used	

Bobcat. June 1, 1990. Engraved, lithographed. BEP.

$2 black (engraved); black, yellow, magenta & cyan (lithographed)

2482a	black (engraved) omitted	*200.00*
	plate block of 4, black omitted	*900.00*
	Quantity: 300-400 reported	

Many variations in the color of the green leaves occur on this issue. They are not color-omitted errors.

Olympians. July 6, 1990. Se-tenant strip of 5. Photogravure. ABN.

25c black, yellow, magenta & blue

  a) Jesse Owens
  b) Ray Ewry
  c) Hazel Wightman
  d) Eddie Eagan
  e) Helene Madison

2500b	strip of 5, blue omitted	—
	Quantity: 2 panes reported	

American Indian Headdresses. July 6, 1990. Se-tenant booklet pane of 10. Engraved, lithographed. BEP.

25c black (engraved); black, yellow, magenta, cyan & olive (lithographed)

  a) Assiniboine
  b) Cheyenne
  c) Comanche
  d) Flathead
  e) Shoshone

2505b	booklet pane of 10, black (engraved) omitted	*2,500.00*
	any single, black (engraved) omitted	—
	any pair, black (engraved) omitted	—
	strip of 3, black (engraved) omitted	—
	used pair, black (engraved) omitted	—
	Quantity: rare	

Micronesia - Marshall Islands. September 28, 1990. Se-tenant pairs. Engraved, lithographed. BEP.

25c black (engraved); black, yellow, magenta, cyan & blue (lithographed)

  a) Micronesia   b) Marshall Islands

2507b	pair, black (engraved) omitted	*1,400.00*
	single (a), black (engraved) omitted	*600.00*
	plate block of 4	—
	Quantity: 20 pairs, 20 singles (a) reported	

▶ Caution. Often with minute flecks of black. Examine carefully under 30-power magnification.

Sea Mammals. October 3, 1990. Se-tenant block of 4. Engraved, lithographed. BEP.

25c black (engraved); black, yellow, magenta & cyan (lithographed)

  a) Killer Whale   b) Northern Sea Lion
  c) Sea Otter   d) Common Dolphin

2511b	block of 4, black (engraved) omitted	*250.00*
	Zip block of 4, black omitted	*250.00*
	any single, black omitted	*60.00*
	any single, black omitted, used	—
	Quantity: 100-120 blocks of 4	

Flag Over Mt. Rushmore. July 4, 1991. Coil. Photogravure. ABN.

29c blue, red, light brown, medium brown & dark brown

2523Ae medium brown omitted   —
      Quantity: 1 reported

William Saroyan. May 22, 1991. Photogravure. JWF.

29c maroon, black, yellow, magenta & cyan

2538b   maroon, yellow, cyan & magenta
       omitted   *11,000.00*
       Quantity: unique

Eagle & Olympic Rings. September 29, 1991. Photogravure. JWF.

$1 gold, black, dark blue, yellow, red & green

2539a   black omitted   —
       Quantity: n/a

Eagle. July 7, 1991. Engraved, lithographed. ABN.

$2.90 black (engraved); black, yellow red & cyan (lithographed)

2540b   black (engraved) omitted   *750.00*
       Quantity: 20 reported

Of the 20 reported examples, 3 are sound and the balance are faulty.

Express Mail. June 16, 1991. Engraved, lithographed. ABN.

$14 red (engraved); black, yellow, magenta & cyan (lithographed)

2542a   red (engraved) omitted   *750.00*
       Quantity: very rare

Imperforate examples with one or more colors omitted are printer's waste.

NOTE. No. 2544A, the $10.75 Express Mail stamp of 1995, has been reported with cyan omitted; however, the editors are not aware of any examples with cyan 100% omitted. Check under 30-power magnification.

Fishing Flies. May 31 1991. Booklet pane of 5. Photogravure. ABN.

29c black, yellow, magenta, cyan & orange
       a) Royal Wulff
       b) Jock Scott
       c) Apte Tarpon Fly
       d) Lefty's Deceiver
       e) Muddler Minnow

2545a   stamp a, black omitted   —
2546a   stamp b, black omitted   —
2547a   stamp c, black omitted   —
       Quantity: each reportedly unique

World War II. September 31, 1991. Se-tenant block of 10. Engraved, lithographed. BEP.

29c black (engraved); black, yellow, magenta & cyan (lithographed)

a) Burma Road   f) Reuben James
b) Draft   g) Civil Defense
c) Lend Lease   h) Liberty Ship
d) Atlantic Charter   i) Pearl Harbor
e) Arsenal of Democracy   j) Declares War

2559k   se-tenant block of 10, black
      (engraved) omitted   *6,500.00*
      Quantity: 1 pane containing 2 blocks of 10

District of Columbia Bicentennial. September 7, 1991. Engraved, lithographed. BEP.

29c black (engraved); black, yellow, magenta & cyan (lithographed)

2561a   black (engraved) omitted   *85.00*
      plate block of 4, black omitted   *350.00*
      Quantity: 1,000+

Comedians. August 29, 1991. Booklet pane of 10. Engraved, lithographed. BEP.

29c scarlet & violet (engraved); black, red & violet (lithographed)

a) Laurel & Hardy
b) Bergen & McCarthy
c) Jack Benny
d) Fanny Brice
e) Abbott & Costello

2566c   booklet pane of 10, scarlet & violet
      (engraved) omitted   *350.00*
      any single (a, c or e) scarlet
      (engraved) omitted   *60.00*
      any single (b or d) violet (engraved) omitted   —
      first day cover with strip of 5 (a-e),
      red & violet (engraved) omitted   —
      first day cover with any single (a-e),
      red & violet (engraved) omitted   —
      Quantity: 100-150 booklet panes reported;
      6 first day covers with strip; unknown
      number of first day covers with singles

Refer to note following No. 2265a in the Imperforates section regarding first day covers.

Christmas. October 17, 1991. Booklet pane of 10. Engraved, lithographed. BEP.

(29c) red & black (engraved); yellow, magenta, cyan & gold (lithographed)

2578b   red & black (engraved) omitted   2,250.00
      Quantity: 9 sound examples;
      1 faulty example

Eagle & Shield. September 25, 1992. Pane of 17 plus label. Photogravure. Self-adhesive. Straight die cut. BCA.

29c brown (engraved); black, yellow, magenta & cyan (lithographed)

2595c   brown (engraved) omitted   *250.00*
      Quantity: 75-150 reported

Stock Market. May 17, 1992. Engraved, lithographed. ABN.

29c black (engraved); red & green (lithographed)

2630b   black omitted   *4,000.00*
      Quantity: 28 stamps

Twenty-four examples of No. 2630b occurred on 2 panes (12 from each pane) that also contained examples with the black engraved portion of the design inverted (see No. 2530c in the Inverts section). In addition, four examples occurred on a pane that did not contain invert errors.

Space Accomplishments. May 29, 1992. Se-tenant. Photogravure. BEP.

29c black, yellow, magenta & cyan

a) Cosmonaut, Space Shuttle
b) Astronaut, Space Station
c) Apollo Command Module, Sputnik
d) Soyuz, Mercury & Gemini Spacecraft

2634b   block of 4, yellow omitted   *4,750.00*
        plate block of 4, yellow omitted   —
        single stamp (c or d), yellow omitted   —
        Quantity: 10 blocks of 4;
          5 singles of stamps c and d

Alaska Highway. May 30, 1992. Engraved, lithographed. BEP.

29c black (engraved); black, yellow, magenta, cyan & dark brown (lithographed)

2635a   black (engraved) omitted
          well centered   *575.00*
          poorly centered   *325.00*
          used on cover, black omitted   *125.00*
        Quantity: 220

Of the 220 stamps, 100 are poorly centered and 120 are well centered. Cover value is for contemporaneous commercial usage.

Kentucky Statehood. June 1, 1992. Photogravure. JWF.

29c dark blue, black, yellow, red & cyan

2636a   dark blue omitted   —
        Quantity: n/a

2636b   dark blue & red omitted   —
        Quantity: n/a

World War II. August 17, 1992. Se-tenant block of 10. Engraved, lithographed. BEP.

29c black (engraved); black, yellow, magenta & cyan (lithographed)

a) Tokyo Raid   f) Secret Code
b) Ration Stamps   g) Yorktown Lost
c) Battle of Coral Sea h) Women in War
d) Corregidor   i) Guadalcanal
e) Aleutian Island   j) North Africa

2697k   block of 10, red (litho) omitted   *4,000.00*
        Quantity: 1 pane containing 2
        blocks of 10

Minerals. September 17, 1992. Se-tenant block of 4. Engraved, lithographed. BEP.

29c black (engraved); black, yellow, magenta, cyan & silver (lithographed)

a) Azurite   b) Copper
c) Variscite   d) Wulfenite

2703b   strip of 4, silver (litho) omitted   *6,000.00*
        Quantity: 2 strips of 4 containing a-d

The strips of 4 of No. 2703b with color omitted are contained in blocks of 8 stamps that also contain 4 normal stamps.

▶ Examples with magenta (lithographed) ostensibly omitted exist; however, we are of the opinion that they are changelings.

Juan Rodriguez Cabrillo. September 28, 1992. Engraved, lithographed. SVS.

29c black (engraved); black, yellow, magenta, cyan, dark red & tan (litho)

2704a   black (engraved) omitted   *1,750.00*
        Quantity: 10 reported

Sports Horses. May 1, 1993. Se-tenant block of 4. Engraved, lithographed. SVS.

29c black (engraved); black, yellow, magenta & cyan (lithographed)

a) Steeplechase   b) Thoroughbred Racing
c) Harness Racing   d) Polo

2759b   block of 4, black (engraved) omitted   *500.00*
        plate black of 4, black omitted   —
        any single (a-d), black omitted   *125.00*
        Quantity: 56-68 blocks of 4

Garden Flowers. May 15, 1993. Booklet pane of 5. Engraved, lithographed. BEP.

29c black (engraved); black, yellow, magenta & cyan (lithographed)

a) Hyacinth
b) Daffodil
c) Tulip
d) Iris
e) Lilac

2764b   booklet pane, black (engraved)
        omitted   *135.00*
        Quantity: 250+ panes reported

Individual panes usually contain a tab fault. Value is for pane with tab fault.

National Postal Museum. July 30, 1993. Engraved, lithographed. ABN.

29c maroon & black (engraved); black, yellow, magenta, cyan, tan & dark blue (lithographed)

a) Ben Franklin   b) Pony Express
c) Charles Lindbergh   d) Stamps & Barcode

2782b block of 4, maroon & black
       (engraved) omitted   2,500.00
       hz strip of 4, maroon & black
       (engraved) omitted   —
       pair, maroon & black (engraved)
       omitted   —
       Quantity: 8-16 blocks of 4, 2 strips of 4

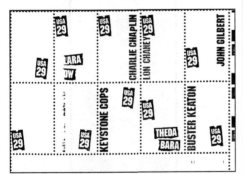

Stars of the Silent Screen. April 27, 1994. Se-tenant block of 10. BEP.

29c red & pale violet (engraved); black, red & bright violet (lithographed)

a) Rudolph Valentino   f) Zasu Pitts
b) Clara Bow   g) Harold Lloyd
c) Charlie Chaplin   h) Keystone Cops
d) Lon Chaney   i) Theda Bara
e) John Gilbert   j) Buster Keaton

2828b block of 10, black (litho) omitted   —
       Quantity: 2 blocks of 10

2828c block of 10, black (litho),
       red & bright violet (engraved) omitted —
       Quantity: 2 blocks of 10

Garden Flowers. April 28, 1994. Booklet pane of 5. Engraved, lithographed. BEP.

29c black (engraved); black, yellow, magenta & cyan (lithographed)

a) Lily
b) Zinnia
c) Gladiola
d) Marigold
e) Rose

2833c booklet pane, black (engraved)
       omitted   125.00
       Quantity: 250-300 panes

Individual panes usually contain a tab fault. Value is for pane with tab fault.

Cranes. October 9, 1994. Se-tenant pair. Engraved, lithographed. BCA.

29c black & magenta (engraved); black, yellow, magenta & cyan (lithographed)

a) Black-necked Crane b) Whooping Crane

2868b pair, black & magenta (engraved)
       omitted   1,250.00
       single (a or b), black & magenta omitted —
       plate block of 4, black & magenta omitted —
       Quantity: 30-40 pairs

Auto – Bulk Rate. March 10, 1995. Coil. Photogravure. Water activated. JWF.

(10c) black, red brown & brown

2905c single, on piece, plate No. S33,
       brown omitted   400.00
       Quantity: unique

Flag & Porch. May 21, 1996. Coil. Photogravure. Self-adhesive. Serpentine die cut. Red 1996 date. BEP.

32c tan, dark brown, blue & dark blue

2915Ai   used, tan omitted   —
          Quantity: 2 reported

NOTE. Dummy simulations bearing the design of the 32c Flag Over Porch coil stamp, but lacking the "USA 32," were included as leaders in a refrigerator-magnet stamp dispenser sold at some Wal-Mart stores in the spring of 1999. They are not color-omitted error stamps.

Flag & Porch. April 18, 1995. Booklet pane of 20. Photogravure. Self-adhesive. Serpentine die cut. Blue 1995 date. BEP.

32c tan, dark brown, blue & dark blue

2920j   dark blue omitted   *2,100.00*
       Quantity: unique

The discovery pane includes some stamps with dark blue partially omitted. No. 2920j is located at lower left on the pane. Some stamps on the pane just beneath the error stamp were used before the error was noticed.

Love. February 1, 1995. Booklet pane of 20. Engraved, lithographed. Self-adhesive. Straight die cut. BCA.

(32c) red (engraved); black, yellow, magenta & cyan (lithographed)

2949b   single, red (engraved) omitted   *100.00*
       Quantity: 40-60 stamps

2949c   booklet pane, red (engraved)
       omitted   *2,000.00*
       Quantity: included above

Richard Nixon. April 26, 1995. Engraved, lithographed. BCA.

32c red (engraved); black, yellow, magenta & cyan (lithographed)

2955a   red (engraved) omitted   *800.00*
       Quantity: 70 reported

Transition multiples exist and sell for a premium.

Recreational Sports. May 20, 1995. Se-tenant strip of 5. Lithographed. BCA.

32c black, yellow, magenta & blue

a) Volleyball   b) Softball
c) Bowling   d) Tennis
e) Golf

2965c   strip of 5, yellow omitted   *1,600.00*
       Quantity: 12 strips reported

Designs in strips of Nos. 2965c and 2965d may vary in arrangement due to layout of pane.

2965d strip of 5, yellow, blue & magenta
    omitted   *1,600.00*
    Quantity: 8-16 strips reported

Women's Suffrage. August 26, 1995. Engraved, lithographed. APU.

    32c black (engraved); black, yellow, magenta & cyan (lithographed)

2980a black (engraved) omitted   *275.00*
    plate block of 4   *1,000.00*
    Quantity: 40-60 reported

▶ Caution. This issue was prone to printing problems. Many varieties exist with colors partially omi tted. Certificate recommended. Many examples of No. 2980a are poorly centered. Value is for a fine example. Very fine examples sell for much more.

Note. The Jazz Musicians compact pane, Nos. 2982-2992, issued September 1, 1995, exists with the dark blue marginal inscription "Jazz Musicians," which is normally located on the top margin, omitted. The dark blue color used to print the inscription does not normally appear on any of the stamps; therefore, it cannot be considered to be omitted from any of them.

Madonna. October 19, 1995. Engraved, lithographed. BEP.

    32c black (engraved); black, yellow, magenta & cyan (lithographed)

3003c black (engraved) omitted   *200.00*
    Quantity: 100+ stamps

Cherub. January 20, 1996. Booklet pane of 20. Engraved, lithographed. Self-adhesive. Serpentine die cut. BCA.

    32c red (engraved) ; black, yellow, magenta & cyan (lithographed)

3030c single, red (engraved) omitted   *75.00*
    Quantity: n/a

3030h booklet pane, red (engraved)
    omitted   *1,200.00*
    Quantity: n/a

Coral Pink Rose. April 7, 2000. Double-sided booklet pane of 20. Photogravure. Self-adhesive. Serpentine die cut. SSP.

    33c black, pink & green

3052Eg black omitted   *350.00*
    Quantity: 24-36 reported

3052Eh booklet pane, black omitted
    on side with 12 stamps   —
    Quantity: several

Examples of No. 3052Eg occur on the 12-stamp side of the double-sided booklet pane. Stamps on the 8-stamp side are normal.

Yellow Rose. August 1, 1997. Coil. Photogravure. Self-adhesive. Serpentine die cut. Black 1997 date. BEP.

32c black, magenta, yellow & green
3054b	black, yellow & green omitted	—
	Quantity: 50-100 stamps	

3054d	black omitted	*250.00*
	Quantity: 14 stamps	

The discovery roll of Nos. 3054b and 3054d is miscut. It contained 5 normal stamps, 14 black omitted, and 1 black, yellow and olive green omitted. Refer to Nos. 3054c and 3054e in the Imperforates Section for combination die-cutting omitted and color-omitted Yellow Rose errors. Since the discovery roll appeared, several additional partial rolls containing No. 3054b errors have surfaced. They exist for plate Nos. 2233, 3344 and 5555. Plate Nos. on these error strips appear as single magenta digits, "2," "3," and "5" respectively.

Jacqueline Cochran. March 9, 1996. Engraved, lithographed. BEP.

50c black (engraved); black, yellow, magenta & cyan (lithographed)
3066a	black (engraved) omitted	45.00
	plate block of 4	190.00
	Quantity: several thousand	

▶ Caution. Beware of examples with black partially omitted.

Madonna and Child. November 1, 1996. Lithographed, engraved. Self-adhesive. Serpentine die cut. BEP.

32c black (engraved); magenta, yellow, cyan & black (lithographed)
3107a	black (engraved) omitted at bottom	*600.00*
	Quantity: n/a	

On No. 3107a, an albino impression of the lettering at bottom is present, but there is no trace of black ink.

Swan. February 4, 1997. Booklet pane of 20. Lithographed. Self-adhesive. Serpentine die cut. BCA.

32c black, yellow, magenta & cyan
3123d	booklet pane, black omitted	—
	single, black omitted	—
	Quantity: n/a	

Computer vended postage (CVP) stamps exist with the denomination omitted. The denomination is added by the vending equipment at the point of sale and is not part of the initial production process. Some denomination omissions have been intentionally created by customer manipulation of the vended strip. Therefore, CVP stamps with omitted or misplaced denominations have not been listed as errors. Their existence is mentioned here as a matter of record.

Celebrate the Century 1900s. February 3, 1998. Se-tenant pane of 15. Engraved, lithographed. APU.

32c red (engraved); black, yellow, magenta & cyan (lithographed)
3182p	pane of 15, red engraved omitted	*3,000.00*
	Quantity: possibly unique	

Engraved red appears on only one stamp, the Gibson Girl. Engraved red was the only color used to print the Gibson Girl stamp. Its omission creates a blank stamp.

Holiday Wreaths. October 15, 1998. Se-tenant pane of 20. Lithographed. Self-adhesive. Serpentine die cut. BCA.

32c black, yellow, magenta, cyan, red & green

a) Evergreen Wreath b) Chili Wreath
c) Colonial Wreath d) Tropical Wreath

3252f	block, red omitted	*625.00*
	strip, red omitted	—
	Quantity: 2-3 panes reported	
3252g	block of 4, red & green omitted	—
	strip, red & green omitted	—
	Quantity: 1 pane reported	

Dedicated printing plates were used to print the red or green denominations and salutations. Red and green appearing in the wreaths arises from plates used in process color printing and, therefore, is not part of the color omission. The se-tenant designs vary in order of appearance from block to block within a pane. By virtue of the layout, each of the blocks of 4 contains plate numbers in the salvage.

Weather Vane. November 9, 1998. Lithographed. APU.

(1c) black, yellow, blue, red & dark blue

3257a	black omitted	125.00
	plate block, black omitted	—
	Quantity: 100-150 reported	

Hat & H. November 9, 1998. Coil. Photogravure. Self-adhesive. Serpentine die cut. BEP.

(33c) black, red, blue & gray

3265b	single, red omitted	*300.00*
	strip, red omitted, plate No. 222	*1,600.00*
	Quantity: 100 reported	

On the discovery roll, the gray and blue portions of the design are shifted right. No. 3265b can be collected as a single stamp or a pair. The listing is for a single stamp.

3265c	black omitted	*1,400.00*
	Quantity: 35 reported	

Of the 35 examples, 17 have normal die cuts between stamps and 18 possess trace die-cut impressions analogous to blind perfs.

Refer to Nos. 3265d and 3265e in the Imperforates section for listings of either red omitted or black omitted on die-cutting omitted examples.

3265f	single, blue omitted	—
	Quantity: 46	

The red portion of the design is shifted to the right. The gray portion of the design is also shifted to the right, but to a lesser degree.

Flag Over City. February 25, 1999. Coil. Photogravure. Self-adhesive. Serpentine die cut. BEP.

33c dark blue, light blue, red & yellow

3281b	single, light blue & yellow omitted	*275.00*
	pair, light blue & yellow omitted	*550.00*
	strip, as above, plate No. 6666	—
	Quantity: 95 stamps	

The dark blue and red portions of the design are misregistered in relation to one another, separated by about an eighth of an inch. In addition, the design is shifted to the right, resulting in die cutting appearing to be misplaced. Only dark blue and red digits appear on plate number strips. Often collected in pairs.

Margaret Chase Smith. June 13, 2007. Pane of 20. Engraved, lithographed. Self-adhesive. Serpentine die cut. APU.

58c black (engraved); red (lithographed)
3427b   black (engraved) omitted   *400.00*
       plate block of 4   —
       Quantity: 1 pane reported

Lithographed black was also used in printing, but only for marginal markings and inscriptions, and thus appears only in the selvage.

James Michener. May 12, 2008. Lithographed. Self-adhesive. Serpentine die cut. BCA.

59c blue, magenta, yellow, black & red
3427Ac   blue, magenta and yellow omitted   *1,500.00*
Quantity: 1 pane reported

3427Ad   Blue and yellow omitted   —
         Quantity: 4 reported

On No. 3427Ad, traces of magenta are present.

Jonas Salk. March 3, 2006. Engraved, lithographed. Self-adhesive. Serpentine die cut. BCA.

63c black (engraved); red & black lithographed
3428a   black (litho) omitted   *275.00*
       Quantity: 20

Apple & Orange. March 6, 2001. Booklet pane of 20. Photogravure. Self-adhesive. Serpentine die cut. BCA.

34c black, yellow, magenta & cyan
3492c   pair, black omitted   —
       Quantity: 4 pairs initially reported

Apple and orange designs alternate; their order is reversed from row to row. The discovery examples consist of 4 pairs at right on a pane of 20.

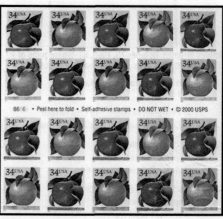

3492f   pane, yellow omitted   *3,500.00*
       Quantity: n/a

The omission of yellow occurs on the right vertical column of 4 stamps (2 pairs) on the discovery pane.

U.S. Flag. June 7, 2002. Booklet pane of 20. Lithographed. Self-adhesive. Serpentine die cut. BCA.

37c black, yellow, magenta & cyan
3635b   pane, black omitted on 2 stamps   *3,000.00*
       Quantity: unique

The discovery pane contains two stamps with black omitted and four stamps with black partially omitted. Three stamps at lower right were removed and presumably used by the original purchaser.

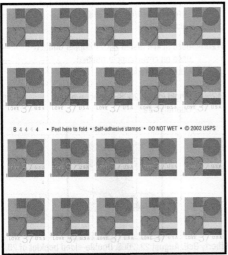

Year of the Monkey. January 13, 2004. Photogravure. Self-adhesive. Serpentine die cut. APC.

37c magenta, yellow, cyan & green

3832a yellow omitted —
Quantity: n/a

Modern American Architecture. May 19, 2005. Se-tenant pane of 12. Offset. Self-adhesive. Serpentine die cut. APU.

37c black, green, orange, purple, red, blue & orange yellow

a) Guggenheim Museum	b) Chrysler Building
c) Vanna Venture House	d) TWA Terminal
e) Disney Concert Hall	f) 860-880 Lake Shore
g) National Gallery	h) Glass House
i) Yale Art	j) High Museum
k) Exeter Academy	l) Hancock Center

3910m pane of 12, orange yellow omitted *400.00*
Quantity: several panes reported

Orange yellow is omitted on the second (denominations) and fourth (first word of building names) vertical rows.

Love. August 16, 2002. Lithographed. Booklet pane of 20. Self-adhesive. Serpentine die cut. BCA.

37c black, yellow, magenta, cyan & silver

3657b pane, silver omitted on top row
of 5 stamps *750.00*
Quantity: 1 pane

3657c hz strip of 5, silver omitted on
one stamp *1,000.00*
Quantity: unique

Snowy Egret. October 24, 2003. Coil. Photogravure. Self-adhesive. Serpentine die cut. AVR.

37c black, gray blue, gray & yellow
3829b black omitted —
used on cover, black omitted —
strip, on liner, uncanceled —
Quantity: 23 unused, 2 used on
cover, uncanceled strip of 5
affixed to liner

The five examples affixed to liner were peeled off a package and were used but not canceled.

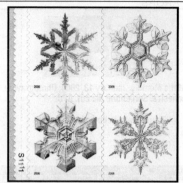

Snowflakes. October 5, 2006. Lithographed. Se-tenant booklet pane of 20. Self-adhesive. Serpentine die cut. BCA.

39c black, blue, red & green

4108c   block of 4, red & green omitted   —
          Quantity: unique

The color blue on the error block is partially, but not completely, omitted.

Liberty Bell. April 12, 2007. Double-sided booklet of 20, dated 2007. Photogravure. Self-adhesive. Serpentine die cut. SSP.

Forever (41c) black, yellow, magenta, cyan & copper

4125d   booklet (dated 2008, large
          microprinting), copper omitted   *1,000.00*
Quantity: several panes

4125e   booklet (dated 2008), copper omitted
          on the side with 12 stamps   —
          Quantity: n/a

4125h   used single (dated 2007), copper omitted   —
          used on cover, copper omitted   —
          Quantity: 1 reported

4125j   Single (dated 2008), copper omitted   50.00
          Quantity: n/a

Liberty Bell. August 22, 2008. Double-sided booklet of 20, dated 2008. Photogravure. Self-adhesive. Serpentine die cut. SSP.

Forever (42c) black, yellow, magenta, cyan & copper

4126f   used single on piece (dated 2008,
          small microprinting), copper omitted   *1,400.00*
          Quantity: 1 reported

Air Force One. June 13, 2007. Engraved, lithographed. Self-adhesive. Serpentine die cut. APU.

$4.60 black (engraved); black, yellow magenta, cyan & gray (lithographed)

4144a   black (engraved) omitted   225.00
          Quantity: 50-60 reported

Flag. August 15, 2007. Coil. Photogravure. Self-adhesive. Serpentine die cut. AVR.

41c tan, gray, red, blue, light blue

4188c   used single on cover, light blue
          ("41 USA") omitted   —
          Quantity: 1 reported

4262b   single (c) light green omitted   —
        single, plate No. V111111,
        light green omitted   —
        Quantity: 8 singles, 1 plate single,
        and a strip of 54

Nine singles were removed from the coil and individually placed on liner paper. The strip of 54 contains one plate number strip. The plate number on a normal example contains a letter and 7 digits. The error example contains 6 digits, one having been omitted.

Circus Posters. May 5, 2014. Lithographed, engraved. Self-adhesive. Imperforate. BCA.

        $1 multicolored (1 stamp), 50c red (2 stamps)
4905f   imperf sheet of 3, gold omitted
        in sheet margin   —
        Quantity: 12 reported (1 press sheet)

Flag. January 29, 2016. Coil. Lithographed. Self-adhesive. Serpentine die cut. BCA.

        Forever (49c) cyan, magenta, yellow, black, grayish blue
5052b   imperf pair, grayish blue (inscription and
        date) omitted   —
        Quantity: 2 rolls of 100 reported

USA and Star. February 10, 2017. Coil. Lithographed. Self-adhesive. Serpentine die cut. APU.

        (5c) multicolored
5172a   red (star) omitted   —
        Quantity: n/a

The discovery example of No. 5172a is on piece, uncanceled.

AIR MAIL STAMPS

HINGING. Prices for airmail color-omitted stamps are for never-hinged examples. Hinged examples sell for less.

First Man on the Moon. September 9, 1969. Engraved, lithographed. BEP.

        10c black, red, & dark blue (engraved); yellow, rose red, light blue, ultramarine & gray (lithographed)
C76a   rose red (litho) omitted   *500.00*
        pair, one with rose red omitted   *600.00*
        Quantity: 250-300

▶ Caution. Many examples exist with red shoulder patch omitted but with litho dots of red present in the visor and yellow area of the lunar lander. All traces of red must be absent in order for the stamp to qualify as the error. Careful inspection under magnification is necessary. Also, note that the European standard for color-omitted errors differs from the accepted U.S. standard; the European standard requires only that the shoulder patch be omitted to qualify as an error. Value for an example with patch omitted, but other red litho dots present: $300.

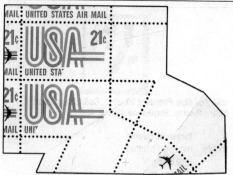

USA & Jet. May 21, 1971. Engraved, lithographed. BEP.

    21c black & dark blue (engraved);
    light blue & red (lithographed)
C81b   black omitted   *2,750.00*
       Quantity: 2

This error occurs as the result of a foldover at the bottom right
of a pane yielding 2 black omitted stamps. The value listed is for
the intact pane.

**National Parks Centennial. May 3, 1972. Engraved,
lithographed. BEP.**

    11c black (engraved); yellow, blue,
    orange & green (lithographed)
C84a   blue & green omitted   *600.00*
       as above, used   *900.00*
       as above, plate block of 4   —
       Zip block of 4, blue & green omitted —
       used single, blue & green omitted —
       Quantity: 92 reported

**Progress in Electronics. July 10, 1973. Engraved,
lithographed. BEP.**

    11c black & deep red (engraved);
    black, vermilion, brown, olive
    & light violet (lithographed)
C86a   vermilion & olive (litho) omitted   *800.00*
       Quantity: 100

C86c   olive green (litho) omitted   *1,000.00*
       Quantity: n/a

No. C86c is similar in appearance to No. C86a due to vermilion
being nearly completely omitted and present only as small specks.
The discovery examples are contained in a plate block of 4.

**Wright Brothers. September 23, 1978. Vertical se-tenant
pair. Engraved, lithographed. BEP.**

    31c ultramarine & black (engraved); black,
    yellow, magenta, blue &
    brown (lithographed)

    a) Wrights & Biplane
    b) Wrights, Biplane & Hanger

C92b   pair, ultramarine & black (engraved)
       omitted   *475.00*
       Quantity: 150 pairs reported

C92c   pair, black (engraved) omitted   *1,750.00*
       Quantity: n/a

C92d   pair, black, yellow, magenta,
       blue & brown (litho) omitted   *1,750.00*
       as above, plate block of 4   —
       Quantity: 15 pairs

Transition multiples exist and sell for a premium.

Octave Chanute. March 29, 1979. Vertical se-tenant pairs. Engraved, lithographed. BEP.

21c ultramarine & black (engraved); black, yellow, magenta, blue & brown (lithographed)

a) Large Portrait
b) Small Portrait

C94b   pair, ultramarine & black (engraved)
     omitted   *4,000.00*
     plate block of 4, colors omitted
       as above on right pair   *5,000.00*
     Quantity: 5 pairs reported

Transition multiples exist and sell for a premium.

Glenn Curtiss. December 30, 1980. Photogravure. BEP.

35c black, blue, light blue, yellow & red
C100a light blue omitted   *2,000.00*
        Quantity: 2 reported

The two discovery examples are at left in a top left Zip block of 4.

Igor Sikorsky. June 23, 1988. Engraved, lithographed. BEP.

36c red, dark blue & black (engraved); black, yellow, magenta, cyan & pale blue (lithographed)
C119a red, dark blue & black (engraved)
       omitted   *1,250.00*
       plate block of 4   —
       Quantity: 50, including those
        in the plate block

No. C119, the Sikorsky 36c airmail stamp, is known with the red engraved inscriptions omitted in varying degrees. However, red specks (visible under magnification) are present on all stamps seen to date, so it is not considered to be a true 100% color-omitted error. Nevertheless, it is considered a collectible variety: price $125 to $150, depending on the degree of red omitted.

20th UPU Congress. November 28, 1989. Se-tenant block 4. Perf 11. Engraved, lithographed. BEP.

45c light blue (engraved); black, yellow, magenta & cyan (lithographed)

a) Spacecraft   b) Hovercraft
c) Lunar Rover   d) Space Shuttle

C125b block of 4, light blue
       (engraved) omitted   *500.00*
       block of 4 with hz gutter   —
       plate block of 4   —
       any single, a-d   *115.00*
       Quantity: 60-80 blocks of 4

POSTAGE DUE STAMPS

HINGING. Prices for postage due color-omitted stamps are for never hinged examples. Hinged examples sell for less.

Numeral of Value. June 19, 1959. Engraved, typographed. BEP.

J89a	single stamp, black omitted	150.00
	plate block of 4, black omitted	—
	Quantity: several hundred	

The red background for postage due stamps of this series were printed from common engraved plates. Denominations were added in black as demand required. When black is omitted, it is not possible to identify the denomination of an error, except in the case of pairs containing a normal stamp. Likewise, it is not possible to attribute black-omitted plate blocks to any specific denomination because denominations share plate numbers. Panes of postage due color-omitted errors usually contain a row of 10 pairs of one normal stamp and one error stamp. The balance of the pane consists of varying quantities of normal stamps and color-omitted stamps. Once the remaining color-omitted stamps have been detached from the pane, they are impossible to identify by denomination, and are listed above. Transition multiples also exist with black partially omitted from some stamps. They sell for a premium.

Numeral of Value. June 19, 1959. Engraved, typographed. BEP.

1c carmine rose (engraved); black (typographed)

J89b	pair, one with black omitted, one normal	350.00
	Quantity: 50+ pairs	

Numeral of Value. June 19, 1959. Engraved, typographed. BEP.

3c carmine rose (engraved); black (typographed)

J91a	pair, one with black omitted, one normal	550.00
	Quantity: 40-60 pairs	

Numeral of Value. June 19, 1959. Engraved, typographed. BEP.

5c carmine rose (engraved); black (typographed)

J93a	pair, one with black omitted, one normal	1,100.00
	Quantity: 10 pairs reported	

Numeral of Value. June 19, 1959. Engraved, typographed. BEP.

6c carmine rose (engraved); black (typographed)

J94a	pair, one with black omitted, one normal	700.00
	Quantity: 20 pairs	

Numeral of Value. June 19, 1959. Engraved, typographed. BEP.

8c carmine rose (engraved); black (typographed)

J96a   pair, one with black omitted,
        one normal   *750.00*
        Quantity: 20 pairs

STAMPED ENVELOPES

Prices are for unused entire envelopes unless otherwise noted.

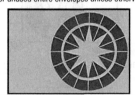

Compass. October 13, 1975. Typographed, embossed.

10c brown & blue (light brown paper)

U571a   brown omitted   *125.00*
        Quantity: n/a

Quilt Design. February 2, 1976. Typographed, embossed.

13c brown & blue green (light brown paper)

U572a   brown omitted   *125.00*
        Quantity: n/a

Wheat Sheaf. March 15, 1976. Typographed, embossed.

13c brown & green (light brown paper)

U573a   brown omitted   *125.00*
        Quantity: n/a

Mortar. June 30, 1976. Typographed, embossed.

13c brown & orange (light brown paper)

U574a   brown omitted   *125.00*
        Quantity: n/a

Tools. August 6, 1976. Typographed, embossed.

13c brown & carmine (light brown paper)

U575a   brown omitted   *125.00*
        Quantity: n/a

Golf. April 7, 1977. Photogravure, embossed.

13c black, blue & yellow green

U583a   black omitted   *500.00*
        Quantity: n/a

U583b   black & blue omitted   *500.00*
        Quantity: n/a

Energy Conservation. October 20, 1977. Photogravure, embossed.

    13c black, red & yellow

U584a	red & yellow omitted	*190.00*
	Quantity: n/a	
U584b	yellow omitted	*150.00*
	Quantity: n/a	
U584c	black omitted	*135.00*
	Quantity: n/a	

U584d	black & red omitted	*350.00*
	Quantity: n/a	

U.S.A. July 28, 1978. Photogravure, embossed.

    16c blue; black "Revalued to 15c"

U586a	black surcharge omitted	*225.00*
	used, black surcharge omitted	1,000.00
	Quantity: n/a	

Auto Racing. September 2, 1978. Photogravure, embossed.

    15c red, blue & black

U587a	black omitted	100.00
	Quantity: n/a	
U587b	black & blue omitted	*170.00*
	Quantity: n/a	

U587c	red omitted	100.00
	Quantity: n/a	
U587d	red & blue omitted	*170.00*
	Quantity: n/a	

Exists albino.

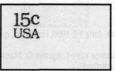

Veterinary Medicine. July 24, 1979. Photogravure, embossed.

    15c brown & gray

U595a	gray omitted	*425.00*
	Quantity: very rare	

U595b	brown omitted	*500.00*
	Quantity: 5-7 reported	

U595c	gray & brown omitted	*325.00*
	Quantity: n/a	

The embossed seal is present on No. U595c.

Olympics 1980. December 10, 1979. Photogravure, embossed.

    15c red, green & black

U596a	red & green omitted	*150.00*
	Quantity: n/a	
U596b	black omitted	*150.00*
	Quantity: n/a	

U596c   black & green omitted   *150.00*
      Quantity: n/a

U596d   red omitted   *325.00*
      Quantity: n/a

   Exists albino.

Bicycle. May 16, 1980. Photogravure, embossed

15c blue & rose claret

U597a   blue omitted   100.00
      Quantity: n/a

Honeybee. October 10, 1980. Photogravure, embossed.

15c brown, green & yellow

U599a   brown omitted   *100.00*
      Quantity: n/a

U599b   green omitted   *100.00*
      Quantity: n/a

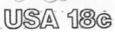

Blinded Veteran. August 13, 1981. Photogravure, embossed.

18c blue & red

U600a   blue omitted   *300.00*
      Quantity: n/a

U600b   red omitted   *210.00*
      Quantity: n/a

Great Seal of the United States. June 15, 1982. Photogravure, embossed.

20c dark blue, black & magenta

U602a   dark blue omitted   *175.00*
      Quantity: n/a

U602b   dark blue & magenta omitted   *175.00*
      Quantity: n/a

   Exists albino.

The
Purple
Heart
1782
1982
USA 20c

Purple Heart. August 6, 1982. Lithographed, embossed.

20c purple & black

U603a   black omitted   *80.00*
      Quantity: very rare

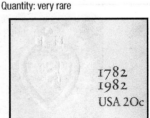

U603b   purple omitted   *200.00*
      Quantity: n/a

   Exists albino.

Paralyzed Veterans. August 3, 1983. Photogravure, embossed.

20c red, blue & black

U605a   red omitted   260.00
         Quantity: n/a

U605b   blue omitted   260.00
         Quantity: n/a

U605c   red & black omitted   125.00
         Quantity: n/a

U605d   blue & black omitted   125.00
         Quantity: n/a

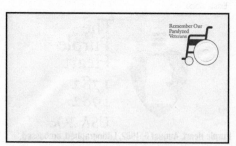

U605e   black omitted   125.00
         Quantity: n/a

USA 25. March 26, 1988. Photogravure, embossed.

25c dark red & deep blue

U611a   dark red omitted   50.00
         Quantity: 160+

Often with printed corner card "Magnificat High School."

Frigate Constitution. April 12, 1988. Typographed, embossed.

8.4c black & bright blue

U612a   black omitted   500.00
         Quantity: 8-12 reported

USA & Stars. March 10, 1989. Typographed

25c dark red & deep blue

U614b   dark red omitted, entire   125.00
         Quantity: n/a

USA & Stars. July 10, 1989. Typographed.

25c dark red & deep blue

U615a   dark red omitted   425.00
         Quantity: n/a

Love. September 22, 1989. Lithographed.

25c dark red, bright blue & pale blue

U616a   dark red & bright blue omitted   150.00
         Quantity: n/a

U616b   bright blue omitted   150.00
         Quantity: 5 reported

Space Station. December 3, 1989. Lithographed, hologram.

25c ultramarine & multicolored hologram
U617a   ultramarine omitted   400.00
         Quantity: 8-10 reported

Star & USA. January 24, 1991. Lithographed, embossed.

29c ultramarine & rose
U619a   ultramarine omitted   300.00
         Quantity: n/a

U619b   rose omitted   250.00
         Quantity: n/a

Love. May 9, 1991. Lithographed.

29c light blue, purple & bright rose
U621a   bright rose omitted   200.00
         Quantity: scarce

U621b   purple omitted   400.00
         Quantity: scarce

Star, USA & Bars. July 20, 1991. Lithographed.

29c ultramarine & rose
U623a   ultramarine omitted   350.00
         Quantity: n/a

U623b   rose omitted   200.00
         Quantity: n/a

Football. September 17, 1994. Typographed, embossed.

29c black & reddish brown
U631a   black omitted   325.00
         Quantity: n/a

Liberty Bell. January 3, 1995. Typographed, embossed.

32c greenish blue (bell) & blue
U632a   greenish blue omitted   *400.00*
        Quantity: n/a

U632b   blue omitted   *200.00*
        Quantity: 75 reported

No. U632b occurs on a No. 10 envelope with a printed Credit Union corner card. Exists tagged and untagged. The tagged variety is scarcer.
Exists albino.

Old Glory. January 12, 1995. No. 10 envelope. Typographed.

G (32c) blue & red
U634a   red omitted   *325.00*
        Quantity: n/a

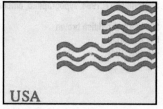

U634b   blue omitted   *325.00*
        Quantity: n/a

Liberty Bell. May 6, 1995. Typographed.

32c greenish blue & blue
U638a   greenish blue omitted   *175.00*
        Quantity: n/a

Paralympic Games. May 2, 1996. Lithographed.

32c black, blue, gold & red
U641a   blue & red omitted   *260.00*
        Quantity: n/a

U641b   blue & gold omitted   *550.00*
        Quantity: n/a

U641c   red omitted   *260.00*
        Quantity: n/a

U641d   black & red omitted   *450.00*
        Quantity: n/a

U641e   blue omitted   *300.00*
        Quantity: 2 initially reported

U.S. Flag. January 11, 1999. Typographed, embossed.

33c yellow, blue & red
U642b   used entire, blue omitted   *200.00*
        Quantity: n/a

▶ Caution. Examine carefully for traces of color. Exists albino.

U642c   yellow omitted   *175.00*
        Quantity: n/a

U642d yellow & blue omitted   *175.00*
       Quantity: n/a

U642e blue & red omitted   *175.00*
       Quantity: n/a

U642g red omitted   *450.00*
       Quantity: n/a

U642h red & yellow omitted   —
       Quantity: n/a

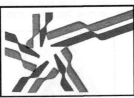

Federal Eagle. January 7, 2001. Typographed.

34c blue gray & gray
U646a blue gray omitted   175.00
       Quantity: n/a

U646b gray omitted   —
       Quantity: n/a

Ribbon Star. June 7, 2002. Typographed.

37c red, blue & gray
U649a gray omitted   —
       Quantity: n/a

U649b blue & gray omitted   —
       Quantity: n/a

AEROGRAMMES

Values are for complete aerogrammes unless otherwise noted.

Jet Aircraft. May 1959. Inscription on reverse (type I, in 3 lines; type II, in 2 lines). Typographed.

10c blue & red (blue paper)
UC32b red omitted, type II   *625.00*
       Quantity: very rare

UC32c blue omitted, type II   *600.00*
       Quantity: scarce

UC32d red omitted, type I   *700.00*
       Quantity: very rare

Jet Aircraft & Globe. June 16, 1961. Typographed.

11c red & blue (blue paper)
UC35a red omitted   *750.00*
       Quantity: n/a

UC35b blue omitted   *950.00*
       Quantity: n/a

John F. Kennedy. May 29, 1967. Typographed.

13c red & dark blue (blue paper)
UC39a red omitted   *600.00*
       Quantity: very rare

UC39b dark blue omitted   *500.00*
       Quantity: n/a

Human Rights Year. December 3, 1968. Photogravure.

13c gray, brown, orange & black (blue paper)

UC42a	orange omitted	800.00
	Quantity: n/a	

UC42b	brown omitted	375.00
	Quantity: n/a	
UC42c	black omitted	700.00
	Quantity: rare	
UC42d	gray & black omitted, used	—
	Quantity: n/a	

Birds in Flight. May 28, 1971. Photogravure.

15c gray, red, white & blue

UC44b	red omitted	300.00
	Quantity: n/a	
UC44c	red omitted	—
	Quantity: n/a	

No. UC44b is without the inscription "Aerogramme." No. UC44c is with the inscription "Aerogramme."

U.S.A. January 4, 1974. Photogravure.

18c red, white & blue (blue paper)

UC48a	red omitted	200.00
	Quantity: n/a	

U.S.A. December 29, 1980. Photogravure.

30c blue, red & brown (blue paper)

UC53a	red omitted	70.00
	Quantity: 150	

U.S.A. May 21, 1985. Photogravure.

36c black, blue, magenta & yellow (blue paper)

UC59a	black omitted	600.00
	used entire, black omitted	—
	Quantity: 3 reported, 1 used entire	

POSTAL CARDS

Values are for unused entire cards unless otherwise noted.

▶ Caution. Many postal cards were available from the Postal Service in large uncut sheets. It is possible to cut individual cards from such sheets with the stamp design appearing in virtually any position. Occasionally intentionally miscut cards are offered to the unsuspecting as errors. They are not errors and have no philatelic value.

FIPEX. May 4, 1956. Lithographed.

2c deep carmine & dark violet blue

UX44a	dark violet blue omitted	525.00
	with first day cancel	—
	used, dark violet blue omitted	600.00
	Quantity: n/a	

Artmaster and Farnham cachets exist on some first day canceled cards.

UX44e dark violet blue omitted, double impression
of deep carmine   *500.00*
Quantity: n/a

UX44g dark violet blue omitted from
rose pink variety   *750.00*
Quantity: n/a

The reddish area of the design on No. UX44g appears as rose pink
instead of deep carmine.

World Vacationland. August 30, 1963. Lithographed.

8c blue & red
UX49a blue omitted   *7,500.00*
Quantity: 3 reported

U.S. Customs. February 22, 1964. Lithographed.

4c red & blue
UX50a blue omitted   *550.00*
used entire, blue omitted   —
Quantity: n/a

UX50b red omitted   —
Quantity: n/a

Social Security. September 26, 1964. Lithographed.

4c dull blue & red
UX51a red omitted   —
Quantity: n/a

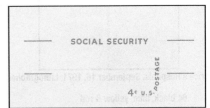

UX51b dull blue omitted   *625.00*
used, dull blue omitted   *625.00*
Quantity: n/a

U.S. Coast Guard. August 4, 1965. Lithographed.

4c blue & red
UX52a blue omitted   *4,000.00*
Quantity: 3 reported

Weather Services. September 1, 1970. Lithographed.

5c blue, yellow, red & black
UX57a yellow & black omitted   *1,250.00*
used, black & yellow omitted   *750.00*
Quantity: n/a

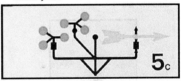

UX57b blue omitted   *750.00*
used entire, blue omitted   *5,000.00*
Quantity: rare

UX57c black omitted   *1,250.00*
used, black omitted   *850.00*
Quantity: n/a

America's Hospitals. September 16, 1971. Lithographed.

6c black, blue, yellow & red

UX60a   blue & yellow omitted   *1,000.00*
       Quantity: n/a

UX60b   yellow omitted   *500.00*
       Quantity: n/a

UX60c   red & black omitted   —
       Quantity: n/a

UX60d   red omitted   —
       Quantity: n/a

UX60f   black omitted   *3,500.00*
       Quantity: n/a

Figurehead. January 4, 1974. Lithographed.

12c black, yellow, magenta & blue

UX67a   yellow omitted   *1,000.00*
       Quantity: n/a

Federal Courthouse, Galveston, Texas. July 20, 1977. Lithographed.

9c black, yellow, magenta & cyan

UX71a   black omitted   *6,000.00*
       Quantity: very rare, possibly unique

George Rogers Clark, Vincennes, 1779

George Rogers Clark. February 3, 1979. Lithographed.

10c black, yellow, magenta & blue

UX78a   yellow omitted   —
       Quantity: n/a

Landing of Rochambeau, 1780

Rochambeau. July 11, 1980. Lithographed.

10c black, yellow, magenta & blue

UX84b   magenta & blue omitted   *3,000.00*
       Quantity: very rare, possibly unique

No. UX84 also exists normally printed on the front and with the additional printing of the colors black and yellow on the back. Value *$4,000.*

Nathanael Greene, Eutaw Springs, 1781

Eutaw Springs. September 8, 1981. Lithographed.

12c black, yellow, red & blue

UX90a   red & yellow omitted   *2,900.00*
       Quantity: 2-4 reported

Philadelphia Academy of Music. June 18, 1982. Lithographed.

13c brown, red & cream (buff paper)

UX96a   brown & cream omitted   *1,000.00*
       Quantity: 4 reported

Olympics. August 5, 1983. Lithographed.

13c black, blue, yellow & red

UX100a yellow & red omitted   *5,500.00*
Quantity: 1 unused; 1 used

▶ Caution. Expert certificate essential. At least one example
exists with deceptively faded yellow and red.

Rancho San Pedro. September 16, 1984. Lithographed.

13c black, blue, yellow, & magenta
UX104a black & blue omitted   *1,500.00*
Quantity: 5 reported

Buffalo. March 28, 1988. Lithographed.

15c black, yellow, magenta & blue
UX120a black omitted   *1,750.00*
Quantity: 2 reported

UX120d black & magenta omitted   *1,000.00*
Quantity: 3 reported

UX120e black, yellow & blue omitted   *1,250.00*
Quantity: 4 reported

UX120f black & blue omitted   *1,750.00*
Quantity: 1 reported

UX120g black, magenta & yellow omitted   *1,750.00*
Quantity: 4 reported

Yorkshire Packet. June 29, 1988. Lithographed.

28c black, yellow, magenta & blue
UX122a black & blue omitted   *850.00*
Quantity: 2 reported

UX122b black, blue & yellow omitted   *1,250.00*
Quantity: 1 reported

UX122c black & magenta omitted   *1,000.00*
Quantity: 4 reported

UX122d black, yellow & magenta omitted   *1,000.00*
Quantity: 4 reported

UX122e black omitted   *2,000.00*
Quantity: 2 reported

Settling of Ohio. July 15, 1988. Lithographed.

15c black, yellow, magenta & blue
UX124a black, blue & yellow omitted   *1,150.00*
Quantity: 1 reported

UX124b black & magenta omitted   *750.00*
Quantity: 4 reported

UX124c black & blue omitted   *900.00*
Quantity: 4 reported

UX124d black omitted   *2,000.00*
Quantity: 2 reported

UX124e black, magenta & yellow omitted   *1,500.00*
Quantity: 4 reported

Hearst Castle. September 20, 1988. Lithographed.

15c black, yellow, magenta & blue
UX125a black & magenta omitted   *750.00*
Quantity: 1 reported

UX125b black, blue & yellow   *2,000.00*
Quantity: 2 reported

UX125c black, magenta & yellow omitted   *1,000.00*
Quantity: 4 reported

UX125d black omitted   *2,000.00*
Quantity: 2 reported

UX125e black & blue omitted   *1,000.00*
Quantity: 4 reported

AIRMAIL POSTAL CARDS

Virgin Islands. March 31, 1967. Lithographed.

6c blue, yellow, black & red
UXC6a red & yellow omitted   *1,700.00*
Quantity: 2 reported

World Jamboree. August 4, 1967. Lithographed.

6c blue, yellow, black & magenta
UXC7a blue omitted   —
Quantity: very rare

UXC7b blue & black omitted   *7,500.00*
Quantity: 2-3 reported

UXC7c red & yellow omitted   *11,000.00*
Quantity: n/a

Eagle Weather Vane. January 4, 1974. Lithographed.

18c black, yellow, red & blue
UXC15b black & yellow omitted   *7,500.00*
Quantity: 1 reported

Angel Weathervane. December 17, 1975. Lithographed.

21c black, yellow, red & blue
UXC16a blue & red omitted   *7,500.00*
Quantity: 3 reported

BIRD HUNTING STAMPS

Refer to the Back Inscription Omitted section for additional bird hunting stamp errors.

Canvasbacks. July 1, 1982. Engraved, lithographed. BEP.

$7.50 black (engraved); green, violet, pale yellow & orange
RW49a orange & violet omitted   *10,000.00*
Quantity: 5 reported

▶ Caution. The orange and violet colors are fugitive when exposed to UV light or sunlight. Each of the colors bleaches at a different rate, creating a variety of ostensibly color-omitted errors. Bleached examples are abundant. Expert certificate is essential.

Cinnamon Teal. July 1, 1985. Engraved, lithographed. BEP.

$7.50 multicolored
RW52a light blue (litho) omitted *20,000.00*
       plate block of 4 .... —
       Quantity: 5

The error exists in three vertical strips of 6 (top stamp the error) and in a plate block of 12 (2x6, top 2 stamps the error).

Fulvous Whistling Duck. July 1, 1986. Engraved, lithographed. BEP.

$7.50 black (engraved); yellow, pale blue, brown, gray green & light gray
RW53a black (engraved) omitted *1,900.00*
       Quantity: 62

King Eiders. June 30, 1991. Engraved, lithographed. BEP.

$15 black (engraved); black, yellow, magenta & cyan (lithographed)
RW58a black (engraved) omitted *20,000.00*
       Quantity: 6-10 reported

Canvasbacks. June 30, 1993. Engraved, lithographed. BEP.

$15 black (engraved); black, yellow, magenta, cyan & tan (lithographed)
RW60a black (engraved) omitted *2,100.00*
       as above, used *1,500.00*
       Quantity: 120-150

Transition multiples exist with black partially omitted.

HOLOGRAM-OMITTED ERRORS

▶ Caution. Holograms are affixed to souvenir sheets with an adhesive. It may be possible to remove a hologram by dissolving the adhesive with a solvent. Therefore, caution is advised, and an expert certificate is strongly recommended.

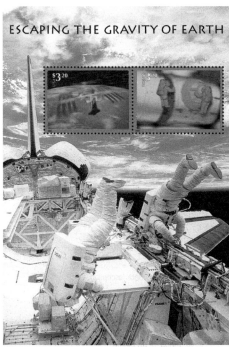

Earth. July 7, 2000. Circular pane of 1. Photogravure & hologram. SSP.

$11.75 multicolored & hologram
3412b   hologram omitted   —
        Quantity: 3-4 reported

Landing on the Moon. July 8, 2000. Souvenir sheet of 1. Photogravure & hologram. SSP.

$11.75 multicolored & hologram
3413d   hologram omitted   —
        Quantity: 1 reported

Escaping the Gravity of Earth. July 9, 2000. Souvenir sheet of 2. Photogravure & hologram. SSP.

$3.20 multicolored & hologram

a) Satellite with Solar Array   b) Astronaut EVA

3411c   hologram omitted from right stamp (b)   —
        Quantity: likely unique

A perforated pane of No. 3410 exists with hologram "b" erroneously affixed at top center. It sold at auction for $3,740 in October 2002.

X-Plane. March 17, 2006. Lithographed & hologram. Self-adhesive. Serpentine die cut. BCA.

    $4.05 multicolored & hologram "X"
4018a silver hologram "X" omitted   —
      Quantity: 8

▶ Caution. Stamps with partially omitted "X" exist.

BACK-INSCRIPTION ERRORS

BACK INSCRIPTION OMITTED

> **YOUTHFUL HEROINE**
> On the dark night of April 26, 1777,
> 16-year-old Sybil Ludington rode
> her horse "Star" alone through the
> Connecticut countryside rallying
> her father's militia io repel a
> raid by the British on Danbury.
> Back Inscription

Sybil Ludington. March 25, 1975. Photogravure. BEP.

    8c multicolored, green back inscription
1559a back inscription omitted   *110.00*
      Quantity: 100-150

▶ Caution. Green back Inscription is printed in partially water-soluble ink. Used examples without expert certificates should be regarded with suspicion.

> **GALLANT SOLDIER**
> The conspicuously courageous
> actions of black foot soldier
> Salem Poor at the Battle of
> Bunker Hill on June 17, 1775,
> earned him citations for his
> bravery and leadership ability.
> Back Inscription

Salem Poor. March 25, 1975. Photogravure. BEP.

    10c multicolored, green back inscription
1560a back inscription omitted   *110.00*
      Quantity: 300+ reported

▶ Caution. Refer to note following No. 1559a.

> **FINANCIAL HERO**
> Businessman and broker Haym
> Salomon was responsible for
> raising most of the money
> needed to finance the American
> Revolution and later to save
> the new nation from collapse.
> Back Inscription

Haym Salomon. March 25, 1975. Photogravure. BEP.

    10c multicolored; green back inscription
1561a back inscription omitted   *110.00*
      as above, used single   —
      Quantity: 400+ reported

▶ Caution. Refer to note following No. 1559a.

[Olympics se-tenant pane of 20 with back inscription quotes and event descriptions]

"What is important in the Olympic Games is not winning, but taking part. What is important in life is not the triumph, but the struggle."

Olympics. May 2, 1996. Se-tenant pane of 20. Photogravure. SVS.

32c multicolored; black back inscription

3068v pane of 20, back inscription
omitted on the leftmost vertical row
of stamps (positions 1, 6, 11 & 16) —
Quantity: unique

No. 3068v is due to a shift in printing of the back inscriptions so that the description for "Decathlon" (the top leftmost stamp) is shifted right one stamp and appears on the back of the "Men's Canoeing" stamp (the second stamp from the left on the top row). Each of the 16 non-inscription-omitted stamps contains a shifted inscription.

Richard P. Feynman
(1918-1988)
developed a new formulation of quantum theory based, in part, on diagrams he invented to help him visualize the dynamics of atomic particles. In 1965, this noted theoretical physicist, enthusiastic educator, and amateur artist was awarded the Nobel Prize in Physics.

John von Neumann
(1903-1957)
made significant contributions in both pure and applied mathematics, especially in the areas of quantum mechanics, game theory, and computer theory and design. In 1956, the U.S. government presented the Enrico Fermi Award to this eminent mathematician.

Josiah Willard Gibbs
(1839-1903)
formulated the modern system of thermodynamic analysis. For this and other extraordinary achievements, Gibbs received some of the most prestigious awards of his era, including the Rumford Prize from the American Academy of Arts and Sciences.

Barbara McClintock
(1902-1992)
conducted maize plant research that led to her discovery of genetic transposition—the movement of genetic material within and between chromosomes. In 1983, this pioneering geneticist was awarded the Nobel Prize in Physiology or Medicine.

American Scientists. May 4, 2005. Se-tenant pane of 20. Lithographed. Self-adhesive. Serpentine die cut. BCA.

37c multicolored

a) Barbara McClintock
b) Josiah Willard Gibbs
c) John von Neumann
d) Richard Feynman

3909c block or hz strip of 4, back
inscription omitted —
Quantity: 1 pane reported

Super Heroes. July 20, 2006. Se-tenant pane of 20. Photogravure. Self-adhesive. Serpentine die cut. AVR.

39c multicolored

4084u pane of 20, back inscription omitted *2,000.00*
Quantity: 1 pane reported

BIRD HUNTING STAMPS

▶ Caution. Back inscriptions are printed on top of the gum. Beware of regummed examples offered as inscription-omitted errors. It is possible to simulate this type of error by washing gum off (along with the inscription) then regumming a stamp. Expert certificate strongly advised.

DUCK STAMP DOLLARS
BUY WETLANDS
FOR WATERFOWL.

IT IS UNLAWFUL TO HUNT
WATERFOWL UNLESS YOU
SIGN YOUR NAME IN INK
ON THE FACE OF THIS STAMP.

Back Inscription

Pintails. July 1, 1962. Engraved, lithographed. BEP.

$3 multicolored

RW29a back inscription omitted —
Quantity: Unique

BUY DUCK STAMPS
SAVE WETLANDS

SEND IN ALL BIRD BANDS

SIGN YOUR DUCK STAMP

Back Inscription

Hooded Mergansers. July 1, 1968. Engraved, lithographed. BEP.

$3 multicolored

RW35a back inscription omitted —
Quantity: unique

Wood Ducks. June 30, 1974. Engraved, lithographed. BEP.

$5 multicolored

RW41a   back inscription omitted   4,750.00
        Quantity: unique

The error stamp is the upper left stamp in an upper left plate block
of four and results from a foldover in which the back inscription is
partially printed on the front.

> TAKE PRIDE IN AMERICA
> BUY DUCK STAMPS
> SAVE WETLANDS
> •
> SEND IN ALL BIRD BANDS
> •
> SIGN YOUR DUCK STAMPS
> IT IS UNLAWFUL TO HUNT WATERFOWL OR USE THIS STAMP
> AS A NATIONAL WILDLIFE ENTRANCE PASS UNLESS YOU
> SIGN YOUR NAME IN INK ON THE FACE OF THIS STAMP
> Back Inscription

**Black Bellied Whistling Duck. June 30, 1990. Engraved,
lithographed. BEP.**

$12.50 multicolored

RW57a   back inscription omitted   300.00
        plate block   —
        Quantity: 150, including 3 plate blocks

> INVEST IN AMERICA'S FUTURE
> BUY DUCK STAMPS AND
> SAVE WETLANDS
> _____
> SEND IN OR REPORT ALL
> BIRD BANDS TO
> 1-800-327-BAND
>
> IT IS UNLAWFUL TO HUNT WATERFOWL OR USE THIS STAMP
> AS A PASS TO A NATIONAL WILDLIFE REFUGE UNLESS
> YOU SIGN YOUR NAME IN INK ON THE FACE OF THIS STAMP.
> Back Inscription

Snow Geese. June 30, 2003. Water activated gum. APU.

$15 multicolored

RW70c   back inscription omitted   4,500.00
        Quantity: 12 reported

BACK INSCRIPTION INVERTED

Back inscriptions are normally oriented with the top of the
inscription at the top of a stamp. Inverted inscriptions appear to
be upside down when turning a stamp in the same fashion as
turning the page of a book.

Blue Geese. July 1, 1955. Engraved. BEP.

$2 dark blue

RW22a   back inscription inverted   5,500.00
        used, back inscription inverted   4,500.00
        Quantity: 2 mint, 1 used

The used (signed) example possesses partial original gum, which
allows the error to be authenticated. Refer to the note preceeding
No. RW29a in the preceeding section regarding gum.

American Eiders. July 1, 1957. Engraved. BEP.

$2 emerald

RW24a   back inscription inverted   5,000.00
        Quantity: 6-8

Labrador Retriever & Mallard. July 1, 1959. Engraved,
lithographed. BEP.

$3 multicolored

RW26a   back inscription inverted   27,500.00
        as above, used   15,000.00
        Quantity: 2 reported

INVERT ERRORS

In this section, centers are described as inverted, without regard to the order in which the plates were printed. The visual relationship of design elements to one another is the most convenient way to describe an error: the inverted Jenny, the inverted candle flame, etc.

NOTE. Prices for classic errors vary widely according to condition and may be substantially higher or lower than values listed.

Columbus Landing. 1869. Engraved.

15c brown & blue

119b	center inverted	1,000,000.00
	used, center inverted	22,500.00
	Quantity: 3 unused (1 with original gum, 2 without gum); 87-88 used	

Used examples almost always contain faults. Used value is for an example with faults; sound examples sell for a premium of 100% or more. An unused example, reported to be the finest known, sold at auction for $920,000 in October 2013.

119c	used, center double printed, one inverted	80,000.00
	Quantity: 3 used examples	

One stamp is quite faulty and extensively repaired. Value is for the finer of the two sound examples.

Declaration of Independence. April 7, 1869. Engraved.

24c green & violet

120b	center inverted	750,000.00
	used, center inverted	37,500.00
	used pair, centers inverted	110,000.00
	used block of 4, centers inverted	737,500.00
	used on cover	130,000.00
	Quantity: 4 unused; 85-90 used	

Used examples usually contain faults. Value is for an example with faults. Sound examples sell for a premium of 100% or more. Of the unused examples, one is sound and three are faulty. The sound example sold for $1,271,250 in February 2008. The example on cover is unique. No. 120b also exists misperfed.

One hundred sets of plate proofs on card of the 1869 Series (15c, 24c, 30c & 90c) exist with centers inverted. The 90c value exists as an invert in proof form only. Market value per set of 4 single proofs is $7,500-$10,000. Plate blocks exist: 24c, two plate blocks of 8; 30c, one plate block of 4 and one plate block of 8; 90c, two plate blocks of 8.

Eagle and Shield. May 15, 1869. Engraved.

30c ultramarine & carmine

121b	flags inverted	750,000.00
	used, flags inverted	90,000.00
	Quantity: 7 unused, 37-40 used	

Almost all examples contain faults. Only 3 sound examples are known. Used value is for an example with faults; sound examples sell for a premium of 100% or more. The unused example valued above is reported to be the finest example extant.

Steamship. May 1, 1901. Engraved.

1c green & black

294a	center inverted	12,500.00
	block of 4, centers inverted	75,000.00
	bottom margin strip of 4 with plate No. 1139	167,500.00
	used, center inverted	25,000.00
	used pair, centers inverted	—
	used on cover	—
	Quantity: 250+; 3 used on cover	

Typically, unused examples are poorly centered, have disturbed gum and small faults. Value is for an example with typical small faults. Sound examples sell for a premium ranging from 100% to 300% or more. A nice unused example sold at auction for $34,500 in October 2013. A particularly fine used example sold at auction for $51,750 in June 2008. The used pair may be unique.

Train. May 1, 1901. Engraved.

2c carmine & black

295a	center inverted	50,000.00
	used, center inverted	55,000.00
	intact block of 4	900,000.00
	Quantity: 75-85 unused; 7 used; 2 blocks of 4 listed above	

Both unused and used examples almost always contain faults. Value is for an example with faults; sound examples sell for a premium of 100% or more. A select unused example sold at auction for $218,500 in October 2013.

Antique Automobile. May 1, 1901. Engraved.

4c deep red brown & black

296a	center inverted	85,000.00
	block of 4, centers inverted	400,000.00
	plate strip of 4	450,000.00
	Quantity: 97	

Usually encountered with small faults or disturbed gum (from being stuck down to a Post Office archive book prior to dispersal). Value is for an example with usual small faults. Fault free examples sell for a premium ranging from 100% to 300%. A particularly choice unused example with bottom plate No. 1145 sold at auction for $149,500 in October 2013.

296a-S	center inverted and with SPECIMEN overprint	11,500.00
	Quantity: 106	

Distributed by the Third Assistant Postmaster General and marked with the word "Specimen." Additional examples were traded by the National Museum for stamps needed for their collection. Most examples with "Specimen" overprint are centered toward the bottom. Often with disturbed gum or small faults. Catalogue value is for an example with small faults; fault-free examples sell for a premium of 50%-200% or more.

Dag Hammarskjold. October 23, 1962. Engraved.

4c black, brown & yellow

1203a	yellow background inverted, used on first day cover postmarked New York, NY, October 23, 1962	3,000.00
	used on cover postmarked Brooklyn, NY, Vanderveer Sta., October 26, 1962	2,000.00
	used on cover postmarked Cuyahoga Falls, November 14, 1962	—
	pane of 50, signed per note below	—
	Quantity: 25-30 FDCs; see note	

The pane of 50 discovered by Leonard Sherman was signed in its margin by ten well-known philatelists, among them George W. Linn, Leo August and Ernest A. Kehr. It was donated to the American Philatelic Society in 1987 by Mr. and Mrs. Sherman and remains in the society's possession. The covers machine-postmarked Cuyahoga Falls, Ohio, November 14, 1962, are notarized in the lower left corner by George W. Swartz, Notary Public.

After the discovery of the Hammarskjold error, the government reissued the stamp, intentionally inverting the yellow. Inverted examples of No. 1203 are identical to the re-issued stamp (No. 1204, issued November 16, 1962). Aside from the autographed discovery pane, the only positive way to identify the actual error is by use on cover postmarked prior to November 16, 1962.

First day covers are on uncacheted, unaddressed covers bearing a New York, NY, "First Day of Issue" hand-cancel slogan postmark. Forty-two first day covers are reported to have been made; however, some are thought to have been lost. First day covers bearing Artmaster cachets were contrived using examples of No. 1204.

▶ Caution. Faked first day covers exist made by substituting used examples of No. 1204 for No. 1203 on first day covers of No. 1203. Expert certificate absolutely essential.

Candle Holder. July 2, 1979. Engraved, lithographed. BEP.

$1 brown (engraved); orange, yellow & tan (lithographed)

1610c	candle flame inverted	17,000.00
	as above, white vertical stripe	17,000.00
	block of 4, candle flame inverted	70,000.00
	ZIP block of 4, candle flame inverted	77,750.00
	Quantity: 95	

The discovery pane contained 95 error stamps, including eight white-stripe varieties. Five stamps from the pane had been used before its discovery and are presumed to be lost to philately.

Washington Crossing the Delaware
From a Painting by Emanuel Leutze / Eastman Johnson

Washington Crossing the Delaware. May 29, 1976. Souvenir sheet of 5. Lithographed. BEP.

24c multicolored

1688k	white (USA 24c) on "d" & "e" inverted	12,500.00
	Quantity: 2 reported	

Note. The 24c and 31c souvenir sheets of the Bicentennial issue exist with perforations inverted in relation to the design.

Examples of the 32c Nixon stamp with the lithographed portion of its design (Nixon's bust and the denomination) inverted in relation to the engraved (Richard Nixon) legend found their way onto the marketplace in 1996, having been stolen by an employee of one of the printing plants. The employee was subsequently arrested, tried and convicted of theft of government property. The Postal Service ordered all "inverts" seized; however, one or two examples are not accounted for.

Stock Market. May 17, 1992. Engraved, lithographed. ABN.

29c black (engraved); green & red lithographed

2630c	black center vignettes inverted	*17,000.00*
	pair, 2630c & 2630b	*22,500.00*
	Quantity: 56	

The 56 examples of No. 2630c arise from 2 panes, one in the lower left position and one in the lower right position. Each pane also contains 12 examples with black center omitted (No. 2630b, which appears in the Color Omitted section). The discovery pane (LR position) sold at auction for $488,750 in June 2002 and has since been broken up. A second pane (LL position) sold at auction for $373,750 in November 2005.

AIR MAIL

Biplane. May 13, 1918. Engraved. BEP.

24c carmine rose & blue

C3a	center inverted	*450,000.00*
	block of 4, centers inverted	*2,000,000.00*
	center line block, centers inverted	*2,000,000.00*
	margin block of 4 with blue plate	
	number	*5,000,000.00*
	Quantity: 100	

Market prices for this stamp vary substantially according to condition. Each example must be valued according to its merits. The finest graded example (extra fine-superb 95) sold for $1,351,250 in May 2016. A never-hinged example, graded extra fine 90, sold for $1,593,000 in November 2018.

In 2013, the Postal Service issued a reprint of the famous inverted Jenny (No. C3a) in a souvenir sheet of six stamps (No. 4806). At the same time, they issued 100 sheets with the aircraft in its normal flying position (No. 4806d). The "uninverted inverts" were distributed randomly to postal outlets in sealed packets that were outwardly identical to the regularly issued stamp. Despite the fact that they differ from the issued inverts, they are not errors because they were intentionally issued, whereas true errors are unintentionally released.

POSTAL CARD INVERTS

Olympics 1984. April 30, 1984. Lithographed.

13c black, blue, yellow & magenta

UX102a	yellow & black inverted & to the	
	left of basic design	*7,000.00*
	Quantity: 5 reported	

REVENUE STAMP INVERTS

Revenue stamps exist with pen cancels, metal or rubber stamp cancels, and various types of cut cancels. Catalogue values are for canceled examples with small faults unless otherwise noted. Market prices vary widely according to condition. Faults are endemic; sound examples are the exception.

▶ Caution. Deceptive forgeries exist.

Internal Revenue. September 1871. Engraved.

1c blue & black

R103a	center inverted	*1,600.00*
	pair, centers inverted	*3,500.00*
	block of 4, centers inverted	—
	Quantity: n/a	

Internal Revenue. September 1871. Engraved.

2c blue & black
R104a center inverted — 5,000.00
pair, centers inverted — —
block of 4, centers inverted — —
Quantity: 35

Internal Revenue. September 1871. Engraved.

5c blue & black
R107a center inverted — 4,000.00
Quantity: 42

Internal Revenue. September 1871. Engraved.

10c blue & black
R109a center inverted — 2,000.00
pair, centers inverted — 5,250.00
Quantity: 52 singles; 1 pair

Internal Revenue. September 1871. Engraved.

20c blue & black
R111a center inverted — 8,000.00
pair, centers inverted — 17,000.00
Quantity: 13 singles; 1 pair

Internal Revenue. September 1871. Engraved.

25c blue & black
R112a center inverted — 13,000.00
Quantity: 17 singles

Internal Revenue. September 1871. Engraved.

50c blue & black
R115a center inverted — 1,050.00
pair, centers inverted — 2,750.00
on document — 1,750.00
2 singles on piece — 1,850.00
Quantity: singles scarce; 5 pairs

Value for an example with cut cancel, $650.

Internal Revenue. September 1871. Engraved.

70c blue & black

R117a   center inverted   *4,000.00*
        Quantity: 27

Value for an example with cut cancel, $1,250.

Internal Revenue. September 1871. Engraved.

$1 blue & black

R118a   center inverted   *6,000.00*
        Quantity: 60

Value for an example with cut cancel, $1,500.

Internal Revenue. September 1871. Engraved.

$5 blue & black

R127a   center inverted   *3,000.00*
        Quantity: approximately 40

Value for an example with cut cancel, $1,500.

Internal Revenue. November 1871. Engraved.

2c orange & black

R135b   center inverted   425.00
        pair, centers inverted   *1,850.00*
        block of 4, centers inverted   *4,250.00*
        block of 6, centers inverted   *7,250.00*
        vertical strip of 5 with right
          margin imprint   *7,600.00*
        Quantity: several hundred including
          2 pairs and 3 blocks of 4

Internal Revenue. December 1871. Engraved.

5c orange & black
R137a   center inverted   *5,000.00*
        L-shaped block of 3 on
          partial check   *15,000.00*
        Quantity: 17 singles; 3 on document

Internal Revenue. January 1872. Engraved.

15c brown & black

R139a	center inverted	*16,000.00*
	pair, center inverted LRS (6/09)	*15,000.00*
	Quantity: 13 singles; 1 pair	

The used pair has average centering and has manuscript and waffle-iron grid cancels.

Internal Revenue. January 1872. Engraved.

30c orange & black

R140a	center inverted	*3,500.00*
	Quantity: approximately 36	

Value for an example with cut cancel, $1,750.

Internal Revenue. January 1872. Engraved.

$1 green & black

R144a	center inverted	*12,500.00*
	block of 4 on full document	*85,000.00*
	single on document	*11,500.00*
	Quantity: 21-22; the 2 examples on document listed above	

Value is for an example with cut cancel, $10,000.

Internal Revenue. January 1872. Engraved.

$2.50 claret & black

R146a	center inverted	*22,500.00*
	Quantity: 14	

Internal Revenue. October 1874. Engraved.

2c orange & black (green paper)

R151a	center inverted	800.00
	hz pair	1,750.00
	block of 4	—
	Quantity: several hundred; 3 blocks of 4	

Internal Revenue - Proprietary. Engraved.

1c green & black

RB1ad	center inverted (violet paper)	*5,250.00*
	Quantity: 23-24	

Internal Revenue - Proprietary. Engraved.

2c green & black

RB2ac	center inverted (violet paper)	*40,000.00*
	Quantity: 2	
RB2bc	center inverted (green paper)	*8,000.00*
	Quantity: 12-14	

Internal Revenue - Proprietary. Engraved.

3c green & black

RB3ad   center inverted (violet paper)   *14,000.00*
        Quantity: 7 (all are faulty)

Internal Revenue - Proprietary. Engraved.

4c green & black

RB4ac   center inverted (violet paper)   *15,000.00*
        Quantity: 7 (6 of which are faulty)

Internal Revenue - Proprietary. Engraved.

5c green & black

RB5ac   center inverted (violet paper)   *155,000.00*
        Quantity: unique

PRINTER'S WASTE

Printer's waste refers to error-like items that have reached the market through the back door rather than across a post office counter. An error sold across the counter is deemed legitimate. Printer's waste is not. The term "printer's waste" implies that is was misappropriated from a printing plant or wastepaper destruction facility and illicitly sold into the hobby. The term invariably carries a negative connotation. Most collectors do not consider printer's waste to be errors—and rightly so, because they are not.

Beginning in the late 1980s and lasting until the mid-1990s, a surprising amount of printer's waste surfaced for issues printed by private subcontractors. Not all of it reached the marketplace right away, and so-called "newly discovered" items from that period continue to surface. They are invariably touted as "rare," but in reality there is no way of knowing how many exist. It is prudent to take such claims with a grain of salt. Many, but not all, so-called "newly discovered errors" from that period are printer's waste and contain telltale mishandling faults or fingerprints on gum.

George Washington. January 22, 1903. Engraved.

    2c carmine
301   margin single, imperf   —
    Quantity: 4

Without gum and typically faulty. Four examples are known: an upper right margin single, a lower left margin single, a lower right margin single, and a bottom margin single.

George Washington. April 14, 1912. Engraved. BEP.

    7c black
407   imperf block of 7   —
    Quantity: unique

The block is irregular and missing parts of 3 stamps. It is without gum and contains creases. It sold at auction for $23,000 in October 2007.

The 1½c, 2c, 4c, 5c, 6c and 8c denominations of the 1922-23 series exist imperforate with various degrees of smearing or underinking. They are the result of impressions made during the cleaning of printing plates with solvent and are reported to have originally come on the market from a waste paper company. They are not recognized as postage stamps. They are mentioned here as a matter of record only.

U.S. Flag. May 10, 1971. Coil. Engraved. BEP.

8c dark blue, red & slate green

1338G   imperf pane   —
         Quantity: n/a

The pane contains plate Nos. 32974 and 32808, which were used only to print coil stamps. The only way it can exist in pane form is as printer's waste.

Apollo 8. May 5, 1969. Engraved. BEP.

6c multicolored

1371   imperf pair   —
         Quantity: 50 pairs

Pairs have traded in the marketplace in the $1,500-$2,000 range.

Dwight D. Eisenhower. January 28, 1972. Booklet pane. Engraved.

8c deep claret

1395   block of 4 (incl label "Use Zip Code"),
           imperf hz between   —
         booklet pane of 7 + 1 label,
           imperf hz between   —
         Quantity: n/a

The label "Use Zip Code" appears at the bottom left corner on normal booklet panes. Printer's waste of No. 1395 occurs from press sheets or partial press sheets of perforated booklet panes that were separated along the perforations instead of being cut apart in the normal places. Error pairs resulting from a foldover exist; see No. 1395e in the Imperforates section.

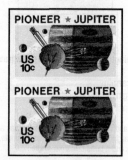

Pioneer Jupiter. February 28, 1975. Engraved, lithographed. BEP.

10c multicolored

1556   imperf pair   —
         Quantity: 50 pairs

Pairs have traded in the marketplace in the $1,500-$2,500 range.

Collective Bargaining. March 13, 1975. Photogravure. BEP.

10c multicolored

1558   imperf pair   100.00
         Quantity: n/a

Recent auction prices have been in the $50 range.

Apollo-Soyuz. July 15, 1975. Se-tenant pair. Photogravure. BEP.

10c multicolored

a) Spacecraft & Globe
b) Spacecraft & Emblem

1569-1570
imperf pair —
Quantity: 10 pairs reported, but more
may exist

All known pairs are faulty and without gum.

Liberty Bell. October 31, 1975. Booklet pane. Engraved. BEP.

13c brown
1595 booklet pane of 7 + 1 label —
vrt pair, imperf between —
Quantity: scarce

These so-called error booklet panes and pairs were separated from uncut sheets along perforations instead of being severed in the normal fashion along the imperforate space between panes. Hence, the panes contain perforations all around the outside edges. The slogan label on printer's waste panes appears at lower left rather than upper left, where it would normally appear. Value for pairs: $35-$50. A few vertical pairs, imperforate between, result from foldovers. They are listed as No. 1595e.

Roses. July 11, 1978. Booklet pane of 8. Engraved. BEP.

15c multicolored
1737 imperf vrt pair —
Quantity: n/a

This item possesses selvage at top, an oversized margin at bottom, and the rose color is partially omitted.

Benjamin Bannecker. February 15, 1980. Photogravure. ABN.

15c multicolored
1804 imperf pair —
Quantity: 500+ pairs

Richard Russell. May 31, 1984. Engraved. BEP.

10c Prussian blue
1853 imperf pair —
imperf strip of 3 used on cover —
Quantity: at least 10 pairs
and likely more

▶ Both tagged and untagged imperf examples of No. 1853 are known. Both types are printer's waste.

American Wildlife. March 15, 1981. Se-tenant booklet pane of 10. Engraved. BEP.

18c dark brown

1880-1889

imperf pair —
Quantity: n/a

Se-tenant pairs exist with images of various animals transposed. For example, on a normal pair the elk would appear at left and the moose at right. On the illustrated example, the positions are reversed.

Flag & Seashore. April 24, 1981. Coil. Engraved. BEP.

18c red, blue & brown

1891   vertical pair, imperf —
block of 4, imperf
Quantity: n/a

Family Unity. October 1, 1984. Photogravure. BEP.

20c multicolored

2104   imperf single, untagged, used —
Quantity: very rare

This item arises from the theft of imperfectly prepared stamps taken by employees of a contractor responsible for hauling away spoiled accountable paper from the Bureau of Engraving and Printing for destruction. The employees were caught and most of the stolen items recovered.

▶ Caution. Beware of tagged used singles trimmed to resemble imperforates.

Pheasant. April 29, 1988. Booklet pane of 10. Engraved, lithographed. ABN.

25c multicolored

2283   vrt pair, imperf between —
Quantity: several hundred

See also No. 2283d in the Imperforates section, which occurs as the result of a foldover. Non-foldover pairs and multiples are printer's waste and common. Value: $25-$35.

2283   vrt pair, imperf hz —
booklet pane, imperf hz —
Quantity: several hundred

▶ Caution. Be aware that vertical pairs or blocks imperforate horizontally can be fabricated by trimming perforations from the top and bottom of printer's waste that is imperforate between. Value: $25-$35.

2283   imperf vertical pair —
Quantity: several hundred

▶ Caution. Be aware that imperforate vertical pairs can be fabricated by trimming exterior perforations from printer's waste that is imperforate between. Value: $25-$35.

William Faulkner. August 3, 1987. Engraved. BEP.

22c green

2350   imperf single, untagged, used —
Quantity: rare

▶ Caution. Beware of tagged used singles trimmed to resemble imperforates. Exists tagged and untagged.

Montana. January 15, 1989. Engraved, lithographed. BEP.

25c multicolored

2401   imperf pair, without gum —
Quantity: a few hundred pairs

All known examples are without gum. Value: $25-$35. At least one block of 4 exists with the postmark "First Day of Issue." It is contrived.

Boat. August 8, 1991. Coil. Photogravure. ABN.

19c multicolored

2529	imperf pair with gum	—
	imperf pair without gum	—
	imperf strip with plate No. A1112	—
	imperf strip with plate No. A7767	—
	Quantity: few thousand pairs	

Exists drastically miscut with printer's registration marks and color bars at bottom. Pairs and strips from plate number A1112 are without gum and exhibit moisture damage. Pairs without gum sell for $10-$20. Pairs with gum sell for $15-$25. Plate strips bearing No. A7767 sell at auction in the $100 range.

Switzerland. February 22, 1991. Photogravure. ABN.

50c multicolored

2532	imperf pair	—
	Quantity: not yet established	

Express Mail. June 16, 1991. Engraved, lithographed. ABN.

$9.95 multicolored

2541	imperf pair, black omitted	—
	Quantity: n/a	

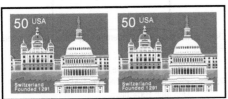

Express Mail. June 16, 1991. Engraved, lithographed. ABN.

$14 red (engraved); black, yellow, magenta & cyan (lithographed)

2542	imperf pair, red (engraved) omitted	—
	Quantity: n/a	

Imperforate examples may exist with one or more colors other than red omitted.

Fishing Flies. May 31, 1991. Booklet pane of 5. Photogravure. ABN.

29c multicolored

a) Royal Wulff
b) Jock Scott
c) Apte Tarpon Fly
d) Lefty's Deceiver
e) Muddler Minnow

2547	hz pair, imperf vrt	—
	two panes of 5, imperf vrt	—
	Quantity: n/a	

Desert Storm. July 2, 1991. Booklet pane of 5. Photogravure. ABN.

29c multicolored

2552	vrt pair, imperf hz	—
	Quantity: n/a	

No. 2552 measures 21½mm wide and can thus be distinguished from the sheet stamp error No. 2551a, which measures 21mm wide.

Santa in Chimney. October 17, 1991. Booklet pane of 4. Photogravure. ABN.

(29c) multicolored

2581	booklet pane, imperf	—
	Quantity: n/a	

Santa & Package. October 17, 1991. Booklet pane of 4. Photogravure. ABN.

(29c) multicolored

2583	booklet pane, imperf	—
	Quantity: n/a	

Santa & Sack. October 17, 1991. Booklet pane of 4. Photogravure. ABN.

(29c) multicolored

2584	booklet pane, imperf	—
	Quantity: n/a	

Santa & Sleigh. October 17, 1991. Booklet pane of 4. Photogravure. ABN.

(29c) multicolored

2585	booklet pane, imperf	—
	Quantity: n/a	

Love. February 14, 1994. Booklet pane of 10. Photogravure. ABN.

29c multicolored

2814	hz pair, imperf between	—
	Quantity: n/a	

Exists in unusual multiples. The exact number extant is not known; however, the item appears at auction with some regularity.

Dove, G Make-Up Rate. December 13, 1994. Lithographed. ABN.

(3c) tan, bright blue & red

2877	imperf pair, bright blue omitted	—
	Quantity: 100+ pairs	

▶ Some exist with traces of blue.

OFFICIAL STAMPS

Official Mail. May 24, 1991. Pane of 100. Lithographed. BEP.

23c red, blue & black

0148	imperf pair	—
	block of 4, imperf	—
	plate block of 4, imperf	—
	Quantity: several hundred pairs	

Imperforate gutter pairs and blocks exist. Perforated gutter pairs and blocks also exist and are printer's waste. Imperforate pairs have sold at auction in the $13-$25 range.

BIRD HUNTING STAMPS

Mallards. July 1934. Engraved. BEP.

$1 blue

RW1   vrt pair, imperf — \
       vrt pair with plate No. 129199 — \
       vrt strip of three, imperf — \
       imperf single — \
       Quantity: 28 stamps \
       vrt block of 8, imperf hz — \
       Quantity: unique

It is almost certain that examples of No. RW1 offered as imperforate vertical pairs or as vertical pairs imperforate horizontally are from printer's waste. Additionally, it is almost certain that all imperforate vertical pairs are pairs imperforate horizontally that have had the vertical perforations trimmed off. No horizontal imperforate pairs are known. All recorded pairs are vertical, with narrow side margins. Most examples exist without gum and with faults. Some pairs have gum on the front (which in some cases appears to have been removed).

The stamps imperforate vertically are recorded as a unique vertical block of eight, with the other recorded varieties being the manufactured imperforate vertical pairs.

FREAKS, ODDITIES & OTHER UNUSUAL STAMPS

Tens of thousands of imperfectly prepared stamps exist. Flawed stamps are a normal part of stamp production. It is called "waste" and security printers make every effort to detect and destroy it. But with literally billions of stamps being produced, some will inevitably get out. What causes waste? Equipment does not always work perfectly. When it starts and stops, waste is created. People are fallible and people operate the presses, perforators, booklet forming machines, etc. The miracle is that there is so little that escapes. Imperfections make them unusual in appearance—often strikingly so. Some fall into the major error category. Others, containing irregularities such as misaligned perforations or color(s), paper folds or creases, overinking or underinking, and so forth, are commonly referred to as freaks. They are far too numerous to list or price individually. Even a reasonably modest discussion of freaks could easily fill a book. What follows is a generalized overview of the most commonly encountered types together with a few representative illustrations and some basic price guidelines.

Because so many freaks are unique, and because no reliable population statistics exist for the rest, rarity is often not the primary factor in pricing. Visual appeal and topical appeal are most often the key elements in pricing freaks. The element of scarcity comes more into play in pricing non-unique freaks, where a definite quantity is known. The best way to get a handle on the prices of freaks is to check retail price lists for comparables, study prices realized from public auctions, and talk to dealers and collectors.

Collecting freaks is one of the most fascinating areas of philately. A growing number of collectors find their peculiar appearance irresistible. And in a day and age where the Postal Service is flooding the market with hundreds of new issues whose primary—and often sole—purpose is to boost revenue, many find it appealing to collect the very items that the Postal Service goes to such great lengths to keep from the public—improperly prepared stamps. There is something magical about owning the uncommon and the offbeat, about owning something few others own or choose to appreciate.

To the uninitiated the distinction between major errors and freaks is not always clear or logical. Historically, the way in which an error was created had a lot to do with how it was regarded. Major errors generally were considered to be the result of a complete omission of one of the steps of production (for example, perforations or color), the unintentional reversal of a sheet passing through the printing press (i.e., an invert), or the use of the wrong color ink to print a stamp. Freaks were generally considered to be the result of random flukes in production, for example misperfs, foldovers, misregistrations of color, smears, underinking or overinking, odd shades resulting from ink-fountain contamination and so forth, and not deemed as important or as valuable as major errors.

Before the 1960s, major errors surfaced rarely—only a handful of inverts, a couple of color-omitted stamps, and precious few imperfs during the previous hundred years. Discovery of a new major error became a celebrated event. Collectors prized them for their rarity and value, and stamp catalogues accorded them individual recognition. By contrast, freaks—although never common—turned up much more frequently but were largely ignored by mainstream philately, which regarded them as little more than curiosities. Their sheer number and randomness of physical appearance made impossible any attempt to individually record each one or form a comprehensive collection.

Since the late 1960s, hundreds of new imperforates and color-omitted errors have been discovered. The newfound abundance of major errors spawned a phenomenal rise in the popularity of error collecting and all types of error material—both major errors and freaks. Freaks have come into their own, and are now seriously studied, collected and appreciated by a growing number of error enthusiasts.

Despite attempts to precisely define categories for errors and freaks, gray areas inevitably crop up. Some items, by their very nature, defy easy classification. And among stamp catalogue editors, differences of opinion and philosophy exist. It seems that in the taxonomy of EFOs, there is always room for question about which phylum, class, order, family, genus or species an item belongs. Differences of opinion regarding nomenclature also exist (i.e., what should properly be called an error, a variety, a freak, and so forth). The foregoing is mentioned for the benefit of those new to the hobby, who may find all this confusing and difficult to understand at first. In the final analysis, definitions and classification should never be allowed to stand in the way of appreciating an error for what it is—something unusual, intriguing, and exquisite in its own right. And many freaks are arguably as eye-arresting and fascinating as major errors. Beauty—as the old saying goes—truly lies in the eye of the beholder.

The website of the Errors, Freaks, & Oddities Collectors' Club (www.efocc.org) is an excellent resource for those who want to learn more about this field. It includes a listing of what material fits under each category, detailed explanations of how EFO material can be created, and links to useful EFO literature.

MISPERFS

Misperfs (misperforated, also known as misplaced perforations, also used to refer to misplaced die cuts) and perforation shifts occur when stamps are misaligned with perforating or die-cutting equipment or when part of a sheet of stamps (typically, a corner) has been folded over during production (see **foldovers**). Misset rows of perforating pins also can cause misperfs. They can occur on any perforated or die-cut stamp: sheet stamps, coil stamps, and booklet panes. Misperforated commemorative stamps are generally priced higher than misperforated

definitive stamps, and misperforated sheet definitives are generally (but not always) priced higher than misperforated coil stamps. Too many misperfs exist to list individually or attempt to price. Value is generally a function of topical appeal and degree of misperforation. Usually, the more visually striking (the more severe or unusual the misplacement of perforations) and topically popular an item, the greater its relative value.

Misperfs range from barely misaligned to dramatically misaligned, as illustrated by the two coil stamps shown here. The 25-cent flag coil is only slightly misperfed; the 10-cent crossed-flag coil is perforated exactly down the center of the stamp. Misperfed coils are most commonly collected in pairs or strips. Misperfed modern coil pairs, such as those illustrated, range in retail price from $2 to $5 for slightly misperfed to $10 to $20 per pair for those perforated down the center. Occasionally an older or scarcer item sells for more.

Misperfed commemorative stamps are generally scarcer than misperfed coils. Slightly misperfed modern commemoratives, such as the First Man on the Moon commemorative illustrated above, usually range in retail price from $15 to $25 per stamp depending on age and topic. The illustrated stamp trades nearer the high end of the range because aerospace is a popular topic. A similar perf shift on a less popular topic might sell more toward the lower end of the price range. Pairs and blocks are priced proportionally. Older (pre-1940) or rarer misperfs also sell for more.

Some stamps exist misperfed only slightly, shifting a legend or denomination from top to bottom or from one side to another, resulting in an outwardly normal-appearing "change of design." This effect is illustrated by the Thomas Gallaudet strip shown above. The stamp on the far right is normal; the two stamps on the left are changed designs by virtue of the inscriptions moving to the opposite side of the stamps as a result of a malfunction of the electric eye at the start of a run. The electric eye adjusts the rows of perforating pins and die wheels to the stamps being perforated. This happens as the stamps begin to go through the perforator. Thus the leading edge of a web will always be waste, and will be destroyed. The second stamp from the right is "narrow," which removes Gallaudet's name from the stamp. Such strips retail for $40 to $75.

The Kennedy stamps of the Prominent Americans series illustrate another type of change of design. A normal 13-cent stamp is seen on the left; a "3-cent" variety is seen on the right, created by a very slight perforation shift. In most cases, a stamp with such a slight perforation shift would be unsalable. This "changed design," however, possesses eye-appeal and retails for about $10-$15.

Misperfed "change of design" stamps are generally worth more than other slightly misperfed items in which no change of design occurs. Misperfed joint line pairs and strips also are worth more.

The Frederick Douglass definitive shown above is an example of a modest misperforation that yields a nice effect—you can read part of the design at bottom that normally appears at the top of the stamp. Again, pricing is a function of degree of misperforation and visual effect. This stamp has a retail value of $20 to $25.

Dramatically misperfed modern commemoratives such as the Seattle World Fair stamps usually range in retail price from about $30 to $50 per stamp. Occasionally a rare or expensive item will command a price of as much as $125 or more per stamp.

Stamps with drastically angled misperfs, such as the illustrated 2-cent Liberty series definitive, whose appearance is striking (it almost makes you dizzy to look at it), retail for $100 to $150 per stamp or more.

Misperfs are sometimes collected as singles. Multiples often reveal the misperforation more dramatically, as illustrated by the block of 1-cent Washington-Franklin stamps. The block's perforations slant as a result of having gone through the perforator at a slight angle. Slightly angled misperfs tend to sell at prices similar to those for non-angled slight misperfs. Sharply angled misperfs, especially on high denomination definitives or on commemoratives, sell for more.

FOLDOVERS

As the name implies, foldovers occur when part of a sheet of stamps (most often a corner) is inadvertently folded during production, then subsequently trimmed, resulting in an odd-shaped piece, often with an unusual perforation pattern (commonly known as crazy perfs). A foldover can occur prior to printing and perforating, or it can occur after printing but prior to perforating. Foldovers often contain extra portions of selvage (known as appendages) that normally would have been trimmed off. Foldovers are occasionally responsible for creating a major error such as the imperforate error Scott C60b or the color-omitted error Scott 702a. Major errors resulting from foldovers are rare. Usually a foldover results in a freak. Each foldover is unique.

Foldovers are often collected in multiples, which are usually more visually striking and better illustrate an error. The 10¢ Washington-Franklin block shown here is a good example of a foldover resulting in crazy perfs. Its retail value is $150 to $200. As with other freaks, the range of value for crazy-perf foldovers varies and is a function of topical appeal and appearance, along with the catalog value of the stamp affected and the number of stamps affected.

Foldovers resulting in crazy perfs typically range in value from $10 to $150, with many retailing in the $20 to $50 range, such as the example illustrated nearby. Older examples and eye-arresting examples sell for more, occasionally hundreds of dollars.

MISCUTS

Miscuts occur when the production sheets of stamps become misaligned with cutting equipment. Miscuts often occur on imperforate coil stamps, and mention is made of them in the listings for imperforate stamps. Dramatically miscut imperforate coil stamps usually sell for a premium. Slightly miscut imperforate coils do not. Miscuts also occur on perforated coil stamps. Generally, the more dramatic the miscut, the greater its value. Miscut pre-1981 coil stamps often occur with partial plate numbers or marginal markings. The greater the amount of partial number or marginal marking showing, the more valuable the item. Miscuts also occur on sheet stamps, and they occur on booklet panes, yielding portions of adjoining stamps or in some cases selvage or gutters. Miscuts often occur in combination with misperfs, yielding uncommonly large selvage or, in some cases, gutters and portions of adjoining panes. Slightly miscut perforated coils (showing 15 percent to 25 percent of the adjoining stamp) typically retail in the $15 to $25 a pair range; those drastically miscut (half each of two stamps) retail in the $75 to $100 a pair range.

Most collectors prefer to collect miscut booklets in the form of intact panes. Miscut booklet panes that result from a simple shift often sell in the $10 to $30 range, depending upon the severity of the miscut. Slight miscuts sell toward the lower end of the range, dramatic miscuts toward the high end. The 13¢ Liberty Bell pane illustrated here is a mid-range example.

COLOR SHIFTS

Color shifts (also known as misaligned color or misregistered color) occur when one or more of the plates used to print multicolored stamps is out of register with the others, or when sheets are improperly fed on one or more of the multiple passes through a press. Refer to sections on **lithography** and **photogravure** in the introduction for information on multicolor printing. Color shifts range from mundane to dramatic. Value is generally a function of topical appeal and appearance. Usually, the more visually striking (the more pronounced the misregistration of color) and topically popular an item, the greater its value. On rare occasions, color shifts occur in combination with misperfs. And on occasion, a color shift is mistaken for a misperf.

Color shifts generally range in retail price from $10 to $40 per stamp. Those with slight shifts sell toward the lower end of the range.

Those with more dramatic shifts, such as the stamps illustrated, sell toward the higher end of the range. Stamps with minute or barely discernable color shifts generally command little or no premium.

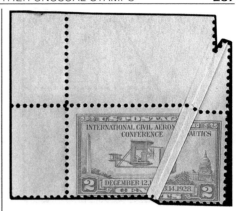

Occasionally, dramatic and visually striking color shifts, such as the 8-cent Liberty definitive shown here, sell for as much as $100 to $250. As with other freaks, there is no hard and fast rule; price is a function of eye-appeal and demand.

GUTTER PAIRS & GUTTER SNIPES

Postage stamps are usually printed in press sheets yielding either four, six or more finished panes of stamps when trimmed apart. The spaces between panes on a press sheet are known as gutters. Gutter pairs and gutter snipes occur when press sheets are miscut so that a pane contains a portion of an adjacent pane, including the gutter separating the two. Gutter pairs and gutter snipes can also result from pre-trimming foldovers.

To be considered a full gutter pair, the pair must contain at least one complete stamp on either side of the gutter. Gutter pairs on issues available from the Postal Service in configurations that normally contain gutters (such as certain of the Farley sheets and modern uncut press sheets) are not considered errors. Pairs (or multiples) with full gutters between are rare and usually retail for hundreds of dollars, typically in the range of $250 to $750.

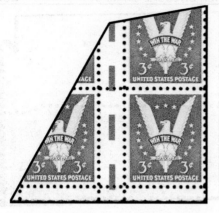

Items with less than a complete stamp on either side are known as gutter snipes and sell for considerably less, the price determined by the size of the incomplete stamp and the issue. The illustrated Seaway commemorative is much scarcer than the Win the War stamp. Some slight gutter snipes can be purchased for less than $25. Those with larger portions of stamps showing sell for more, usually in the $50 to $125 range. The illustrated Seaway pair retails in the $75 to $150 range. The Win the War pair retails for $45 to $60. Again, it's a matter of eye-appeal, and prices range broadly across the spectrum. Stamps showing only perforations from an adjoining pane (and no part of an adjoining stamp) are also called gutter snipes and typically sell for 50¢ or so per stamp.

OPEN CREASES

Preproduction open creases result from paper bunching or folding over on itself prior to receiving a printed impression or perforations. Such stamps should normally be left in the largest multiple possible. Typically, the folded or creased portion of the affected stamp can be gently pulled apart, revealing an unprinted (or open) area. The determining factors of value are: the size of the opening, the underlying catalogue value of the stamp, and the age of the stamp. Generally, the larger and more pronounced the crease, the greater its value. Ironically, open creases are more common on pre-1940 stamps than on later issues, and prices reflect this situation. Many open-creased stamps fall in the $40 to $100 price range. However, a fair number sell for more than $100, especially mint examples and stamps with high underlying catalogue value, which can boost the price to as

much as $1,000 or more. Mint examples sell for more than used examples of the same stamp. Of those illustrated, the one at top would be expected to sell for $100 to $125, while the one at bottom would fetch $125 to $150.

ALBINOS AND BLANK STAMPS

Albinos and blank stamps result from the omission of all printed colors. An albino stamp is generally understood to have a blind, intaglio plate impression embossed on its surface, which is often enough to permit identification of the stamp in the absence of its colors. Such a stamp is considered a color-omitted error. A blank stamp results when all colors are omitted from a stamp printed by lithography or photogravure and no intaglio blind impression occurs. Blank stamps are usually impossible to identify unless attached to a normally (or partially) printed stamp of the same design. Blank stamps are collected in pairs or strips containing both normal (or partially normal) stamps and stamps with all color omitted. Blank stamp combination pairs and strips retail for $250 and up. Albinos likewise retail for $250 and up.

Albino impressions are much more common on stamped envelopes, where color is omitted but the embossed part of the design remains. Pre-1960 albino stamped envelopes typically sell for $2 to $10 each. Recently issued albino stamped envelopes are much scarcer and sell for more, especially used copies.

MISCELLANEOUS

Smears, blobs and blotches are caused by excess ink, by cleaning solvent or other chemicals on a printing plate at some point during production. Solvent smears are usually collected in blocks, strips, or panes large enough to show the entire smear pattern.

Minor overinking on wet-printed stamps (such as the Jefferson stamp on the left) command only a nominal premium; heavily inked wet-printed stamps (such as the one on the right) usually sell in the $5 to $15 per stamp price range. Again, price is a function of eye-appeal. Ink blobs and blotches on stamps usually sell for more than smears. Again, it's a matter of eye-appeal.

Underinked stamps (sometimes known as dry prints) are caused by too little ink being applied to a plate during printing. The stamp on top is normal; the one on the bottom is underinked. Those sufficiently underinked to be considered collectible typically retail from $3 to $15 per stamp depending on severity of the effect. The illustrated 2-cent Presidential retails about mid-range, $7.50 or so.

The two examples shown here are severely underinked and retail in the $10 to $20 per stamp range. Slightly underinked stamps have little value. On occasion, truly startling examples sell for as much as $50. Underinked examples of stamps with odd or high face values sell for for more.

Offsets. The most pronounced examples, known as "in-press offsets," are caused by a printing plate leaving a fully inked impression on an underlying roller when the press skips a sheet of paper. Subsequent sheets then receive a normally inked impression on the top side, as well as a reversed impression on the gummed side, where it has come in contact with the roller. The illustrated examples were created in this fashion. The first sheet passing through after a skipped sheet receives the most vivid impression.

Subsequent impressions fade as ink on the roller is exhausted, and after a few sheets there is no evidence that a skip ever occurred. Impressions made by in-press offsets are characteristically overall and uniform in appearance. Generally, the more bold and pronounced the offset, the greater its value.

A second type of offset, known as a "sheet stacking offset," occurs as a result of flat-plate printed sheets being stacked atop one another while the intaglio ink was still damp. Stacking occurred during production, but prior to gumming, which was a separate operation on pre-1940 flat plate printed stamps. Sheet stacking offsets lack the uniform overall impression of in-press offsets.

As with other freaks, the price of offsets varies with the intensity of the offset image and topical appeal. Prices for in-press offsets typically range from $50 to $100 per stamp, and can range higher depending on the item. Sheet stacking offsets are much more common and sell for much less.

Offsets are occasionally simulated by normally printed stamps sticking together due to high humidity. When pulled apart, they can give the appearance of an offset. They are not true offsets and have no philatelic value.

Imperforate Margins. Occasionally stamps occur with perforations omitted between the design and the margin. They should not be confused with stamps issued with natural straight edges. Although not considered major errors because the omission of perforations does not occur between stamps, imperforate margined stamps, nevertheless, are collectible. Usually, they're worth only a fraction of the value of an imperforate error.

Partial or Blind Perforations. Blind perfs are incompletely or partially impressed (or ground) perforations (or die cuts), often barely indented into the paper, giving a stamp the appearance of being imperforate. They are usually worth little, unless the perforations are so slightly impressed as to be barely noticeable. Occasionally, blind perfs are shifted into a stamp's design making their presence even more subtle and giving the item the appearance of being imperforate. Such shifted blind-perfed stamps usually range in price from $15 to $25 per pair.

Plate Varieties. This term applies to a large class of small flaws that trace to the platemaking process or from damage to the plate during printing, which results in individualized flaws unique to one stamp or on an issued pane. Plate varieties occur more frequently on older engraved stamps than on modern engraved or photogravure stamps. Gripper cracks and double transfers are examples of plate varieties. Retail values tend to be modest, typically three to five times the retail value of a normal example.

Design errors, as opposed to production errors, typically exist on all stamps of an issue. Design errors consist of things such as the wrong number of stars on a flag or the misspelling of a name. Because all stamps of the issue contain the error, no premium is attached to the "error."

The Postal Service rarely attempts to correct design errors once issued. The 1994 Legends of the West issue, a se-tenant pane of 20 designs, which initially included the wrong portrait of Bill Pickett, is an exception. When the Pickett design error was discovered, the Postal Service ordered all post offices to return stocks of the error pane. The discovery and recall were made before the scheduled first day of issue. Several panes, however, reached public hands before the recall.

The Postal Service reprinted the pane with the correct portrait of Bill Pickett and released it in due course. Subsequently, it sold 150,000 panes containing the design error (the incorrect portrait of Bill Pickett, known as the "recalled" pane) by lottery. The recalled error pane is more valuable than the regular pane, only by virtue of the fact that it was released in limited quantity—150,000 panes—and because many collectors regard it as essential to completing a general collection of U.S. stamps.

Error collectors generally consider design errors to fall within the scope of the oddity collecting field. In philatelic vernacular, the term "error" almost always refers to a production error: imperforate, color omitted, invert, freak, and so forth.

ADVERTISER INDEX